About Island Press

Since 1984, the nonprofit organization Island Press has been stimulating, shaping, and communicating ideas that are essential for solving environmental problems worldwide. With more than 1,000 titles in print and some 30 new releases each year, we are the nation's leading publisher on environmental issues. We identify innovative thinkers and emerging trends in the environmental field. We work with world-renowned experts and authors to develop cross-disciplinary solutions to environmental challenges.

Island Press designs and executes educational campaigns, in conjunction with our authors, to communicate their critical messages in print, in person, and online using the latest technologies, innovative programs, and the media. Our goal is to reach targeted audiences—scientists, policy makers, environmental advocates, urban planners, the media, and concerned citizens—with information that can be used to create the framework for long-term ecological health and human well-being.

Island Press gratefully acknowledges major support from The Bobolink Foundation, Caldera Foundation, The Curtis and Edith Munson Foundation, The Forrest C. and Frances H. Lattner Foundation, The JPB Foundation, The Kresge Foundation, The Summit Charitable Foundation, Inc., and many other generous organizations and individuals.

The opinions expressed in this book are those of the author(s) and do not necessarily reflect the views of our supporters.

CITIES FOR LIFE

Cities for Life

How Communities Can Recover from Trauma and Rebuild for Health

Jason Corburn

◯ ISLANDPRESS | Washington | Covelo

Library of Congress Control Number: 2021934516

All Island Press books are printed on environmentally responsible materials.

Manufactured in the United States of America
10 9 8 7 6 5 4 3 2 1

Keywords: Advance Peace program; Adverse Childhood Experience (ACE);
benign neglect; citizen science; climate justice; energy justice;
environmental justice; flooding; food security; gun violence; healing
infrastructure; Health in All Policies (HiAP); health equity; inclusive urban
policy; informal settlement; institutionalizing equity; intergenerational trauma;
the Iron Triangle; Makuru; Medellín, Colombia; Nairobi, Kenya;
neighborhood health centers; place-based trauma; Pogo Park;
police violence; public health; racial bias; racial segregation; racialized
poverty; redlining; resiliency hubs; Richmond, California; slum scientist;
street science; toxic stress, trauma; urban acupuncture; water access

This work is dedicated to all the community activists struggling to be heard, to heal, and to hold power accountable. I appreciate you, and thanks for letting me listen and learn.

Contents

Preface

This book emerged over my own twenty-plus-year career working with communities on environmental health issues. The chapters here reflect events and experiences over the last ten years in Richmond, California; Nairobi, Kenya; and Medellín, Colombia. I want to emphasize that this book didn't spring from a neatly organized research project—I didn't set out to study these three places or to document how activists and city leaders are helping traumatized communities in these places heal. I partnered with organizations in these cities to support their own ideas and initiatives for healthy change. I learned by doing, in hours of contentious public meetings, community workshops, and field visits observing and participating in projects. Through it all, I learned that it was the people-to-people connections in places, not necessarily the project, program, or plan, that mattered most for supporting community healing.

The cases in this book can be traced to my early career as a community organizer, helping to mobilize residents in neighborhoods impacted by polluters to join civil-action lawsuits to hold the corporate and negligent governments accountable. During one controversial case, I was being interviewed on a talk radio program. After I had presented the data and the reasons for the lawsuit, a resident from the impacted community called in. On the live broadcast, the resident questioned my accent and where I was from, since I "didn't sound like I was a local." I admitted that I was an outsider, and after a few more public shaming experiences, I learned how critical it is for traumatized communities to speak for themselves, because being an active agent in diagnosing the stressors you experience and generating solutions that resonate with your experiences are essential aspects of healing.

I soon accepted an internship with the United Nations Environment Program, where I met many nongovernmental organization (NGO)

activists from around the world fighting for the same respect and healing I experienced as an organizer. While at UNEP I met "civil society"
activists pushing back against global environmental agendas that were
ignoring local cultural and Indigenous knowledge. That experience,
combined with the environmental justice organizing, revealed how
the urban living conditions that to me seemed like the foundations
of health—such as affordable housing, public safety, food security, and
dignified employment—were absent from the environmental agenda
in the late 1990s.

After graduating from MIT, I returned to my hometown and
worked as an environmental planner for New York City. I spent countless hours in neighborhoods like East New York, Bedford-Stuyvesant,
Harlem, and the South Bronx, using my power inside government to
center the voices of activists from these communities in planning and
decision-making forums. After relocating to UC Berkeley, I joined
Bay Area environmental justice activists, such as Urban Habitat and
Communities for a Better Environment, to support their local work.
As a board member of the latter, I became intimately familiar with
the environmental health issues in Richmond, California. In 2006 I
became an adviser to Richmond's Community Health and Wellness
Element, which was the first time health equity had been integrated
into a land-use plan in the state of California. I spent the next 14 years
in Richmond, working with nonprofits and advising the City on ways
to implement and evaluate policies, programs, and practices focused on
improving health equity. The chapters in this book document the ways
in which community activists and the City of Richmond have continued to innovate by making people-first community redevelopment a
health and healing issue.

In 2007 a friend from MIT, who was leading the World Bank's Kenya program, helped connect me with Muungano wa Wanavijiji (or
Muungano), which is a civil society group that organizes the urban
poor living in the "slums" of Kenya. Muungano was seeking academic partners to help them prevent evictions in the Mathare informal
settlement in Nairobi. The evictions were due to a UNEP-sponsored
river cleanup program, and since I was familiar with the UN agency,
they asked me to join the community-led efforts. I went to Nairobi

and worked with Muungano and their global NGO network partner called Slum/Shack Dwellers International (SDI). We trained residents to survey themselves and map their community. My students and I helped Muungano devise a plan to stop the evictions and make "visible" the ignored and "invisible" suffering they were facing, from unsafe and undignified toilets to extrajudicial killings of youth. The plan and advocacy efforts stopped the evictions, and word spread to other threatened informal settlements. Our collaboration with Muungano continues, and since 2012, I have been partnering with "citizen scientists" in Mukuru to help them diagnose the traumas they face and to generate solutions.

I began working in Medellín in 2012 after meeting Sergio Fajardo who was visiting UC Berkeley. I was already aware of the dramatic changes occurring there and since 2011 had graduate students in my Healthy Cities course document the different roles activists and local government were playing in the ongoing transformation of Medellín. Through this work, I connected with academics in Medellín, including those at the Universidad de Antioquia (UdeA), who were working to define the *ciudad saludable* (healthy city). In January 2016, Aníbal Gaviria contacted me with an interest to come to Berkeley for a year to reflect on his recently completed term as mayor. I welcomed him to Berkeley, and since that time Aníbal and I have become friends and collaborators. I also deepened my collaborative research with UdeA and NGOs and participated in drafting the healthy city components of the most recent Metropolitan Strategic Plan, known as the PEMOT.

This book shares the frustrations, learning, and beauty I experienced during this journey. My research with communities revealed an all too frequent disconnect; residents in poor and BIPOC (Black, Indigenous, People of Color) communities were saying, "I feel the stress of insecure housing, working two jobs, and unsafe streets," while planners, public health departments, and health care professionals were saying, "We have this program to help you get more exercise and improve your diet." The disconnect was not new for the poor and BIPOC, who are too often ignored or blamed for the traumas they experience, even though the origins of their stress are out of their control and arising from discriminatory and racist public policies and institutional neglect.

I wrote this book to join others in calling for a collective response to chronic trauma, since no pharmaceutical medication or individual behavioral change alone can support healing. Community healing, as I show here, must begin with, and in, community, through positive social connections, including creating spaces and opportunities for interactions and trust building with our neighbors. The stakes are high, and the moment is critical as global suffering, anxiety, depression, hopelessness, and fear are on the rise. One antidote is creating cities and communities that support social connection, which can be as healing and health promoting as quitting smoking, improving one's diet, and exercising regularly. We cannot treat our way out of the crises of inequality and poor urban health. Only through investing in and creating healthy social relations, which demand simultaneous attention to improving the physical conditions of our urban neighborhoods along with new, public policies that redistribute resources to those that have been traumatized, can cities truly promote life.

I owe the insights I share in this book to tens of colleagues, friends, and partners who opened their homes and neighborhoods to me, shared their intimate stories, and also argued with me and called me out when I was off base.

First and foremost, Judea has been my partner and rock, intellectual interlocutor, and greatest champion. Azure and Satya graciously allowed their dad to be away too often.

My heartfelt thanks extend to my friends and colleagues in Richmond: Dan Reilly, Kimberly Aceves-Iñiguez, Gabino Arredondo, DeVone Boggan, Shasa Curl, Kanwarpal Dhaliwal, Joe Griffin, Brandon Harris, James Houston, Toody Maher, Sam Vaughn, and countless others; in Nairobi: Joseph Kimani, Jack Makau, Joseph Muturi, Baraka Mwau, Peter Ngau, Patrick Njoroge, Kilion Nyambuga, Nelmo Nyeri, Jane Wairutu, Jane Weru, and so many others at Muungano, SDI, the University of Nairobi, Strathmore University, and Stockholm Environment Institute; in Medellín: Aníbal Gaviria, Jorge Pérez Jaramillo, Carlos Cadena, Eliana Martinez, Joan Benach, David Hernandez, Yesly Lemos, Camila Rodríguez, Juan Camilo Molina-Betancur, Casa Kolacho, and again, too many others to name here.

Thanks to Heather Boyer at Island Press for insights and editorial guidance. Finally, I could not have done this without my team at UC Berkeley, and most importantly Amanda Fukutome-Lopez and Marisa Asari. They offered expertise, dedication, insights, and practical help with footnotes, data gathering, and images.

Introduction

Designed for Life or Death

I t can be a rare event when you get to see a dream come true. In the summer of 2017, young people and staff from the RYSE Center in Richmond, California, were working to turn their dreams for a new community center into reality. Over a dozen young people came together over five weeks to codesign a proposed "community campus" space, to be called RYSE Commons. The RYSE Youth Center is a community-based organization founded in 2008 in response to young residents who were demanding a safe space where they could recover from the traumas and the everyday violence they faced, such as under-performing schools, food insecurity, dehumanizing policing, immigration roundups, and homelessness.

"It needs to have a music and dance studio, maybe also a movie theater, oh yeah and all-day ice-cream," shared Ciera, one of the youth leaders. Breezy, who had been quiet most of the day, shared, "We need it to feel like RYSE now. Safe from the streets, where we can just breathe. But I want a big garden and kitchen and an outdoor art space. How about a swimming pool?"

Jaime, another youth participant, described how it was hard to capture his dream for the future RYSE Commons: "For me, every day is different, but I'm always lookin' out, know what I mean? RYSE is like my second home. I might need a place to sleep or help with my family one day, next day I need to make some money. Around here you just never know."

Dan Reilly, director of innovation at RYSE, captured all the ideas, encouraged the young people to dream big, and took them outside to build a to-scale model of the future RYSE Commons using cardboard boxes.

"Label each box as something you want to see in or around the building," Dan explained, "like the kitchen, art studio, and swimming pool." The young people labeled the boxes and then negotiated with one another about the layout and how each space ought to relate to the other. They debated whether the art studio should be near the music space and if the swimming pool should be close to the kitchen. Some grappled with how to separate quiet spaces from performance and play, and how to ensure privacy to those that used the health clinic and counseling services. They emphasized open spaces and that there should be as few closed doors as possible to ensure that everyone was in it together. By the end of the summer, the 3D layout had turned into a set of architectural drawings and a site plan.

Kanwarpal Dhaliwal, cofounder and associate director of RYSE, described the significance of having young people codesign a development project in their own community: "The youth in Richmond are oversurveilled and underserved. They don't get the opportunities to dream since their everyday resilience means constantly hustling to manage the atmosphere of trauma around them. What we do at RYSE is create space for them to build safe, supportive connections to one another and healthy adults. We need to be responsive to their immediate priorities and needs, as they define them, but to also adapt when things change. It's all about meeting and loving them where they are and being there with and for them on their journey."

Over two hundred young people participated in the codesign of the proposed RYSE Commons. Once the vision was nearly complete, dozens of paid interns from RYSE spent the next year-and-a-half sharing the vision with government officials and private philanthropy. The final design includes a theater, outdoor play spaces, an art studio, a media lab, a garden and teaching kitchen, mental health counseling, a health clinic, a makerspace, and a pop-up small business incubator space.[1] They decided not to include the swimming pool, but the youth demanded that the space house a new "restorative justice" program where RYSE will partner with the Contra Costa County district attorney's office. This program will allow Richmond youth who are caught committing nonviolent crime to meet with a team of family members or guardians, professional counselors from RYSE, and the crime victims themselves to cocreate a path for the offender to make amends, understand how their actions impacted others, and learn ways that they can right their wrong. The final design and programming concepts won the Fast Company 2019 World Changing Ideas Award (Fig. Intro.1).

"In the midst of trauma, our young people have shown that they have a vision and knowledge to help themselves and their community heal," said Kimberly Aceves-Iñiguez, cofounder and executive director of RYSE.

The work of creating and now operating the RYSE Commons is helping youth and the entire city of Richmond, California, heal from trauma. It accomplished this by centering the voices and knowledge of those most traumatized—the city's youth. RYSE also paid these youth planners to be interns and bring their knowledge to the institutions and decision makers that for too long have not served communities like Richmond. The project is, as this book shows, healing centered since it focuses on building healthy relationships with those most harmed, and cocreating new places that can act as the connective tissue for urban healing.

This book reveals how all cities should and can work more actively to promote the health and healing of all their residents. Borrowing from RYSE and others in Richmond, California, and similar organizations and initiatives in Medellín, Colombia, and Nairobi, Kenya, I refer to cities that are implementing this approach as cities for life. Cities for life acknowledge their part in creating the traumas that cause unhealthy stress, such as segregated neighborhoods, insecure housing, too few playgrounds, environmental pollution, and unsafe streets, particularly for the poor and Black, Indigenous, People of Color (BIPOC). Cities for life invest more in peacemaking and parks than in policing; more in community decision making than in data surveillance.

Figure Intro.1 The RYSE Commons project nearing completion.

They use their land-use powers to permit more libraries than liquor stores and more affordable housing than highways. They redistribute tax revenues to residents, the arts, and youth, rather than to real estate developers.

You might be thinking that cites for life are a utopian dream. But some cities around the world are doing just these things. By investing in people *and* places, while also changing decision-making processes that have contributed to urban trauma, cities are leading the charge in promoting better health for their citizens and for the planet. These cities are approaching human health as something that happens in our neighborhoods and communities, not just at a doctor's office or hospital. While health care is critical for everyone, it often comes too late to prevent disease, and it surely comes too late to address the traumas and related stress from living in a segregated, violent, and disinvested-in community. Cities for life are declaring racism a public health and climate change crisis, and are taking the lead in generating equitable outcomes.[2]

The three cities featured in this book—Richmond, California; Medellín, Colombia; and Nairobi, Kenya—are cities for life. This book is the result of over 10 years of work in each of the three cities, as I partnered with community groups, residents, and decision makers. In all three places, community activists have utilized their expertise to acknowledge how history and modern-day practices have contributed to their trauma and related poor health. In all three places, community groups are leading efforts to address traumas, and government is following their lead with the resources needed to have an impact at scale. In each place, residents are not only cocreating their healing, they are being employed to participate, thereby gaining some economic reparations from the harms inflicted upon them. In all three places, small-scale projects in one place are contributing to policy and planning changes across the city focused on institutionalizing health and healing in the everyday functions of city government.

Richmond, with a population of 111,000, is a formerly industrial city across the Bay from San Francisco. It is one of the most racially and ethnically diverse cities in the Bay Area, and it remains a home for new immigrants. It has a long history of political activism, including African Americans challenging housing segregation in the 1940s and '50s. It is the birthplace of the Black Panther Party and the environmental justice movement. Richmond was once one of the most violent cities in America, with the city council considering bringing in the National Guard to keep the peace in 2005. Instead activists pushed the City to invest in peacemaking, improving economic and environmental conditions, and creating new places to gather and heal. A new government agency works to promote peace through everyday engagement with the most at-risk people in Richmond. Residents redesigned a new neighborhood park and a community group has reinvested millions of dollars from grants into the local economy. The city became the first in the US to adopt a Health in All Policies ordinance, which aims to make health equity and addressing structural racism an explicit aspect of all its decisions. By 2020, murder rates in Richmond had reached thirty-year lows, and life expectancy had improved by over 5 years since 2005. Asthma hospitalizations have gone from impacting over 20 percent of the population in 2000 to 10 percent in 2017. In 2019, twice as many people reported their health as good than in 2007, over 80 percent of residents in one of the poorest neighborhoods reported trusting their neighbors, and twice as many residents rated their quality of life as good or excellent. (For more background on Richmond, see Box 1.)

Medellín is a city of over 2.5 million that sits in the Aburrá Valley in the Department of Antioquia in Colombia. Infamously known as the most violent city in the world in 1995, today it is more often recognized as the world's most innovative city. Medellín, is no longer in the top 100 most violent cities in the world. Much of that improvement has come from innovative, community-driven planning processes that have invested the city's resources and newest, most beautiful infrastructure in the poorest neighborhoods. In the early 2000s a series of new mayors and active civil society organizations reimagined what a public–community partnership could be. Instead of the state bringing the military into impoverished hillside communities (which they did from the 1950s to the 1990s), they adopted a process called social urbanism, which is a commitment to resident-driven problem identification, planning, and coimplementation of solutions with government—starting with the most violent and poorest neighborhoods. As a result, new public transportation connects previously isolated communities, and new schools, community centers, libraries, parks, and social programs have been developed in the poorest areas. Not only is violence down, but poverty is too, and social interactions and people's trust in government have increased. While Medellín is still a work in progress, residents and municipal officials are facilitating healing from decades of militarism, violence, and social stratification in the city. (For more background on Medellín, see Box 2.)

Nairobi is a city of about 4.5 million with a growing middle class and one of the strongest and fastest-growing economies in sub-Saharan Africa. Home of many international organizations, including the headquarters of the UN Environment Program, the city has a deep network of civil society organizations and history of resident activism. Nairobi is also wrestling with its colonial history, as the British left a legacy of racial land segregation. For decades, only Europeans were allowed to own land in the city. Today, many of the areas in Nairobi where colonists allowed Africans to live are the city's largest slums. Over 65 percent of the city's population lives in these slums on only about 10 percent of the land area. The slums have been largely ignored by the State and do not have public services, such as running water, sewers, or waste collection. Yet residents have innovated, and the informal sector represents over 65 percent of Nairobi's economy. In one Nairobi slum, Mukuru, residents have organized with the support of the Kenyan Federation of the Urban Poor, called Muungano wa Wanavijiji. Mukuru residents and Muungano have used data collection, mapping, organizing, music, video, and a host of other strategies to diagnose the traumas they are facing, identify some of the root causes, and propose solutions. They lobbied the government of Nairobi County to designate Mukuru a Special Planning Area in 2017, which empowered residents to devise an improvement plan that the government would finance. Residents worked to develop the plan, and today Mukuru is undergoing a transformation with new roads, water service, safer toilets, formal electricity, waste collection, and flood protection, and a new hospital is under construction. Like Richmond and Medellín, residents in Mukuru defined the traumas they faced, came up with solutions, and are working with government to implement many of those solutions, and they are being paid to do it. (For more background on Nairobi, see Box 3.)

Cities for Life argues that the solutions for addressing and reversing urban trauma must come from those most impacted by harms. This might mean those victimized by gun crime, those displaced from their homes, or those struggling to find their next meal. Too often, urban solutions are the exclusive domain of experts disconnected from the everyday realities of living with trauma and the hustle to survive. We have to acknowledge that this lived experience is a valuable form of expertise, and in many cases more valuable than that of the professionals crunching big data and spitting out analyses devoid of local culture and context.

For example, in Richmond, California, a community-centered violence prevention program has reduced gun violence by more than half in less than 10 years. Even while crime is down in most cities, the degree and pace of gun violence reductions in Richmond are unmatched by other similarly violent cities in the region or nationally.[3] Of the hundreds of young people enrolled in this program, many have gone from homelessness and street life to college and raising families. This work is also saving taxpayers an average of $20 million a year by reducing the law enforcement, criminal justice, health care, and other costs related to urban gun violence. Importantly, the City of Richmond is doubling down and investing in other health-related strategies, such as improving housing and parks, employment training, funding college tuition, and cleaning up its air pollution and toxic dump sites. Not only is this innovative public safety approach helping to reduce crime in communities that have long suffered from violence in Richmond, but, as I will show in later chapters, it is helping to change government policy and practice to be more trauma informed and healing focused.

What Is Urban Trauma?

Maybe you live outside a metropolitan area and have chosen to avoid the stress and high costs of urban living. Yet more and more of the planet's population now lives in cities. In fact, by 2020, close to 60 percent of the planet's population was living in cities. In some places that number is much higher, as in Europe and Latin America, where over 75 percent of the population lives in cities. The twenty-first-century city is not just the megalopolises of Tokyo, Shanghai, New York, Mexico City, or Mumbai. Around the world, but especially in sub-Saharan Africa, Asia, and increasingly in North America, people are living in rapidly growing small to medium-sized cities of less than 500,000. But whether cities are small, medium, large, or mega, they are fundamentally made up of people in communities or neighborhoods. It is these "urban villages"—the social networks we create on street corners, in barbershops, or through attending public events—as the legendary urban sociologist Herb Gans described them, where we have our best chance to support health and healing in the twenty-first-century city.

It is in community, connecting with others, that the village can be a place of collective recovery from trauma and healing. And, according to Bessel van der Kolk, author of *The Body Keeps the Score: Brain, Mind and Body in the Healing of Trauma*, "Trauma is now our most urgent public health issue, and we have the knowledge necessary to respond effectively. The choice is ours to act on what we know."[4]

When I use the word *trauma* in this book, I am not just referring to the experiences of individuals. Entire communities often experience trauma. Urban events capable of causing trauma span a wide range of situations, including extreme poverty, community and domestic violence, food and housing insecurity, exposure to toxic pollution, broken and poorly maintained parks and public spaces, abandoned buildings and lots, and the like. Urban trauma results in stress, fear, uncertainty, deprivation, and feelings of dehumanization when City decisions fail to address spatial and group-based inequities. The stress that is induced by traumatic experiences can be toxic on our bodies. We all experience stress, but in cases of chronic or toxic stress, there are multiple sources of ongoing stress and an absence of support systems. Toxic stress leads to psychological, emotional, cognitive, and biological wounds. Toxic stress alters our brain architecture and our ability to learn, control impulses, and make decisions. It weakens our immune system, so we are more susceptible to infections and long-term, debilitating autoimmune disorders. It can lead to sleeplessness, premature aging, and death. In short, most major human health issues today, and the inequitable disease burdens experienced by the poor and BIPOC, are linked to toxic stress (see chapter 1).

Centuries of public and private sector decisions have enabled some groups in cities to amass great wealth and resources, while allowing others to be subject to dehumanizing violence. The groups with advantages have used this power and wealth to create spaces or neighborhoods that offer them more buffers from stress and trauma, such as quality housing, safe parks and public spaces, libraries, schools, cultural and community centers, bicycle paths, and services to ensure the young, the elderly, and the disabled can all participate in community life. The absence of such opportunities in our cities is itself a form of violence known as structural violence. Structural violence occurs when the institutions and organizations that influence our cities and communities deny some groups, particularly racial and ethnic minorities, access to those healthy and potentially healing resources. Urban structural violence can seem hidden, but its wounds run deep. Structural violence—not your genetics, your behaviors, or whether or not you have access to health care—is now recognized as the root cause of health inequities between population groups and communities around the world, especially in cities.[5,6,7,8]

COVID-19 has ferociously swept through some urban areas because of preexisting structural violence: the precarity of work; the unaffordability of housing; the depth of racial, ethnic, and class divides; a profoundly unequal global economy; and the failure of many governments worldwide to include everyday people in the decisions that influence their lives. We should all care about these structural inequalities because they are destroying our happiness, and in fact they are killing us. While those with wealth and privilege living in cities tend to live longer than those experiencing structural violence, their quality of life has diminished. According to *The Guardian*, "The British got richer by more than 40% between 1993 and 2012, but the rate of psychiatric disorders and neuroses grew."[9] Wealth has reached astronomical levels for some in cities of the twenty-first century, but so too have rates of depression, obesity, heart disease, and suicides. Depression was the largest single contributor to nonfatal health loss worldwide in 2015, according to the World Health Organization.[10] Furthermore, technology and "smart cities"—where automation, online services, and artificial intelligence influence almost every service and sector—are not leading to happier, healthier, or more fulfilling lives.[11] The social isolation of urban residents due to COVID-19 lockdown policies, such as the closing of schools and public spaces, has exacerbated a mental health crisis in our cities, and actively using social media or being constantly online hasn't been shown to mitigate depression, anxiety, or suicides.[12] Depression is often a response to unaddressed trauma. Being traumatized can make us feel defective, that there is something wrong with us, and our sense of compassion toward ourselves and others can be lost. What we often fail to realize and acknowledge is that trauma is often the result of structural violence; the causes are external, not located within ourselves.

The antidote for depression and unhappiness is often social connections *and* eliminating the structurally violent features of our communities, such as segregation, unsafe housing, and the lack of places to shop, eat, create, learn, and play. Being in meaningful, frequent relations with others is the key to healing, health, and happiness. This must start with people, but it also includes our places, communities, and neighborhoods. Ed Diener and Martin Seligman, in their 2002 article "Very Happy People," found that "very happy people have rich and satisfying social relationships and spend little time alone relative to average people."[13] Of course, economic security offers a foundation for health and happiness, especially the money required to ensure that people are not in poverty, searching for their next meal, fearful of losing their housing or job, or forcing them to work multiple jobs just to make ends meet. Yet having supportive and nurturing social connections, as the Institute of Medicine and National Research Council report *From Neurons to Neighborhoods* stated, can be more health promoting than quitting smoking, changing your diet, and even regular exercise, and the conditions *in our neighborhoods* can shape our opportunities for social connection.[14] Social connections can be fostered, supported, and maintained by the ways we design and manage our cities.

In 1968, civil rights activist Stokely Carmichael told mental health practitioners to move beyond "treating" the individual when addressing the traumas of racial bias and instead to "treat" or change the institutions in society that maintain the racist and inequitable status quo, such as zoning laws, economic exclusion, segregated schools, and a biased legal system. Institutionalized racism, he argued, "is less overt, far more subtle, less identifiable in terms of specific individuals committing the acts, but is no less destructive of human life."[15] This is what is called structural or systemic racism, which is when intersecting and mutually reinforcing laws, policies, entrenched institutional practices, and established beliefs and attitudes overlap to produce, condone, and perpetuate widespread unfair treatment of BIPOC. The antiracism lawyer, academic, and activist john powell has defined structural racism as seemingly neutral policies and practices that function in racist ways by disempowering communities of color, conferring advantage to Whites, and perpetuating unequal historical conditions. He notes that a structural racism lens helps us analyze "how housing, education, employment, transportation, health care, and other systems interact to produce racialized outcomes."[16] Thus urban policy and planning are at the root of much structural racism.

I am concerned with how new urban policy and planning decisions can help us heal. This is necessary because medicine and public health are largely failing to heal the most traumatized people and communities. Precision medicine is pushing health care deeper into the body, at the cellular level, to treat diseases but is paying scant attention to our environments, where traumatic exposures originate. If you are lucky enough to get timely, quality, and affordable medical care, you likely leave the clinic and go back into the living, work, and other environments that are making you sick in the first place. Public health remains overly focused on changing individual behaviors or on one environmental risk at a time, while rarely changing the public policies, laws, and norms that structure our ability to make healthy decisions or avoid risks. As importantly, neither medicine nor public health is serious about letting go of some of its autonomy and granting power to those suffering the most to diagnose the challenges they face and generate their own solutions.

Cities for Life is about confronting the science of public health and the art of city making that for too long has blamed the urban poor and BIPOC for how they have responded to traumas that they didn't create. *Cities for Life* aims to challenge a medical and public health model that continues to treat people and send them back into the living, working, playing, and learning conditions that traumatized them in the first place. *Cities for Life* confronts the science and technology "innovations" that argue for data-driven, genetic, and biomedical responses to trauma, while failing to include BIPOC in the conversation or questioning the social institutions that perpetuate inequalities. *Cities for Life* is about a new way forward with, not for, urban communities that rebuilds our social institutions, practices, and policies to be more focused on healing and health. As I will show, this means not only including those most traumatized in decision making, but confronting historically discriminatory, exclusionary, and racist urban institutions, and promoting practices, place making, and public policies that, as Dr. Martin Luther King Jr., interpreted by Professor Cornell West, has reminded us, puts "love back into public policy."[17]

What Is Urban Healing?

How can cities help communities and individuals to heal? City decision making can help healing when it puts those most traumatized at
the center of defining harms and solutions; acknowledges the historical legacy of urban traumas on communities today; takes a nonclinical,
strengths-based approach to harm reduction and healing; and institu-
tionalizes healing within all aspects of City decision making, not just in
its health sector. The following foundational approaches are necessary
for urban healing.

Speaking for Ourselves

Trauma can rob you of the feeling that you are in charge of yourself and
increase a sense of hopelessness. Actively participating in one's own
healing and the restoration of your community can not only restore
hope but is a critical form of expertise that must drive urban healing. A young activist in Richmond, California, who was participating in a project with the RYSE Center mentioned earlier, stated, "We
know we can't run the city. It's too complex, but our experience and
our voices should count, especially because we're the most affected."
A community organizer in Medellín told me, "We live here. We're
experts too." In Nairobi, Mukuru residents acted as citizen scientists,
defining the risks they faced, diagnosing them through measurement,
and prioritizing healing-focused interventions. As I will show in later
chapters, the residents of Richmond, Medellín, and Nairobi (as well
as those in similarly traumatized communities) have been saying for
a long time that they must be leaders in healing their communities
and that partnerships between disinvested-in communities and professional researchers and policy makers can be invaluable for analyzing
complex challenges and generating innovative solutions. Cities for life
heal when diagnoses and interventions are by and with, not for or on,
urban communities.

Incorporating History

We might imagine processes of healing that try to ignore the past (it
might be traumatic after all) or view history as something that has little

bearing on today's inequities. However, urban healing demands engaging with and understanding the long-term processes and decisions that gave rise to trauma and related health challenges. George Rosen, who served as the editor of the *American Journal of Public Health* from 1957 to 1973, wrote that "every social phenomenon is the result of historical process, that is societal factors operating over a period of time through human interaction."[18] History can undermine the seeming inevitability of the status quo by revealing that the present is a result of past decisions, and new choices can be made today to create a different tomorrow. Acknowledging the past and its present-day manifestations can avoid victim blaming, internalizing failures, reifying stereotypes, and a tendency for professionals to identify "solutions" that overlook root causes of urban trauma. One example is when urban policy works to build more affordable housing in an area but fails to acknowledge the historical legacy of racist banking institutions that denied access to capital for BIPOC. Taking history into account in urban healing can also help identify what interests may want to maintain a status quo that is harmful, such as resistance to restorative justice as an alternative to a city's heavy-handed, militarized policing, or when wealthy communities resist the siting of new community centers, public transit, or public housing. A critical engagement with history can rehumanize those that have been harmed and communities that have been traumatized and force us to ask, "What happened here, who has been hurt, and who has a stake in the trauma-producing practice?"

Building on Assets

A clinical approach to trauma might ask, "What's wrong with you," while a healing-centered approach asks, "What's right with you?"[19] This is similar to asset-based community development, which starts by focusing on what is working in a community and how redevelopment can lift up and honor those positive characteristics of places and the people living there. Responses to urban trauma must recognize that traumatized communities are more than the worst things that have happened to them; more than the poverty, inequality, and structural violence. Again, this is not to romanticize impoverished, traumatized communities, but it is a call to look deeper, perhaps in the shadows, for the beauty, ingenuity, genius, and humanity that exist in all places. In these ways, the urban healing approach moves beyond the clinical, even trauma-informed approach of treating symptoms to identifying strengths and investing in possibilities.

Institutionalizing Equity

When people hear the term *institutionalization* they might cringe or think of public institutions that get a bad rap, like the foster care system, some public schools, and policing. Yet, as Michelle Alexander emphasized in her powerful book, *The New Jim Crow*, it was the institutionalization of racist practices within law enforcement and the criminal justice system that cocreated mass incarceration targeting African American men.[20] In order to reverse these entrenched institutional practices, we need new policies, rules, norms, and laws that address their damage and promote health and healing. Cities for life cannot be created on the backs of nonprofits, private philanthropy, or one-off, boutique projects. As I will show in each of the three cities, new government plans, programs, and policies, created and held accountable by active citizen participation, are necessary to move toward greater health and healing.

The chapters that follow will show you how these cities helped the individuals and community to heal, and how any city can become a city for life.

Box 1
Richmond, California: The Industrial City by the Bay

To fully understand the importance of a racial justice approach in Richmond, it is important to know a little about the city's history. Richmond sits directly across the Bay from San Francisco, with over thirty miles of shoreline. After gold was discovered in California in 1849, thousands moved to the Bay Area, and the burgeoning ports and fertile soil in Oakland and Richmond became highly sought after land. By the end of the nineteenth century, Richmond was a strategic part of California's (and the US's) growing maritime industry. The Santa Fe Railroad made Richmond the terminus of its transcontinental railroad in 1899, where it connected to a ferry to transport passengers and freight to San Francisco. According to Richmond historian Eleanor Ramsey, the Santa Fe Railroad company employed largely Mexican American, Japanese, and Native American workers and housed them in segregated camps. By 1902 they were over half of Richmond's population.[1]

In 1901, Standard Oil built what would become the largest refinery in the western United States on Richmond's peninsula. The refinery only hired Whites and helped stimulate a segregated industrialization, calling itself "the Pittsburgh of the West."[2] Over the next decade, a host of industries that would define America's early industrial period located in Richmond, including the Pullman Coach Company, Ford Motor Company, and Stauffer Chemical Company. Industry lured workers, and the population grew from about 3,000 in 1900 to nearly 30,000 by the 1930s.[3]

The African American population grew to be the largest ethnic group in the city by the 1930s. African Americans from Louisiana and other southern states who worked as Pullman porters commonly moved their families to Richmond to avoid the racism of the American South. Discrimination continued in the labor market in California, but a growing African American workforce was willing to accept lower wages than most other workers, in part because jobs were scarce in the Jim Crow segregated South. So, families of African Americans joined Japanese flower farmers, Chinese fishing families, and the families of the original Mexican rancheros in Richmond.

During World War II, the Kaiser Richmond Shipyards became one of the largest military shipbuilding operations in the United States. Workers, many who were Blacks recruited from the southeastern US, flocked to shipyard jobs and needed a place to live. Atchison Village, built in 1941, was one of the largest defense worker housing projects in the country. It was, like almost all government-built or subsidized housing at the time, only available to White workers. The Black, Mexican, and Japanese populations were forced to live in temporary and older housing. By 1945, Richmond had the largest public housing program in the United States, with 80 percent of Richmond's 90,000 people living in segregated public housing.[4]

Racial Segregation in Richmond

Racial segregation permeated housing and employment in Richmond. In 1945 the *San Francisco Chronicle* reported that unemployed Black former shipyard workers were protesting the Richmond Housing Authority's (RHA's) decisions to deny them access to new housing. They also claimed the RHA was charging Blacks higher rents than Whites and evicting them from older public housing.[5] The Steamfitters and Boilermakers Union, which controlled the majority of shipyard jobs, allowed women and people of color to be hired but denied them membership. Even when African Americans were later allowed to join unions in the mid-1940s, they were not allowed to vote in union elections and were not represented in wage negotiations.[6] These racist housing and employment policies in Richmond were enforced by the city and federal governments and private industry and systematically denied African Americans, Asians, and Latinos access to the wealth and opportunities in Richmond and the Bay Area.[7] African American shipyard workers sued for better wages, were represented by Thurgood Marshall, and won a landmark civil rights case in 1944 called *James v. Marinship*.

The racist incarceration of Japanese Americans during WWII also had a significant impact on the city. Richmond was home to a number of Japanese American families that had owned flower farm land since the 1920s and sold their flowers at San Francisco's flower market. The land and greenhouses of all the Japanese farmers was taken, and the families were incarcerated after President Franklin Delano Roosevelt issued a presidential proclamation calling for the arrest and detention of all "alien enemies." After the war, a few families, including the Fukushimas, Maidas, Oishis, and Sugiharas, returned to rebuild their farms but were forced to purchase the land they had once owned.[8]

Since Richmond's African Americans were shut out from new housing in Richmond and from moving to growing suburbs, they settled in an area called North Richmond, which remains an unincorporated area, meaning it doesn't receive any city services or have any representation within city government. By 1950, the shipyards had closed and 36 percent of Richmond's population was unemployed. The all-White RHA decided to evict all non-White public housing residents with the claim that their buildings were temporary and slated for demolition. Tenants went on rent strikes and the NAACP (National Association for the Advancement of Colored People) joined their protest efforts. By 1953, seventeen of Richmond's public housing projects had been razed as part of the federal Urban Renewal Program.[9] African American families moved into older housing in the city's Iron Triangle neighborhood (Figure Box 1.1).

Racial Justice Activism in Richmond

The Black Panther Party for Self Defense held its first protest against racist policing in Richmond in 1967, after an unarmed, 22-year-old Black man named Denzil Dowell was shot in North Richmond. This launched the national Black Panther Party (BPP), which was fundamentally about delivering essential, life-supporting services to Blacks who were discriminated against by Jim Crow era laws and denied the means to survive.

The BPP has an important health and healing legacy, including advocating for health care as a human right; providing primary health care; operating free food, clothing, and transportation programs; developing urban gardens; advocating for affordable housing; and organizing their own ambulance services since racist segregated hospitals refused to serve Black neighborhoods and patients.[10] Of course, the BPP challenged dehumanizing policing, the unjust murdering of unarmed Black people, and mass incarceration, all issues racial and economic justice social movements have continued with today. Importantly, the BPP organized "survival conferences" where free legal services and seminars about mind, body, and health were offered, where they taught about a holistic approach to well-being that challenged the increasing dominance of the medical model of disease.[11]

In the 1980s, an influx of Laotian, Cambodian, Hmong, and Vietnamese refugees settled in Richmond due to US wars in Southeast Asia. The crack epidemic hit Richmond in the 1980s as did a spike in gun violence. There were sixty-two murders in 1991. The violence was also environmental; there were over 300 reported accidents, fires, spills, leaks, and explosions at the Chevron refinery from 1989 to 1995.[12] Residents in the North Richmond and Iron Triangle neighborhoods—named after the railroad tracks that bordered the community—were particularly impacted by environmental pollution and gun violence.[13]

In the 1990s, nonprofit organizations mobilized to push back against environmental racism and structural violence. The West County Toxics Coalition, formed with the support of the National Toxics Campaign, was created by Dr. Henry Clark to protect the health and well-being of Richmond residents suffering from refinery pollution and related toxic sites in the city. Other groups, such as Opportunity West, the Asian Pacific Environmental Network/Laotian Organizing Project, Youth Together, and the Richmond Equitable Development Initiative, were created to build coalitions of residents to challenge corporate and government neglect. The RYSE Center was founded in 2008 at the request of young people in Richmond, who were demanding a safe space of their own where they could heal from the traumas of violence. New power was being built in the city to push back against long-running corporate (Chevron) control over politics, policing, and government decisions more generally.

In 2019 Richmond was home to about 110,000 people, 37 percent of whom were White, 20 percent African American, 16 percent Asian, and over 40 percent identifying as Latino. As a "sanctuary city," Richmond welcomes immigrants no matter their legal status. The median household income is about $64,000, compared to $71,000 in all of California, but in its poorest neighborhoods households report only $38,000 in annual income. However, many measures of well-being have improved in Richmond over the past fifteen years, including life expectancy, gun violence, and self-rated health.

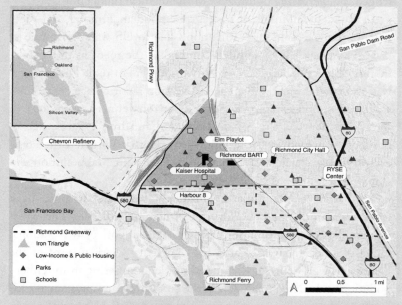

Figure Box 1.1 Richmond, California, with focus on the Iron Triangle.

Box 2
Medellín, Colombia

Once the most violent city in the world, Medellín was recognized in 2013 as the most innovative city in the world by the *Wall Street Journal* and the *Urban Land Institute* and received the Lee Kuan Yew World City Prize in 2016. In the 2000s, when many Latin American cities were struggling with growing levels of urban violence and inequality, Medellín was celebrated as an impressive case study of urban transformation and a model of successful public initiatives that reduced not only gun violence but also poverty, segregation, and inequality.

Medellín is the capital of the Department of Antioquia and the second-largest city in Colombia with a population of about 2.5 million. It sits in the Aburrá Valley, a region with steep mountains on its east and west sides with a river snaking along the valley floor. Within the region are ten other municipalities and a total population of about 3.7 million. Early in its development, Medellín built its wealth on gold mining and coffee exports.[1] Rural violence across the region displaced farmers, and they migrated to the city.

Medellín once had a thriving industrial and manufacturing center, known by some as the Manchester of Colombia.[2] However, by the 1970s there was a steep decline in manufacturing, and once-thriving textile industries left the city seeking less expensive labor in Asian countries. As Medellín's industrial sector declined and the economy slowed, many migrants could not find formal employment, and there was a steep rise in socioeconomic inequality and growth of informal, or community-self-built housing. Large slums grew along the city's hillsides, making life precarious for the urban poor and making it difficult for the city's public infrastructure to reach this growing population.

In 1955, the Medellín City Council consolidated the management of its energy, public water supply, wastewater infrastructure, and telecommunications utilities into a newly formed Public Companies of Medellín (known as Grupo EPM). Owned by the City of Medellín,

EPM is required by law to contribute 30 percent of its annual financial surplus (about USD 400 million in 2018) toward the city's social development investments. This is a unique city–utility–community investment arrangement among cities globally, but particularly those in the Global South.

Colombia has had armed opposition groups, known in Colombia as guerrillas or insurgents, since at least the 1950s. This period in the country's history, known as La Violencia, included an ideological civil war between the Conservative and Liberal parties. During this period, armed groups emerged as strongholds in certain regions, including the now infamous Fuerzas Armadas Revolucionarias de Colombia (FARC, Revolutionary Armed Forces of Colombia) and the Ejército de Liberación Nacional (ELN, National Liberation Army). Other guerrilla groups operated and aimed to control an emerging drug market. By the 1980s the political insurgency and drug trafficking guerrillas were operating in urban areas, using kidnappings, bombings, and other violence to influence politics and control land-use development and the social dynamics within neighborhoods.[3,4] Guerillas operating in the country's mountains began forcing people off their land in an effort to grow more coca. The 1970s and '80s witnessed large-scale internal displacement in Colombia, as millions were driven from rural areas into cities. According to the UNHCR (United Nations High Commissioner for Refugees), Colombia has one of the largest populations of internally displaced people around the world.[5,6]

According to the report, "Medellín: Memories of an Urban War," prepared by the National Center for Historical Memory, the period from 1982 to 1994 was known as the "age of the bombs" in Medellín.[7] This consumed the politics of the city and destabilized neighborhoods and most institutions, both public and private. Elected officials, union leaders, community activists, and others were kidnapped and killed by death squads.

By the 1980s, paramilitary groups and drug cartels fought over control of space and illicit markets, and rates of violence in the city began to spike well above national levels. Poverty, drug trafficking, and the heavy hand of the military combined to give Medellín the infamous title in the 1990s as the murder capital of the world. Pablo Escobar and the Medellín Cartel's activities were at their peak in the late 1980s and early '90s, taking over the city with guerrillas and other gangs.[8] Escobar was killed in 1993, which ended his control over gangs in the city. However, smaller gangs of young people began to claim control over neighborhoods. These gangs ran local drug trafficking, but they also delivered basic services to homes where the city's service did not reach, or refused to go, and enforced their own "extrajudicial" justice to control local disputes.[9]

In 1991 the homicide rate per 100,000 inhabitants in Medellín was 381, the highest in the world and in any other city in the last twenty-five years.[10] Yet, by 2011, Medellín had a murder rate of 70 per 100,000 inhabitants, and by 2015 this figure was reduced to 19, no longer appearing in the top fifty most violent cities in the world. In the 1990s Medellín also had the highest extreme poverty index, equivalent to 19.4 percent of the population, and in 2002, over 36 percent of the population was living in poverty. By 2015, the percentage of the population living in poverty fell to 14.3 percent, and only 3 percent of the population was living in extreme poverty.[11] In the 1990s unemployment reached 22 percent, but by 2014 the city's economy had recovered and unemployment was below 8 percent.

Projects and policies are helping residents heal from decades of violence and inequality. Many point to the new Colombian Constitution in 1991 as a turning point for Medellín.[12,13] The Constitution defined Colombia as a "social state under the rule of law," or *estado social de derecho*, which was accompanied by new rules mandating decentralized municipal governance, participatory democracy, and a recognition of ethnocultural diversity, among other reforms. From 1990 to 1995, a new Presidential Council for Medellín (Consejería Presidencial para Medellín) established public forums where experts, community members, and the private and public sectors came together to discuss the origins of the city's challenges and ways to address them.

The Presidential Council for Medellín was given the charge from the Colombian government to "address the social debt and mitigate the historical absence of the State in the city of Medellín."[14]

The Presidential Council developed a strategic plan for moving forward, and a major slum upgrading program called the Integrated Slum Upgrading Program of Medellín (Programa Integral de Mejoramiento de Barrios Subnormales en Medellín [PRIMED]), was launched. The PRIMED focused on both physical and social integration—physically integrating the peripheral communities into the city and socially integrating residents by providing education, employment, and other opportunities.[15] The program built new housing, delivered land rights to some of the urban poor, and extended water, roads, and sanitary infrastructure to previously excluded barrios. A number of schools and health centers were built, and hillsides were stabilized to prevent landslides.[16]

PRIMED was critical because it emphasized not just physical changes but also improving and transforming relationships within communities, seen as drivers of violence, and between poor communities and the government, also viewed a part of the structural violence experienced by the poor.[17] In the end, PRIMED did improve housing, infrastructure (water, roads, and sanitation), schools, and health centers, and it reduced landslide risks for some of the city's poorest peripheral *comunas* (neighborhoods), particularly one called Popular. However, its work was incomplete. One outstanding challenge was integrating the poorest, hillside areas into the rest of the city (Figure Box 2.1)

After PRIMED, residents, leaders, and the private sector held public dialogues to identify ways to address the crises of violence and rising inequalities. A new mayor in 2004, Sergio Fajardo, introduced the idea of social urbanism, which would enlist the city's poorest residents to identify solutions and invest city resources in the most violent and impoverished communities with the most functional and beautiful projects. Soon the city's first gondola, called the metrocable, was completed in Popular, one of the poorest communities. Electric escalators were built in another poor community, called Comuna 13, to connect hillside residents to the center of the city. A long-range development plan included a strategy for climate change resilience and social justice. The city's former dump site, called Moravia, was cleaned up and turned into an ecopark and garden. New community centers were built on land around water storage tanks that was formerly fenced off from residents. These centers, called Articulated Life Units, or UVAs, brought new jobs, as well as recreational, cultural, and learning spaces to communities that had experienced violence and had been deprived of these amenities. A cleanup of the city's river and a greenbelt along its sprawling hillsides to prevent erosion and landslides were launched (see Figure Box 2.2).

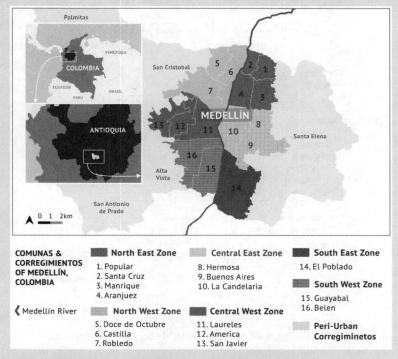

Figure Box 2.1 Medellín and its *comunas* (neighborhoods).

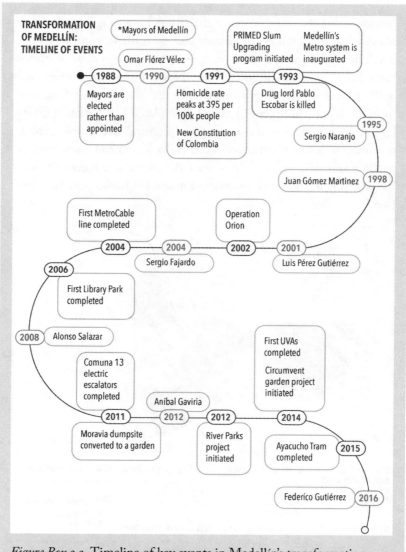

Figure Box 2.2 Timeline of key events in Medellín's transformation.

Box 3
Nairobi, Kenya, and the Mukuru Informal Settlement

Nairobi is a city of about 4.5 million people, where residents are working to dismantle the legacies of its British colonial past. The city was formed as a colonial trading post in 1902 along the Ugandan railway that traversed the region from Kisumu in the west to the coastal city of Mombasa. For decades, the British made it illegal for Africans to live in the city; they were only allowed in during the day for work. Indian workers, also brought by the British Empire, built the railroads and were allowed to live in a small area of the city. Eventually, by the 1940s, the British allowed Africans to live in segregated areas in the city, generally in wetlands, former quarries, and dump sites. In these areas, Africans built their own housing and communities but were largely denied landownership. A 1948 Master Plan for Nairobi, designed by European architects, envisioned the city like Paris and New Delhi, with grand boulevards and completely free of slums. The plan ignored the existing racist land segregation and growing slum populations. Residents within the slums mobilized for resistance to the colonial occupiers and with others across the country. The Mau Mau rebellion eventually defeated the British, and independence was gained in 1963.

Operation Clean Up was one of the first policies passed by the postindependence Nairobi City Council, and it included the removal of "undesirable elements" across the city. Essentially, the postindependence Kenyan government continued some aspects of the British slum clearance, justifying tearing down the shacks by claiming that they were an unhealthy blight. In 1971, over one-third of Nairobi's residents were living in slums, and the new government displaced over 50,000 people. Kenya's National Development Plan in the mid-1970s put a halt to demolitions, and in the early 1980s the World Bank began a "sites and services" loan program that required housing and utility services to be included in development projects. The National Housing Corporation built some social housing in Nairobi in the

1980s, but the supply failed to meet the rapid population growth as rural migrants came to Nairobi seeking economic opportunities, education, and other services. By the 1990s, slum demolitions were common again, displacing an estimated 30,000 residents in 1991 alone. The UN's 2000 Millennium Development Goals (MDGs) campaign was called Cities Without Slums, and while it aimed to improve the lives of 100 million slum dwellers by 2020, it mostly contributed to the Kenyan government's continuing to demolish slums and evict residents to meet these international objectives.

Today, about 65 percent of Nairobi's population lives in informal settlements or slums, which occupy only 10 percent of the city's land area. Many residents of the city's slums work informal day jobs and rent a small 10-foot-by-10-foot shack made of tin, almost none of which have internal running water or a toilet. Yet the informal workers of Nairobi's slums support about 75 percent of the city's economy, and they are increasingly powerful politically (Figure Box 3.1).

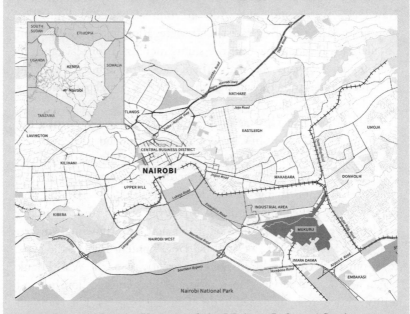

Figure Box 3.1 Nairobi, Kenya, and the Mukuru Informal Settlement.

In Mukuru, the informal settlement discussed in the book, about 300,000 people live on about 600 acres adjacent to the city's industrial area. The area has regularly experienced fires and floods, has a railroad running through it, and gets the brunt of the noxious emissions from neighboring factories and dumpsites. It sits on privately held land, and in the 2000s, women in Mukuru mobilized to demand that the private landowners install life-supporting infrastructure to the tens of thousands of residents now living there. The landowners refused. However, Kenya's revised 2010 Constitution included a new guarantee of access to sanitation for all, and the women again mobilized and filed one of Kenya's first class-action lawsuits on behalf of 10,000 women, demanding that the government enforce their right to safe toilets. The Muungano Alliance, comprising Muungano wa Wanavijiji (the Kenyan federation of slum dwellers), Akiba Mashinani Trust (another nonprofit), and the Kenyan affiliate of the global NGO Slum/Shack Dwellers International (SDI), supported the women's case. In 2011, the residents and Muungano also filed a court case about landownership that resulted in an injunction to stop all evictions in Mukuru. The Muungano Alliance also recognized that Mukuru's residents faced other serious threats to their well-being, including pollution from neighboring industries and frequent flooding from a river that ran along the northern edge of the settlement. River flooding in Mukuru combined with human waste from the lack of sanitation, contributed to some of the largest cholera outbreaks in Nairobi in 2009, 2014, and again in 2017. These conditions contributed to community organizing and local data gathering by a partnership of residents, the Muungano Alliance, and universities, including my team at UC Berkeley. We helped gather the evidence to support the designation of Mukuru as a Special Planning Area (SPA), which provided a structured opportunity for thousands of residents to define the risks they faced and propose solutions. The SPA resulted in an integrated community improvement plan, and by 2020 tens of healing-focused projects, from new recreation spaces and roads, to sanitation and schools, to housing and hospitals, were being constructed.

Chapter 1

Cities of Trauma or Healing?

The fact that many of our cities, or more accurately neighborhoods and communities within our cities, have created environments that have harmed the poor, immigrants, informal workers, and BIPOC (Black, Indigenous, People of Color) is not just about social injustice but also about biological injustice. These places are causing and creating trauma and harm to our brains and bodies. They are making some people more susceptible to disease and causing others to suffer greater disability or to die earlier than they would in different circumstances. Science is increasingly pointing to how the places where we live, learn, and love shape our lives.

The trauma from urban inequities is leaving psychological, emotional, and physical wounds for many urban populations that cannot be easily erased or treated in a doctor's office or clinic. The antidote for urban traumas is cities for life. Cities for life identify the structural or root causes of the trauma, meaning they aim to change political systems, not just treat victims. They value local culture and pursue holistic health, which the World Health Organization defined in 1948 "as a complete state of physical, mental, and social well-being, not merely the absence of disease or infirmity." Cities for life lift up existing assets within communities and cultures, rather than focusing only on

hazards, bad behaviors, or risks. In many ways, most Western medical and public health systems are not focused on healing; rather than
promoting the inherent healing potential of the human body and our
places to live, they focus largely on treating and managing disease and
risks.

Health Is Much More Than Health Care

The world in 2020 seemed particularly focused on health, or perhaps
I should say disease. SARS-CoV-2, the infectious coronavirus that
was linked to COVID-19, emerged as the threat that medicine, public
health, and governments needed to address. Many pointed out that
social and political factors, rather than biological factors, made people
around the world more vulnerable to the virus. Racism had damaged
the bodies of BIPOC, compromising their immune systems and making them more susceptible to adverse health impacts from COVID-19.
People working in dangerous jobs, often not of their choice, were already exposed to unhealthy air or toxic chemicals that also made them
more susceptible to COVID-19. It also became clear in 2020 that living in a dense city like Shanghai or San Francisco (where death rates
from COVID-19 were quite low) did not pose the most significant
risk. Rather, social vulnerability, such as living in overcrowded housing,
working in precarious day labor jobs, and surviving on poverty-level
wages, made people most susceptible to disease.

The vulnerabilities and inequalities found in our living conditions,
public policies, and economic system that can make us sick are referred
to as the social determinants of health. The social determinants of
health suggest that where you live, the economic resources you have,
the degree of autonomy you have at work, the power you have to influence decisions about your life, and the quality of the natural environment you have access to are greater predictors of whether you will get
sick, from almost any cause, than if you have regular medical care. Of
course, these are socially patterned circumstances, since some groups
(primarily those that are White and wealthy) and some places benefit
from historical privileges, such as intergenerational transfers of wealth,
power, and land. So when we talk about who is "healthy" and why we

see persistent patterns of disease distributions and early death among certain groups, we must look to societal stratification for answers.

The example of overweight and obesity can help illuminate the importance of the social determinants concept. We might seek explanations for why entire groups of people or communities are overweight or obese by looking at their diets and lifestyles. We might hear our physician tell us that the key to reducing weight is to eat less, exercise more, drink less alcohol, and get more sleep. We might also be told that the reason we are overweight is due to "bad genetics," and there is little that we can do about it. In this case, we might be advised to take certain pharmaceutical medications to manage any adverse biological impacts from being overweight, such as high blood pressure or diabetes. These explanations constitute what we call the biomedical model of disease.

The biomedical model of disease looks for explanations of why certain groups of people are more sick than others by examining molecular-level pathogens brought about by individual behaviors or hereditary genetics. The implications for treatment and action, according to the biomedical model, are clear: see your clinician often, change your unhealthy lifestyles, be educated about your risks, and if you get sick, be sure to manage your illness with drug treatments. The experts in the biomedical model are doctors and biomedical researchers. This is what I and others call disease management.

Figure 1.1 shows a framework for health equity. The biomedical model is represented by the two columns on the right, Individual Behaviors and Genetics, and Morbidity and Mortality. The biomedical interventions for reducing health risks tend to be education and behavior change, case management, and health care.

An alternative to the biomedical model is to look at the social determinants of health and view the root causes that shape exposures, behaviors, and access to care. This would start with asking those who are overweight if they have the financial resources to afford healthy foods and if such foods are readily available near where they live. Are the foods that are available culturally appropriate? We would also want to know if people live in an area with high concentrations of toxic air pollution or other endocrine-disrupting chemicals (e.g., the pesticide DDT, plastics, detergents, and flame retardants), all of which are suspected of causing damage to the gut microbiome and interrupting the metabolism of fats and carbohydrates.[1,2,3] We might also ask if people live in an area that is inundated with advertising and incentives to purchase inexpensive but highly processed foods, such as those in the dollar-menu at fast-food restaurants. We might ask if there are public policies, domestic and even international trade agreements, that subsidize high-calorie foods, such as grains, but not fruits and vegetables. We would also want to know if a person is working at a high-stress job or not working at all or is housing insecure, perhaps because of discrimination in education and employment based on ethnicity, immigration status, race, disability status, or sexual orientation. We would want to know if people live in fear of violence. These social experiences can lead to chronic stress, which, as I describe in more detail later in the chapter, contribute to the constant release of the hormones adrenaline and cortisol, which can cause fat accumulation, especially in the abdomen. The constant stress-induced release of cortisol can dysregulate glucose and signal the body to crave sugars.[4,5]

This approach is what public health calls the ecological model. The ecological model recognizes the role of our living conditions on our exposures to environmental and social stressors (as shown by the middle column, Living and Working Conditions, in Figure 1.1). The ecological model acknowledges that living conditions are not random; they are actively created by institutions, including government policies and laws, private sector decisions, and pressure by civil society organizations (as shown in the first two columns, Social Values and Institutions, in Figure 1.1). Who has power to influence these institutions is rooted in social dynamics, often with a long history.

The ecological model suggests that the expertise needed to address disease and promote health and well-being is not just held by physicians, but by everyday people living with social and environmental burdens, as well as the organizations that aim to support greater health equity.

Instead of asking the individual to take all the responsibility for their behaviors, we would look to how living conditions shape those behaviors. We would look at ways to change economic conditions that can constrain our choices and behaviors. Changing those living

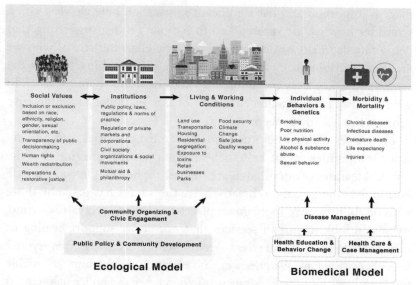

Figure 1.1 A framework for urban health equity.

environments and economic conditions means turning to existing public policies or creating new ones, and particularly policies not in public health and medicine but in areas such as housing, land use, immigration, and education.

When I discuss the ways cities can help us heal in this book, I am looking to the ecological model for ways to create more inclusive and equitable society, not just a healthier version of the current one.

Why Do Our Urban Places Matter for Healing?

Urban place is not just the background or "stage" for individual relations, as much of public health and medicine and the biomedical model might want you to believe. Places shape human relations and human relations can in turn, push back and shape places.

We might think about space as a geographic spot in the universe, and space becomes "a place" as people, practices, representations, and meanings are assigned to it.[6] We make places. In this view, place can both constitute and constrain social relations. The dynamic notion of place is important and has significant impacts on how we view cities. Consider how we are often asked to list our gender, suggesting that being female, male, or nonbinary is a static characteristic of who we are. Yet describing someone as female, male, or nonbinary is not the same as grasping how social relations and institutions are *gendered*. In a similar way, place should be thought of as a relational and interactive process, not a static concept.

How does all this help us to understand how cities and our urban communities might help us heal? First, we can imagine that the physical features of our urban places matter for health. Do we have safe housing? Is the air safe to breathe? Are the streets navigable by those with disabilities? Are there green places to play and recreate? Second, we would look for urban services that can either support healing or contribute to trauma and stress. Are the schools available to everyone? Does everyone have water, sewer, and electricity? Are there affordable food markets? Does public transit stop here? Are the police using racist stop-and-frisk strategies and disproportionately harming young Black men? Are there health care and other services in case of an emergency?

Third, it highlights that the physical design of our place and the presence or absence of services happen through social, sometimes public, processes, not by magic. There are accountable institutions that shape, create, and re-create our places, and when we have the power to shape these decisions, we feel healthier. Healthy urban place making is a process of governance—or the collective decision making about what kind of society we want to be. Urban governance can heal when those who have been harmed by earlier decisions are involved in generating norms, rules, and laws to remedy those harms and deliver justice in their eyes. Some have even suggested that urban decision making can be therapeutic when it is inclusive, well structured, and trauma informed, and when it redresses harms and changes the institutions that created harmful decisions in the first place.[7,8] Yet governance can harm when collective decisions ignore current and past traumas, exclude those who experience trauma, and are dominated by unaccountable, unresponsive, and corrupt government, media, and corporate institutions.

Just as our places shape politics and policy, our urban places can support or constrain cultural expression and social interactions. Are there places for free expression of art and music? Are youth allowed to gather and build connections? Are seniors supported to be active and to navigate the community safely? These social and cultural interactions are mediated through the rules we create and the material forms we design and build; if there is no safe sidewalk or accessible public space in the place where you live, it is unlikely that you can partake in the "sidewalk ballet," as Jane Jacobs the American urbanist characterized those planned and unplanned human-to-human interactions that give communities life in her 1961 classic book, *The Death and Life of Great American Cities*.

Finally, urban places can influence health as they are interpreted, narrated, perceived, felt, understood, and imagined. The reputation of an area influences whether people, and which groups, might come to a place, and whether banks and businesses will invest. It can also stigmatize individuals, particularly when they leave their place (i.e., you are from *there?*). Places' meanings are contested and contingent, and infused with social power dynamics. A place might be labeled "safe" by some but "dangerous" by others.

In all these ways, urban places can help us heal or perpetuate trauma and stress, since poorly designed and managed places can sustain difference and hierarchy in ways that exclude and segregate. Displacement can make people and communities invisible and sever historic connections to sacred places. Yet, as I suggest throughout this book, the healing power of place making and maintaining is in the dynamic ways that places can be inclusive; dismantle hierarchies; provide for cultural, educational, and economic opportunities; encourage supportive social networks; and provide safety and security.

My Postal Code Is More Important Than My Genetic Code

Where I live in Berkeley, California, I can ride the BART train, our regional public transport system, about 15 minutes to the east to the Walnut Creek station. For those who live in the zip code around the Walnut Creek station, life expectancy is over 85 years. A few stops, 20 minutes and about 16 miles away at the 12th Street/Oakland City

Center BART station, life expectancy is less than 73 years (see Figure 1.2). In London, life expectancy around the Tube station Star Lane is about 75.3 years in contrast to 96.4 years for those living near the Oxford Circus Tube station. The differences in life expectancy found along London's Tube, often just a few stops away, were equivalent to those between the UK and Guatemala.[9] Professor Emmanuel Vigneron found similar stark spatial disparities in life expectancy along the RER metro line in Paris.[10] In Sidney, Australia, the wealthy suburbs have an average life expectancy of 87 years, while the districts with life expectancy between 69 and 72 years are in the poorest parts of west and southwestern Sydney.[11]

These spatial differences are health inequities, or what the World Health Organization describes as differences in health status across place and population groups "that are systemic, avoidable, unfair and unjust."[12] Why should the district where you live predict your life expectancy? This isn't just a phenomenon of wealthy America or Europe. In Nairobi, Kenya, the child mortality rate for those living in that city's slums or informal settlements is more than double the rate for those living in other areas of the city. In Latin America more Afro-descendent populations live in informal settlements or slums, and the infant mortality rates for that population exceed the rate for non-Afro-descendants.[13] Of course, life expectancy and mortality rates are important but crude measures, since they can mask the lifelong burdens of poor health, stress, and disability that occur in these same places. So, to understand how urban places can act to harm or heal, it matters where people live, who they are, and, as I will show, how decisions are made to either support or stymie opportunities for both people and places.

Wounded Cities: Some Sources of Urban Trauma

How do our cities wound us, create trauma, and in some cases cause death based on where we live? Cities around the world are marked by structures of violence and exclusion and were never designed to promote healing and health for all, just for an elite few. It is important to understand how history, policy, and institutions cocreate damaging stress and trauma, particularly for the urban poor and BIPOC.

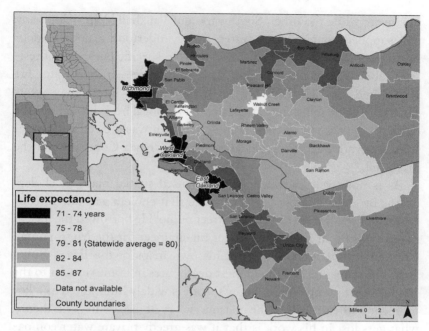

Figure 1.2 Life expectancy in the San Francisco Bay Area, 2010.

Many modern cities emerged from slave labor, particularly in the Americas. Spanish colonialists used the Law of the Indies to design cities that denied indigenous people access to their resources and to protect settler colonists from the "natives." Colonial cities in Africa and Asia were built for extracting people and resources.[14] Smokestacks and crowded workplaces in industrializing Europe were viewed as signs of progress, not danger.

Social reformers began to question the living and working conditions of cities in the nineteenth century. During a cholera outbreak in 1854 in London, the physician John Snow investigated why his patients were dying. He went to Broad Street in Soho, documenting the location of all cases by house, the location of wastewater cesspools, and the water source of the victims. Two competing water companies provided water to Broad Street, and both used water from the Thames that had been contaminated by sewage. However, by 1853, one company, Lambeth Waterworks Company, had moved its intake source farther upstream, while the other, Southwark and Vauxhall Water Company, still supplied contaminated water. Snow undertook a door-to-door investigation of cholera mortality and asked specific questions of residents about the qualities—odor, clarity, and taste—of their water. He also visited the Lion Brewery on Broad Street to interview workers there who went about their work sipping the local beer throughout the day since it was part of their wage. Their beer was brewed with water from a private water supplier called the New River Company, not the local well.

As is now well known, John Snow used spatial maps of cholera deaths by street address to hypothesize that cholera was due to contaminated water from the Broad Street pump. He borrowed the idea of mapmaking from Edmund Cooper, an engineer for the Metropolitan Commission of Sewers, to draft his own maps of the Broad Street area. The maps showed the highest death rates in homes closest to the Broad Street pump. While Snow's work is widely interpreted as a key moment in the shift from the miasma theory of disease to germ theory, what gets lost in his work is that it was greedy private water companies that were ultimately responsible for the deaths. It was the companies' willingness to supply cheap water from the River Thames, which was known to also be part of the city's sewer system. After Snow's findings, the company reluctantly followed the Metropolis Water Act 1852, which regulated water supply companies in London and required them to meet certain water quality standards.[15]

Public health was also used to justify exclusion of immigrants and deny them livelihoods. In 1882, the United States passed the Chinese Exclusion Act, which made it illegal for Chinese workers to come to America and for existing Chinese nationals to become citizens. The act was grounded in racism, xenophobia, and a belief in public health called contagion, or the idea that there could be a direct passage of poison from one person to another. A few years later, Yick Wo, a Chinese American in San Francisco, was told he would have to shut his laundry down since it was in a wooden building, not one made of brick or stone. San Francisco had passed an ordinance that outlawed laundries in wood buildings, citing potential fire dangers and impacts on the sanitary conditions of the surrounding neighborhood. Yet 95 percent of the laundries in San Francisco at the time were in wood buildings owned by Chinese, and the City denied all but one of them a permit to operate under the new ordinance. Yick Wo fought the new law and his challenge reached the Supreme Court. The Court ruled that a law that was seemingly race-neutral was administered in a prejudicial manner, and therefore violated the Equal Protection Clause of the 14th Amendment. The law was overturned, but only after hundreds of Chinese business owners had lost their livelihoods.

Two women activists, Alice Hamilton and Florence Kelley, joined forces in 1890s Chicago to confront unsafe and inequitable labor practices by increasingly powerful privately owned urban industries. Hamilton was a professor of pathology at the Woman's Medical School, Northwestern University, and would go on to become the first woman appointed to the faculty at Harvard Medical School. Kelley had a degree from Cornell. The two met at Hull House in Chicago, a settlement house founded by Jane Adams that served immigrants by offering them a range of services while also doing action research about living and working conditions afflicting the urban poor. Hamilton and Kelley practiced "shoe leather epidemiology," where they went inside factories and sweat shops to document conditions with, not just for, immigrants. The participatory urban health data helped them to successfully advocate for occupational safety standards. They helped to pass the Child Labor Act, preventing children from working in factories, in 1916.[16] Kelley also led a study of poverty in Chicago, "A Special Investigation of the Slums of Great Cities," in which she worked with local residents to document conditions and offer policy and practice suggestions for improving economic status and living conditions.

Racism and the Science of Cities

As cities continued to grow, African Americans from the southern United States migrated north to find jobs. The dual threat of Black and immigrant workers in cities, contributed to White racists promoting a "science" that explained why Blacks and immigrants were inherently inferior to European descendants. Francis Galton published *Natural Inheritance* in 1894, which claimed to prove that there was hereditary transmission of intelligence. Galton and his followers used quantitative measures, such as skull size, to "scientifically prove" that people of African descent were innately inferior to Anglo-Europeans.[17] This pseudoscience was called eugenics, and argued that race was a valid biological category and that the genes which determined race were linked to those that determined health. A eugenic society of biologists gained prominence in cities as leaders looked to blame the poor and non-Whites for their problems rather than seeing these as social responsibilities requiring public resources.[18]

The ground-breaking work of W.E.B. Du Bois, among others, challenged eugenics. In his 1906 edited publication, *The Health and Physique of the Negro American*, Du Bois used statistics from northern and southern cities to argue that health inequities facing African Americans were a consequence of their poorer economic, social, and sanitary conditions, compared to those of Whites. Du Bois noted, "If the population were divided as to social and economic condition the matter of race would be almost entirely eliminated. Poverty's death rate in Russia shows a much greater divergence from the rate among the well-to-do than the difference between Negroes and white Americans.... Even in consumption all the evidence goes to show that it is not a racial disease but a social disease. The rate in certain sections among whites in New York and Chicago is higher than the Negroes of some cities."[19]

Du Bois and an emerging group of urban reformers argued that racialized poverty and discrimination ought to be the priorities for public health. Yet these were controversial positions that were not widely embraced by the emerging field of modern city planning. Nelson Lewis, author of one of the first city planning texts, *The Planning of the Modern City*, captured this tension and suggested that planning be separate from social justice and health:

> There are many who believe that the chief purposes of city planning are social, that the problems of housing, the provision of recreation and amusement for the people, the control and even the ownership and operation of all public utilities, the establishment and conduct of public markets, the collection and disposal of wastes, the protection of public health, the building of hospitals, the care of paupers, criminals and the insane, and all of the other activities of the mod-

ern city are all a part of city planning. All of these, however, are matters of administration rather than of planning.[20]

By the 1920s, there was a profound shift in urban disease distribution in cities of both America and Europe. C. E. Winslow showed that from 1875 to 1925 in New York City, communicable diseases had decreased, and noncommunicable diseases had increased significantly. As Winslow reported, diseases such as scarlet fever, diphtheria, and diarrhea for children under age 5 had declined by 99, 95, and 93 percent, respectively. Winslow also showed that in this same time period in New York City cancer, heart disease, and diseases of the arteries had increased 176, 187, and 650 percent, respectively.[21] It was increasingly recognized that urban environments could shape human health, although place-based interventions that later emerged were only focused on helping the White middle class and on displacing the poor from their neighborhoods.

What had emerged in city planning was the practice of land-use zoning, which specified the type of use for each parcel of land, such as residential, commercial, or industrial. Zoning focused city planning on the functions or activities that could occur in specific districts of cities, but not on the performance or impact of these functions on human well-being. However, legal challenges to zoning, particularly in the United States, were justified in the landmark 1926 *Euclid v. Ambler* Supreme Court case by referring to its ability to promote "health and safety" by separating residential areas from the "dangers of fire, contagion and disorder." In practice, zoning tended to exclude the poor from health-promoting services and increased spatial segregation through such practices as racial covenants and exclusionary clauses that denied BIPOC access to large swaths of urban and suburban areas and forced them to live in increasingly polluted and crowded areas that were poorly served by basic services.[22]

Designed for Discrimination and White Supremacy

In the period before World War II, urban designers were enlisted to help shape "hygienic" communities and cities. Clarence Perry's Neighborhood Unit idea, first offered in 1921, took hold with the American

Public Health Association (APHA) Committee on the Hygiene of Housing. The APHA committee adopted the Neighborhood Unit design scheme as the basis for two reports; one, in 1938, *Basic Principles of Healthful Housing*, and a second in 1948, *Planning the Neighborhood*. The earlier housing guide detailed thirty essential health aims that were believed to be the minimum required for the "promotion of physical, mental, and social health, essential in low-rent as well as high-cost housing, on the farm as well as in the city dwelling." The latter document set standards for the "environment of residential areas," defined as "the area served by an elementary school," and emphasized that "no perfection in the building or equipment of the home can compensate for an environment which lacks the amenities essential for decent living. We must build not merely homes but neighborhoods if we are to build wisely for the future of America. . . . In recent years it has been clearly recognized that the effect of substandard environment extends beyond direct threats to physiological health, and that it involves quite as significant detriments to mental and emotional well-being."[23]

These public health–endorsed housing and neighborhood design guidelines found their way into US housing policies in the 1940s and '50s. Designed into postwar housing policies in the US were three features that worked to traumatize the poor and communities of color; denying People of Color loans for housing, urban renewal that razed existing neighborhoods, and redlining. The New Deal helped create the Federal Housing Administration and included programs for the federal government to subsidize the underwriting of mortgages that were only offered to Whites and reserved for suburban single-family housing, not older inner-city housing.[24] Federal housing policies throughout the 1940s and '50s required that urban "blight" be removed and replaced with modern housing, contributing to the widespread demolition of existing, largely Black communities. This program, what James Baldwin called "Negro removal"[25] displaced once vibrant cultural and social connections, such as in Pittsburgh's Hill District and San Francisco's Tenderloin. This displacement of urban African American communities resulted in what psychiatrist Mindy Fullilove has called "root shock," or the "traumatic stress reaction to the destruction of all or parts of one's emotional ecosystem"[26] that threatens the whole body's ability to function. According to Fullilove, urban renewal contributed to trauma-related mental disorders, stress from losing family wealth and housing, and prolonged grief, all of which can increase hypertension, stroke, heart disease, and other diseases. For Fullilove, urban places can act as a kind of "exoskeleton" that help protect our social and physical well-being.

Redlining and Intergenerational Trauma

The term *redlining* comes from the Home Owners' Loan Corporation (HOLC) categorization, which ranked as "high risk" some neighborhoods whose residents should not be given access to mortgages and thus were colored red on maps.[27] The HOLC also created the City Survey Program, which appointed local bankers and real estate men to appraisal committees. These committees rated each neighborhood as being in one of four financial risk and lending categories, from the most desirable (labeled A and colored green on maps) through the least desirable (labeled D and colored red on maps). The level of desirability was based almost entirely on race, since neighborhoods that were predominantly African American and immigrant were labeled D and colored red (thus redlining) while areas that were predominantly White and nonimmigrant were labeled A and colored in green. The color-coded "residential security maps," were widely adopted by the private banking and mortgage industry and led to residents in redlined areas being denied access to loans by local banks, limiting Black homeownership and making it difficult to improve older housing, create family wealth, and address neighborhood disadvantages. A lack of investment meant houses fell into disrepair, health hazards like mold and lead paint increased, and industrial sites were more likely to be located near redlined neighborhoods since property values remained low without new investments. As areas declined, retailers left, including grocery stores, which meant residents had less access to healthy food.

Though redlining was banned in the US as part of the Fair Housing Act of 1968, a majority of those areas that had been deemed hazardous (and were subsequently redlined) remain low income, communities of color, while those deemed desirable remain predominantly White communities with above-average incomes today.[28] Redlining helped entrench racial residential segregation and the related traumas from persistent poverty and limited wealth creation. Redlining contributed to capital flight from Black neighborhoods, and today redlined neighborhoods are plagued by high-rates of gun violence, have fewer parks, and have higher concentrations of pollution than areas that were not redlined.[29]

My own research looked at the relationships between historical redlining and health outcomes in 2017 in Atlanta, Chicago, Cleveland, Los Angeles, Miami, New York, San Francisco/Oakland metro area, and St. Louis. My coauthors and I used digital HOLC security maps, overlaid them with today's census tracts, and associated those redlined areas with census-tract-level health outcome data from the Centers for Disease Control and Prevention's 500 Cities dataset.[30]

We found that in census tracts today that were redlined in the 1940s, the median household income is significantly lower in red areas ($39,800) than in green or low-risk census tracts ($61,200). The percentage of People of Color was greatest in previously redlined neighborhoods (63.7 percent) compared to 37.8 percent in census tracts that received a green risk grade. Most surprisingly, redlined areas in almost every city we looked at have higher rates of cancer, diabetes, and poor self-reported mental health, but there were variations across metropolitan regions.[31] In Los Angeles, formerly redlined areas have high rates of asthma and diabetes today, while in Miami formerly redlined areas have the highest rates of stroke and poor mental health. As William Faulkner stated, "The past is never dead. It's not even past."

Planned Shrinkage

By the 1960s and early 1970s, American cities had lost much of their White population, and new businesses relocated to the suburbs. As their tax base eroded, cities were faced with declining budgets and very little fiscal help from the federal government. Racial inequalities and protests against these inequities in housing, schools, workplaces, and land-use policies emerged as a powerful civil rights movement. Facing fiscal stress, many cities adopted a policy that came to be known as planned shrinkage. Planned shrinkage was the closing and removal of municipal services, such as police and fire stations, garbage collection, and hospitals, in Black and Brown communities. A 1976 *New York Times* article, "City Housing Administrator Proposes 'Planned Shrinkage' of Some Slums," noted that some activities, such as suspending housing rehabilitation, were already taking place, and "the strategy would involve phasing out services after the city had induced people to move elsewhere."[32] This strategy was linked to one called *benign neglect*, put forward a few years earlier by Daniel Moynihan, then counselor to President Nixon. Benign neglect turned out to be a racist strategy to remove social programs for and municipal services in African American communities.[33] By the mid-1970s, 70 percent of the fire stations in the Black neighborhoods of the South Bronx and Bushwick, Brooklyn, had been closed, many due to modeling by the New York City Rand Institute showing these services were inefficient and ineffective.[34,35]

The impacts of these strategies included fires that burned throughout the night, garbage piling up on city streets, ambulances refusing to pick up patients, and delayed care due to lack of health care facilities. The burned-out, tooth-gapped neighborhoods that emerged from these urban policies, were then inundated with crack, widespread HIV and TB infections, and the destruction of family and community ties.[36]

Policing, Incarceration, and Urban Trauma

The lack of services and heavy-handed police responses to poverty contributed to civil unrest in many cities from Los Angeles to Newark. The 1968, Kerner Commission aimed to understand why poor, largely African American communities were pushing back against dehumanizing practices by police and other urban actors. The Report of the National Advisory Commission on Civil Disorders stated, "What white Americans have never fully understood—but what the Negro can never forget—is that white society is deeply implicated in the ghetto. White institutions created it, white institutions maintain it, and white society condones it." The Kerner Commission recommendations were to invest in housing to improve living conditions for African Americans, create at least two million jobs in 3 years, end the racial segregation of neighborhoods, and increase the racial diversity of urban police forces. However, President Johnson did not act on the commission's recommendations, and instead passed the Crime Control and Safe Streets Act of 1968, which viewed urban police as "frontline soldiers" and increased federal funding and military-style weapons for local police departments.[37] Police increased arrests and incarcerations, in part to justify the increased funding, and sentencing for nonviolent crimes, such as New York's Rockefeller drug laws and California's Determinant Sentencing Act, mandated long prison sentences for drug possession. These policies contributed to the massive removal of vibrant, mostly young, Black men from communities, traumatizing their partners, families, and children. Those that returned from prison often came home with infectious diseases that were widespread in jails and prisons, such as hepatitis C, TB, and HIV. Their felony convictions locked them out of employment, public housing, and voting, among other rights. Returning prisoners have a higher prevalence of hypertension, mental illness, and depression, and women with a family member incarcerated have an increased risk of heart attack, low-birth-weight babies, and dying during childbirth.[38]

From Neighborhoods to Neurons: Trauma, Toxic Stress, and Human Health

In 2000, the US Institute of Medicine and National Research Council convened a workshop to explore the impacts of early life events on the developing child's brain. The workshop's report, *From Neurons to Neighborhoods*, presented a range of evidence about how early life experiences influence brain development and behavior.[39] The report claimed to represent the authoritative science behind human development. In an updated report in 2012, the workshop committee emphatically stated that human development differences were associated with social and economic circumstances and that urgent early-life interventions were necessary to stave off hardships later in life. They stated that harmful prenatal and early postnatal experiences that disrupted nurturing and dependable relations were creating neurotoxic exposures for some children. Human relationships, the report noted, were the building blocks of healthy development. The 2012 Institute of Medicine report called for urgent action, on par with that which had been directed toward smoking cessation, to enhance the quality of those environments and experiences that will promote healthy human development. However, despite the title, nowhere in the original report or in the 2012 update did the committee mention which specific physical and social characteristics of urban neighborhoods were contributing to "toxic exposures" or which features of neighborhoods need to change in order to promote healthy human development.[40]

The brief history of urban policy and planning offered here attempts to fill the gap left by the *Neurons to Neighborhoods* reports by starting with the urban policies and decisions that have shaped neurotoxic traumas in our urban neighborhoods. How do these place-based traumas influence our health? How do the traumas of inequitable urban policies and practices contribute to poor health, and how do we promote healing with impacted communities? These policies and practices have produced toxic stress in the lives of the poor and People of Color, and this chronic stress is responsible for sustained poverty, violence, and poorer health in these communities.[41,42]

There are at least three kinds of stress in our lives. First, there is positive stress, which arises when we face a personal challenge that we are able to overcome. A second type of stress is tolerable stress, which is an adverse life event that is made bearable because we have some ability to buffer the stress, such as supportive relationships, material resources to see a therapist or to take a mediation class, or even the ability to physically escape the source of the stress.

The third and most dangerous type of stress, and the one caused by the traumas experienced in urban communities over the last century or more, is called toxic stress. Toxic stress is more than the everyday anxiety-producing event. It is caused by frequent and sustained adverse events in the absence of buffers and supportive resources. This stress can even occur before a person is born, such as when a pregnant woman experiences racism or poverty. Toxic stress can start early in life and continue as we age. In this situation we are always on alert fearing danger or rejection; we might experience a "brain fog'" that keeps us from staying on task and engaging fully in the task at hand. The body's reaction under constant stress is called allostatic overload.[43]

When the stress is chronic, the brain and body begin to change (Figure 1.3). The constant release of stress hormones cortisol, norepinephrine, and adrenaline deteriorate the hippocampus, the part of the brain associated with learning and spatial memory. The stress hormones overstimulate the amygdala, the part of the brain that regulates emotion, fear, anxiety, and aggression. The same hormones damage the medial prefrontal cortex, the part of the brain responsible for decision making, working memory, impulse control, and mood. Cytokines, or proteins that signal cells to trigger an immune response, produce an internal inflammation response when overstimulated due to toxic stress.[44]

This constant state of internal hypervigilance starts to wear away at the body's systems. It is akin to being in constant overdrive. Researchers have called this process weathering.[45] Under toxic stress circumstances, the oversecretion of cortisol and adrenaline triggers other biological responses, such as poor glucose regulation and constant feelings of hunger that can contribute to chronic diseases, including overweight, obesity, and diabetes. The internal inflammation that is supposed to protect vital organs during an emergency contributes to coronary artery plaque buildup and calcification, which lead to hypertension, cardiovascular disease, and stroke, the leading causes of disease, disability, and death in most places around the world.

Weathering also damages our chromosomes and makes us age prematurely. The stress response damages something called telomeres, which are caplike features at the ends of chromosomes that help protect them when cells divide. Shortening telomeres are an indication of aging and diminishing health overall.[46] The toxic stress response also shapes whether a gene will be turned "on" or "off." This is called epigenetics.[47] Thus our experiences, such as chronic toxic stressors, can rearrange the epigenetic marks that govern gene expression and change whether and how genes release the information they carry.[48] Studies of toxic stress's effects have revealed that our DNA is not our destiny; rather, our social experiences can shape whether and how our genes release the information they carry.[49,50]

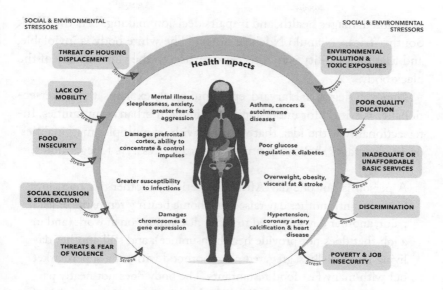

Figure 1.3 Urban toxic stress and health impacts.

The Pair of ACEs

The repeated traumas that happen early in life are called adverse child-hood experiences (ACEs). Many ACEs are racially patterned, meaning that experiences of physical abuse and neglect, parental incarceration, homelessness, and being placed in the foster care system dispropor-tionately burden BIPOC communities not because of personal char-acteristics but due to generations of systemic racism, or laws, norms, and practices that have devalued and dehumanized the lives and living conditions of African Americans.[51] ACEs include childhood physical and sexual abuse, experiences with and witnessing violence, extreme deprivation, homelessness and poverty, and living in a household with a substance abuser or in a home that has lost a person to incarcera-tion. Childhood abuse and exposure to family violence can adversely impact a young person's emotional regulation, aggression, social com-petence, and interpersonal relationships.[52] Racism is another common and too frequently unaddressed form of trauma, both individually and within institutions, that contributes to the dehumanization of People of Color, damages health, and impairs decision making.[53] As the Black South African Njabulo Ndebele notes, "The white body is inviolable, and that inviolability is in direct proportion to the vulnerability of the black body."[54]

Nancy Krieger, a Harvard epidemiologist, explains that intersectionality is critical for understanding trauma in urban communities. Intersectionality is the idea that we carry with us multiple "marginalities" or disadvantages that can contribute to toxic stress. As Krieger notes,

> A person is not one day African American, another day born low birth weight, another day raised in a home bearing remnants of lead paint, another day subjected to racial discrimination at work (and in a job that does not provide health insurance), and still another day living in a racially segregated neighborhood without a supermarket but with many fast food restaurants. The body does not neatly partition these experiences—all of which may serve to increase risk of uncontrolled hypertension, and some of which may likewise lead to comorbidity, for example, diabetes, thereby further worsening health status.[55]

Our bodies do not partition experiences with inequality, and these experiences act cumulatively as stressors on the immune and neurological systems that lead to a range of diseases and premature death.

Yet the urban policies (or lack thereof), such as urban renewal and benign neglect, also produce neighborhood-level traumas. These traumas are in our everyday environment, and can include expensive but poor-quality housing; lack of economic mobility; low-quality schools; dangerous streets; too few parks, trees, or green spaces; street-level violence; chronic noise; toxic air and other environmental pollutants; and what has been described as a general "neighborhood disorder."[56] Neighborhood disorder is an idea that has a long and controversial history in urban sociology.[57] In general it states that "disorder" is the observed or perceived breakdown of social control, contributing to chronic fear, insecurity, and distrust, which can cause residents to withdraw from community life and can break social connections.[58] Neighborhood conditions are especially impactful on the development of children.[59] Thus we can think of a pair of ACEs coproducing traumas in many urban communities: adverse childhood experiences and adverse community environments. In Figure 1.4, the leaves on the tree represent the symptoms more frequently identified in clinical, education, and social work settings. The "roots" that give rise to the childhood experiences are in our communities, public policies, and corporate decisions, and they include segregation, lack of quality education, unemployment, insecure housing, environmental pollution, and heavy-handed policing. These area-level stressors also contribute to trauma (Figure 1.4).[60]

The "pair of ACEs" disproportionately traumatizes urban BIPOC.[61] Policing and mass incarceration have produced intergenerational traumas, particularly for Black men and their families. Black men have a higher number of lifetime police stops than any other population group and are three times more likely to report posttraumatic stress disorder (PTSD) than the general population.[62] In New York City and Baltimore, Black men were three times more likely than others to experience police violence, and over 20 percent of these victims experienced adverse psychological impacts.[63] In Chicago, researchers found that exposure to multigenerational poverty and community violence was associated with aggression, delinquency, and PTSD symptoms, and that Black youth in these communities were emotionally desensitized to community violence as gun conflicts increased.[64]

Trauma of Slow Urban Violence

The author Rob Nixon describes the "slow violence" that occurs when policies and practices contribute to the poor simultaneously struggling to remain in their housing, pay for food and energy, access education and services, and being exposed every day to high levels of toxic pollution.[65] Slow violence leads to what Nixon calls delayed destruction of culture and communities, and turns our attention away from the highly visible events. It points to the incremental and accretive traumas that occur over time and space, such as the genocide of Indigenous peoples around the world, or the ongoing destruction caused by the Chernobyl nuclear disaster.

Eric Klinenberg's book *Heat Wave*, highlights how the everyday disasters present in urban communities are created by policies and can result in fatal consequences. Klinenberg set out to study the Chicago

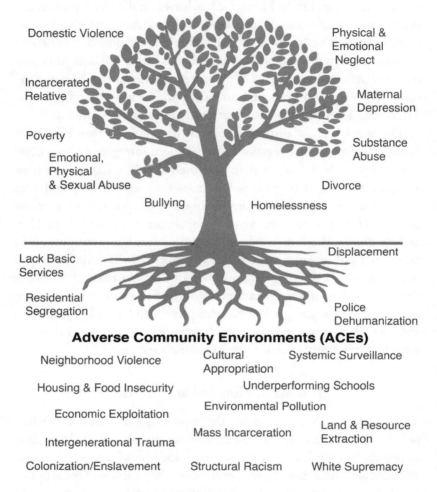

Adverse Childhood Experiences (ACEs)

Domestic Violence

Physical & Emotional Neglect

Incarcerated Relative

Maternal Depression

Poverty

Substance Abuse

Emotional, Physical & Sexual Abuse

Divorce

Bullying

Homelessness

Lack Basic Services

Displacement

Residential Segregation

Police Dehumanization

Adverse Community Environments (ACEs)

Neighborhood Violence

Cultural Appropriation

Systemic Surveillance

Housing & Food Insecurity

Underperforming Schools

Economic Exploitation

Environmental Pollution

Intergenerational Trauma

Mass Incarceration

Land & Resource Extraction

Colonization/Enslavement

Structural Racism

White Supremacy

Figure 1.4 Pair of ACEs. (Source: Wendy R. Ellis and William H. Dietz, "A New Framework for Addressing Adverse Childhood and Community Experiences: The Building Community Resilience Model," *Academic Pediatrics* **17**, no. 7 (2017): S86–S93, https://doi.org/10.1016/j.acap.2016.12.011)

heat wave of 1995, and asked why the African American community of the North Lawndale neighborhood had higher heat-related deaths than the neighboring Latino community of South Lawndale, called Little Village. He performed a "social autopsy," a technique that looked at the history, policies, and migration patterns that impacted these places. He also used spatial mapping, photographs, interviews, oral histories, and a review of social organizations, such as churches and block groups.

The study found that a combination of public policies, including racial residential segregation, policing and incarceration, and redlining, combined to shape physical and social despair in North Lawndale. Elderly African Americans in North Lawndale were stranded among abandoned lots and fearful to leave their homes due to street violence during the heat wave. These same policies did not have the same effect in the largely Latino Little Village neighborhood. Despite high individual and family poverty in Little Village, the community had a robust informal local economy, and cultural and religious activities that contributed to more street life and social interactions. Elderly residents in Little Village were less fearful than those in North Lawndale and got out of their homes to cool off during the heat wave. The social interactions also encouraged social workers and church members to check on vulnerable residents during the heat crisis.

For Klinenberg, "the deep sources of the tragedy were the everyday disasters that the city tolerates, takes for granted, or has officially forgotten," and the heat wave sped up and "made visible the hazardous social conditions that were always present but difficult to perceive." The urban policies he identified created an "emergency in slow motion" that was specific to the African American community. The social autopsy is an important first step in identifying the political organs that have created slow violence and related traumas in urban communities, and moving toward a trauma-informed, but healing-centered approach for rebuilding communities.

From Trauma Informed to Healing Centered

Cities for Life demands a new, trauma-informed and healing-centered approach to rebuilding our communities and cites. We have known for decades about the multigenerational traumas caused by chronic urban poverty, but we still seem content to treat these as clinical or individual issues. A trauma-informed approach involves a commitment to four key principles:

1. *Antireductionism*—is an approach to healing that avoids a focus on single behaviors, diseases, or risk factors, and reifying some social groups or neighborhoods as if they were homogeneous. This is a rejection of the biomedical model of disease and aims to rehumanize those at the center of toxic stress and structural violence. As Audre Lorde reminds us, "There is no such thing as a single-issue struggle because we do not live single-issue lives."[66] This principle also supports healing by acknowledging that if a problem is framed too narrowly, too broadly, or wrongly, the solution will suffer from the same defects. For instance, an urban air pollution control strategy focused on a single pollutant cannot produce adequate knowledge about the environmental health consequences of exposure to multiple pollutants—the reality in many communities. Similarly, violence isn't just something that is interpersonal; it is found in the structures of government, law, capitalism, and racism. As described in this chapter, a deeply historical approach to the urban condition is critical for understanding the multiple and overlapping forces that created and continue to perpetuate urban trauma.

2. *Antideterminism*—rejects the idea that only genetics, behaviors, or physical living conditions influence human health and embraces relational notions of place and "pathogenic exposures." A healing-centered approach recognizes that we and our communities are more than the worst things that may have happened to us. Like the antireductionist idea, antideterminism demands that we reject the tendencies in public health and medicine to only focus on the disease or hazards while ignoring the existing assets and strengths in communities and among population groups. According to Danielle Sered, author of the 2019 book, *Until We Reckon: Violence, Mass Incarceration, and a Road to Repair*, damage-centered narratives reflect a history of deficit-based thinking and pathologizing behaviors that fail to fully account for the complex, and sometimes contradictory, lived experiences of oppression and pathways toward liberation.[67] Antideterminism focuses us on how

communities and cities reconstruct local places even as they participate in transnational networks.

3. *Antipositivism*—demands that practitioners continually question the neutral, disembodied, and placelessness of health science by including contextually specific epistemologies. From a healing perspective, antipositivism means that the statistical probability of some intervention contributing to health or well-being doesn't mean that it actually heals. As I will show in later chapters, just reducing the rate of gun violence in a community does not necessarily mean that those victimized are supported to heal from their trauma. This approach means recognizing, valuing, and centering culture in the healing process, so that symbols, norms, and shared identities can support a sense of belonging when trauma tends to disconnect us. Culture sits in places and our bodies, even if it is not restricted to them. This also recognizes that healing is experienced collectively, such as in restorative justice healing circles, a practice rooted in different Indigenous traditions. An antipositivist approach aims to emphasize the social aspects of urban healing, and to challenge realist ideologies that persistently separate the domains of nature, facts, objectivity, and reason from those of culture, values, subjectivity, and emotion.

4. *Anti-elitism*—acknowledges that urban expertise is always co-produced by "experts" with a diversity of life experiences. It focuses explicitly on reversing privileges obtained through social structural inequalities according to wealth, ethnicity, gender, immigration, disability status, sexual orientation, and other forms of privilege. Shawn Ginwright, a professor of education and African American studies at San Francisco State University, notes, "A healing centered approach to addressing trauma requires a different question that moves beyond 'what happened to you' to 'what's right with you' and views those exposed to trauma as agents in the creation of their own well-being rather than victims of traumatic events."[68] The anti-elitism principle suggests that expert analytic frameworks often create high entry barriers for alternative ideas, and expert claims of objectivity tend to hide the exercise of power so that normative presuppositions are not subjected to general

debate. Processes of healing communities and cities must make explicit the normative that lurks within the technical and to acknowledge from the start the need for plural viewpoints and collective learning.

What Do Cities for Life Look Like in Practice?

There are no drugs that can cure us or vaccines that can inoculate us from the overlapping traumas of housing displacement, police violence, racial segregation, underresourced schools, and other place-based traumas. In the same way that traumatized individuals start to recover through relationships—with families, loved ones, spiritual communities, or clinicians—our communities and cities can only start to promote healing when they dismantle existing barriers to social inclusion and human interactions. Physically and socially inclusive communities are healing centered because they support people-to-people relationships where individuals and groups can feel safe, supported, and valued.

Creating inclusion can also mean very targeted interventions that have widespread benefits. One example is the sidewalk intersection curb cut (the break in the sidewalk that ramps down to become flush with the street). Before curb cuts were part of sidewalk design, people in wheelchairs struggled with mobility. In fact, urban disability justice activists campaigned in the 1970s to require cities to mandate curb cuts at intersections. After much protest and struggle, the activists won, and today, most cities require a curb cut at intersections. And what resulted from this inclusive urban policy? Everyone has benefited. Today people with mobility challenges can more easily and safely navigate intersections, but so too can those pushing a baby stroller, someone delivering packages on a wheeled cart, skateboarders, and the elderly who might be walking gingerly or pushing a walker.

The curb cut lesson is that when policy supports society's most vulnerable, we not only create the possibility for those that have been left behind to fully participate, but we also deliver benefits for everyone else. Today in cities we see the opposite of the curb cut; we are ignoring the traumas experienced by some, and those traumas have been magnified into challenges impacting us all. In short, the curb cut is an equitable and healing practice because it promotes just and fair inclusion

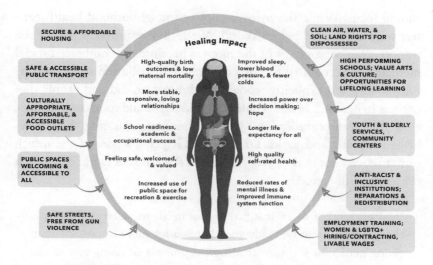

Figure 1.5 City for life policies and practices and their healing impacts.

throughout society and creates the conditions in which everyone can participate, prosper, and reach their full potential. Figure 1.5 provides some examples of policies and practices that cities for life can implement and their related healing impacts.

Neighborhood Health Centers

The creation of the neighborhood health center is another curb cut example, since they were originally started in immigrant neighborhoods and aimed to address the needs of the urban poor. As originally conceived in the 1920s, urban neighborhood health centers combined ambulatory health services with community participation in development and land-use decisions.[69] Health centers were started in predominantly immigrant neighborhoods of Milwaukee and Philadelphia, the Mohawk-Brighton district of Cincinnati, New York's Lower East Side, and the West End of Boston.

To ensure widespread benefits, the health center included block committees where residents participated in decisions about their community, including prioritizing public health issues on which the center should focus. While the 1920s versions of neighborhood health centers were eliminated before World War I, they returned as part of the war on poverty programs of the 1960s. This time they embraced social medicine, which aimed to link economic redistribution to health improvements and explicitly worked to eliminate racial and ethnic disparities in health.[70] Health centers started farms and food cooperatives, as well as transportation and job training programs, and they refurbished housing and parks. Dr. H. Jack Geiger, a leader of the health center movement in the 1960s, described the kinds of work led by each center's health council:

> It is this kind of social institution that needs to be created if social change is going to be made and that is a lot more important than giving penicillin shots, or treating pneumonia or doing any of the other 'let's bail it out after the disaster has occurred' kinds of things that medicine has been focused on for the last 50 years. Our goal is to make change in the social order which will see to it that people stay healthy rather than merely to clean up the human debris. So, our task is to organize people, to help them organize themselves, to encourage them to articulate their own needs, and then to give them the technical assistance to act to meet those needs.[71]

Despite their success in supporting economic improvement and healing, federal funding for community health centers declined in the 1970s. Funding was later tied to clinical, not social, outcomes. However, healing-focused health centers continue to operate. In Lowell, Massachusetts, the Metta Health Center supports Cambodian and Laotian refugees, many of whom were victims of torture and lived through the Khmer Rouge regime before coming to the US.[72] (*Metta* means loving-kindness and compassion in the Buddhist Pali language.) Metta Health Center offers Western family medicine delivered by bilingual and bicultural practitioners who also link Western and traditional healing.

In Boston, the nonprofit organization called the Dudley Street Neighborhood Initiative, or DSNI, organized residents to take back their community after years of illegal garbage dumping and violence.

DSNI rejected a city-sponsored redevelopment plan and created their own plan. After failing to find a developer to rebuild housing and other community amenities, DSNI financed and rebuilt the housing themselves. Like the food and housing cooperatives of the neighborhood health centers, DSNI focused on community wealth building as a key aspect of their healing and well-being strategy.[73] In addition, a youth council of DSNI took back parks and vacant lots by occupying, painting, and programming activities. According to one of the lead organizers of the DSNI effort, their healing-centered work was less about physical building and more about the challenge of building hope: "How do you develop people to have confidence in a community, in individuals, to speak, to stand up for, to strive, to fight and to have hope? I think those are the key challenges. It's not so much, 'what building are you going to build' or 'what social program are you going to change?' But, it's the people part of it. The part that has people investing themselves to make a difference, to make a change, and to see that hope. That's the challenge."[74]

Rebuilding Urban Hope

The challenges for how communities can recover from trauma and rebuild for health include ensuring that any initiative is community led, culturally responsive, and addresses the short- and long-term needs of people and places. In chapter 2, I explore one such program that started in Richmond, California, and is now called Advance Peace.

Chapter 2

Reducing Urban Violence through Street Love

I t was only a few blocks between the community center and the corner store in the Iron Triangle neighborhood of Richmond, California, just across the Bay from San Francisco (for more background on Richmond, see Box 1). One whole block was a deserted ball field with a high chain-link fence running along the sidewalk. The corner store, a two-story building, a market with apartments above, had a broken sign with writing that was visible only on one side. From my vantage point, I could see an empty garbage can, an abandoned shopping cart, and a broken-down car with rusted rims and a patchy paint job parked halfway down the block. The neighborhood looked left behind, but hardly like a potential war zone.

Yet the texts were coming in every few minutes on James Houston's phone. James is a street outreach worker—called a neighborhood change agent (NCA)—with the Office of Neighborhood Safety (ONS) in Richmond. His job is to help keep these streets safe from gun violence, in part by developing caring, trusting, and loving relationships with the young people caught up at the center of gun violence in this city. His phone buzzed again and he turned to me. "These youngsters want a ride to the store. They haven't eaten all day. But they know walking might be deadly since there is an ongoing beef between Central and North Richmond."

We jumped in the car and picked them up. The young guys could not have been more than 15 or 16 years old. They were skeptical of me at first, but James put them at ease. He told them, "You see, even a UC Berkeley professor wants to come out here and find a way to get ya'll opportunities." James asked them about their family and some friends. The typical answer "aight" wasn't enough for James. He probed a little more.

"What are ya'll doing in school?" he asked. They haven't been in school for a few days out of fear of getting jumped, they reply, and one of the guys mentions he's been out of town at his cousin's house.

When we arrived at the store and they didn't immediately jump out, James knew what was up. They didn't have any money for food, so James pulled out some cash and handed it over.

A young man known as J-Mac was recently shot and killed near the market, and everyone around the neighborhood seems to know that a simple walk to the store can be tragic.

They returned a few minutes later and jumped back in the car. We drove to a neighborhood community center. A few more young people were out front, and they recognized James. "Hey, what's good with it, Unc?" one tall youngster said.

James smiled like a father seeing his children. In fact, James later told me that that is sort of how he sees his work, as being the caring, consistent, and ever-present father that many of these young people don't have. His measure of success is ensuring that the group of young people he engages with care about themselves and their community, and aren't willing to take a life or throw their own away. When James grew up on the streets of Richmond, he didn't have many positive male role models. He said that he always felt like he needed to be tougher than everyone else. He tells me that he made some poor decisions as a young man, and one day, at 21 years old, he jumped in the middle of an argument between a neighbor and his girlfriend. The neighbor came for him. James pulled out a gun and shot him in the stomach. James was convicted of second-degree murder and became a "lifer" in prison. After spending 18 years behind bars, James was released after demonstrating to the parole board all the work he had done healing from his own trauma and anger, as well as his commitment to helping others do the same. When he got out, he was given the chance to help others through working with Richmond's ONS.

James described to me that the healing work he was able to do in prison happened because other, older, inmates (some who had done twice as much time as he had), encouraged him and directed him to the resources in prison. They steered him toward a restorative justice program called the Victim Offender Education Group (VOEG). James credits those elder mentors and the VOEG program with giving him self-awareness about the trauma that he had experienced, how it impacted his day-to-day decisions, and how that trauma impacted others in his community.

For the last seven years, James has been part of a team of formerly incarcerated street outreach workers delivering mentorship, support, service referrals, and, most importantly, unconditional love, to those at the center of urban gun violence in Richmond. When the ONS was created over 10 years ago, it was innovative because it established a city agency focused on promoting peace and healing. It was one of the first ONSs in the country to be embedded in city government. A group of street outreach workers like James, NCAs, facilitate the healing and peacekeeping work. According to DeVone Boggan, the creator of the ONS, its first director, and now the chief executive officer of the nonprofit called Advance Peace, which is bringing the ONS model to other cities, "The NCAs are the few with the credibility and skillset capable of reaching the one-percenters, or the small number of people in the city who are likely behind most gun violence. We know these folks are also the most likely to be victims of gun violence. We recognized that if a city doesn't engage meaningfully with these cats, who have remained invisible to most and avoided law enforcement, the cycles of urban violence will never stop. We are either going to survive together, or this is going to bring everyone down."

Today, the Advance Peace model has expanded beyond Richmond to Sacramento, Stockton, and Fresno, California, as well as Ft. Worth, Texas. It is also being considered by dozens of other cities. The ONS and Advance Peace offer an important approach to urban healing and reveal that when we face violence in our communities honestly, courageously, and with profound compassion for the survivors—many of whom are also perpetrators of harm—we can begin to heal, honor everyone's humanity, and break our addiction to caging young people of color.

The Need for Street Love

While crime rates have declined in almost all American cities, low-income, communities of color continue to bear a disproportionate share of American gun violence. This violence is the result of a long history of divestment, dehumanization, and White institutions' disregard toward African Americans.

Perhaps contrary to conventional thought, the reasons for most urban gun homicides are not drug deals or robberies. In the US in 2019, 73.7 percent of all murders occurred by firearm and 88.5 percent of murders occurred in metropolitan areas.[1,2] Sixty percent of the murders in 2019 were because of arguments or "beefs," not robberies or drug-related crimes.[3] According to Boggan, this was what he found in Richmond: "There wasn't a major gang war or shootings over drug turf. It was about a fight over a girl or a dice game or an insult about your neighborhood on social media. The younger brothers were fighting a war they often didn't even know why, or who started it." Those at the center of urban gun violence are often potential offenders and victims, who are grappling with the unaddressed traumas of living in communities with long histories of structural violence and racism, including racial segregation, chronic withdrawal of social services, dehumanization through police violence, and alienation from other government institutions.[4]

Boggan knew that public health approaches to reducing gun violence were increasingly effective alternatives to heavy-handed, dehumanizing law enforcement that had resulted in today's epidemic of mass incarceration of Black and Brown people.[5] A public health approach to addressing gun violence means first identifying the root causes of the "disease," or in this case drivers of violence, working to prevent "exposures" to those causes, and treating the victims with compassion.[6] A key aspect of this public health approach is recognizing and addressing the traumas too often experienced by youth living in impoverished and segregated neighborhoods. The Substance Abuse and Mental Health Services Administration has noted that turning to gun violence to resolve disputes in segregated communities should be seen as a treatable disease, since the behavior is often a reaction to unaddressed traumas. These traumas can be intergenerational and can range from childhood physical and sexual abuse, experiencing and witnessing violence, extreme deprivation, homelessness and poverty, or living with a substance abuser or in a household that has lost a member to incarceration.[7] Racism is another important form of trauma, both individually and within institutions, that contributes to the dehumanization of People of Color, damages health, and can impair decision making, cognitive development, and self-control.[8]

The public health approach to addressing urban gun violence also demands culturally competent clinicians. This idea, that those who have experienced violence are best situated to prevent it, was eloquently captured by Sam Vaughn, now the director of the ONS, who stated, "A vaccine is created by the exact same disease that it is trying to destroy. I have learned that peace can come through those who have been, lived, and understand violence. The way to create a healthy, nonviolent community is by killing the hate in violent young men and then reinjecting them back into that same community with more positive values, such as love, self-respect and a true understanding of the society that they live in."[9]

For Vaughn, that meant directly addressing the stigma of being labeled a "thug" or killer, and being treated as such by every institution and program—from foster care, to schools, to nonprofits, to social services. He told me, "These young people were never allowed to be kids, to be vulnerable, to make mistakes, to see the possibilities of another way besides using a gun." Street love is genuine, heartfelt, mutual support that furthers individual, group, and community development and is crucial for ending cycles of toxic masculinity and surviving in an impoverished community.[10]

As Shawn Ginwright notes in his book, *Hope and Healing in Urban Education*, "In communities ravaged by violence, crime and poverty, care is perhaps one of the most revolutionary antidotes to urban violence and trauma because care ultimately facilitates healing. Care within the black community is as much a political act as it is a personal gesture because it requires black youth to confront racism and view their personal trauma as a result of systemic social problems."[11] Sam emphasized that "they expect you to give up on them, and we refuse to do that."

A New Model of Public Safety and Community Healing

What occurred in Richmond through the creation of the ONS and what is happening now with Advance Peace points to a new model of public safety and community healing, led by community members. It shows how cities can invest in reversing the cycles of violence, poverty, exclusion, and shortened lives that too many communities of color experience today.

In Richmond, James and other outreach workers engage with some of the most traumatized individuals in the city, many of whom experienced neglect and abuse, and are coping with extreme poverty. Their approach suggests that a city's safety cannot simply be determined through the levels of crime and violence, but rather is about reestablishing the humanity of its most traumatized residents and improving their well-being, so that the entire city can heal.

At the heart of the Advance Peace program is what they call the Peacemaker Fellowship. This is an intensive, 18-month program where fellows, or participants, receive 24/7 mentorship, wraparound services, life-skill classes, elder supports, transformative travel opportunities, and, if participants demonstrate a consistent investment in themselves and their communities, an allowance of up to $1,000 per month.[12] According to Boggan, the milestone allowance is only one small aspect of the program, but one he used to purposely send shock waves through the city. "This is controversial, I get it. But what's really happening is that they are getting rewarded for doing really hard work, and it's definitely hard work when you talk about stopping picking up a gun to solve your problems."[13]

As the saying goes, "hurt people, hurt people," and according to

Advance Peace, until that hurt is addressed cities and entire populations will continue to suffer. In Richmond, the ONS approach seems to be paying off. Since the inception of the program in 2009, there has been a 55 percent reduction in gun homicides and assaults (Figure 2.1), a 117 percent increase in residents' positive ratings of their quality of life, and a 131 percent increase in their positive rating of Richmond as a place to live.[14] In 2014, Richmond experienced 13 homicides, its lowest number of homicides in over 30 years, and it has maintained these low rates. As importantly, since 2009, 94 percent of the Peacemaker Fellowship participants were still alive in 2019, 83 percent had no gun injuries or hospitalizations, and 77 percent had not been a suspect in any firearm activity.

In 2007, before the ONS was started, the city of Richmond, California, had 47 homicides, which was ten times the average rate for the state of California. For a city of just over 110,000 people, these homicide numbers made Richmond one of the most violent cities in America. The roots of violence are seen in the city's history, and include racial segregation in its shipyard workforce, discrimination in public housing, and segregated schools that plagued the city throughout much of the twentieth century (I describe these dynamics in more detail in Box 1 and in chapter 6). In 2005 the city council declared a state of emergency because of gun violence and was about to bring in the National Guard to patrol the streets.[15] Boggan was hired as a consultant to help the city explore alternative solutions. He talked with other community leaders, organizations, residents who were imprisoned, the police, and many others.[16] He knew that the lock-'em-up strategies of urban police departments, such as that in neighboring Oakland, had left California with the highest incarcerated population in the US, a majority of whom were Black and Brown young men. The police department budget was close to half the city's overall budget, a reality in many cities. A failing, underresourced school system, in Richmond and throughout California, resulted in one of the nation's highest suspension rates for Black children.[17] "Right when young children, as early as kindergarten, needed support and guidance from adults, they were being kicked out of school, being sent back to homes and neighborhoods without the resources or stability to support them," Tashaka Merriweather, the

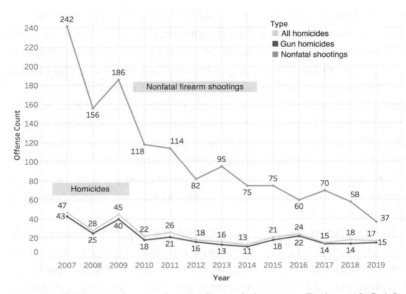

Figure 2.1 All homicides, gun homicides, and shootings, Richmond, California, 2007–2019. (Source: Richmond Police Department)

coordinator of West Contra Costa Unified School District's Comprehensive School Health Programs, told me.

Boggan also knew from an increasingly large body of criminology research that firearm violence was disproportionately burdening 15- to 34-year-old African American men, and that a small number of people were likely responsible for most gun crime in any given city. The victims of urban gun crime are overwhelmingly young Black males between 15 and 34 years old, and as Figure 2.2 shows, this has persisted for decades, even as cities have seen sharp decreases in murder rates. As a *Guardian* news investigation revealed, of the over 13,000 firearm homicides in the US, more than half were in just 127 cities, and in those cities, just 1,200 neighborhood census tracts, equal to about an area of 42 square miles.[18] According to the *Guardian* report, "Though these neighborhood areas contain just 1.5% of the country's population, they saw 26% of America's total gun homicides." The idea that gun crime is highly concentrated among "hot people and hot places" has been well documented in the criminology literature.[19] As Boggan recalled to me,

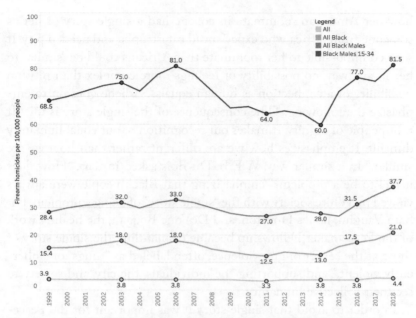

Figure 2.2 Gun homicide rates per 100,000 persons, United States, 1999–2018. (Source: CDC, Web-Based Injury Statistics Query and Reporting System), https://www.cdc.gov/injury/wisqars/index.html.

"I heard from Richmond PD that there were maybe 100–200 people responsible for most of the shootings in that city. I was like, really? OK, we are going to have a laser-sharp focus on those few hundred and see what we can do." So, even in highly racially segregated, impoverished neighborhoods, the majority of residents have nothing to do with gun violence. Sam Vaughn, the current director of Richmond's ONS, described how the streets of Richmond can be thought of as an "urban jungle," where you are either a lion or a gazelle: "No one wants to be a gazelle surrounded by a bunch of lions. So that jungle is full of lions preying on one another to survive."[20]

Disrupting the Single Story of Gun Crime

In "The Danger of a Single Story" narrative so beautifully articulated by the Nigerian author Chimamanda Ngozi Adichie,[21] she recounts how her American roommate in college had a single story of her as someone from Africa who experienced catastrophe and needed pity. It seemed impossible to her roommate that Africans could be "similar to her in any way, no possibility of feelings more complex than pity, no possibility of a connection as human equals." Adiche goes on to emphasize the following: "The consequence of the single story is this: It robs people of dignity. It makes our recognition of our equal humanity difficult. It emphasizes how we are different rather than how we are similar." In a similar way, W.E.B. Du Bois asked in 1897, "How does it feel to be a problem?" emphasizing that Black people were always viewed by White society with the "single story" of being a problem. For Sam Vaughn, James Houston, and DeVone Boggan, the healing work of the Peacemaker Fellowship became dismantling the single story of those at the center of gun violence, often labeled as "thugs" or "inherently violent," and supporting the individuals, the city, and society to see their collective humanity.

In order to avoid that single story it was important for the Peacemaker Fellowship to be unique from other urban gun violence reduction programs. Advance Peace turned to programs such as Operation Ceasefire, which started in Boston in 1996, and its spin-off program Cure Violence, which was started in 2000 by physician Gary Slutkin, for inspiration.[22] Slutkin's work in Chicago was featured in the *New York Times Magazine* in 2008, where he described the public health approach as stopping the infection at its source: "For violence, we're trying to interrupt the next event, the next transmission, the next violent activity. And the violent activity predicts the next violent activity like H.I.V. predicts the next H.I.V. and TB predicts the next TB."[23] A key aspect of Operation Ceasefire, which is frequently referred to as pulling levers and focused deterrence, is changing gang member behaviors. They work closely with law enforcement and the attorney general to "pull every legal lever possible" to lock up offenders. The partnership between outreach workers and law enforcement developed by Operation Ceasefire was unique and is credited with reducing youth homicides in Boston. Cure Violence uses a model of group violence intervention that distanced itself from Ceasefire's cozy partnership with law enforcement, and uses street outreach workers that interrupt gun violence while also engaging gang members and using public education with the larger community in an effort to "denormalize" gun crime. Cure Violence has shown success in reducing gun crime, such as a 25 percent decrease in gun homicides in Chicago and a 30 percent reduction in shootings in Philadelphia.[24]

Boggan recognized that being affiliated with the police or focusing on gang behavior wasn't going to work in Richmond. He also noted that Ceasefire and Cure Violence rarely evaluated their impacts on the individuals at the center of gun violence and the influences, if any, on their lives, their stress, and their overall well-being.[25] When Boggan designed the Peacemaker Fellowship within the ONS, he intentionally set out to disrupt the single story of success for urban gun violence programs, or the idea that outside "experts" had the right formula for success; instead, the Fellowship's "success" wouldn't be primarily measured by whether or not gun crime statistics decreased.[26] He pointed out to me that almost none of the evaluations of community-based gun violence programs like Cure Violence reported on whether or not the lives of the clients were improved, if the communities were healthier, or if the lives of those doing the gun violence interruption and mentoring (almost all formerly incarcerated folks) were changed. Also surprising to Boggan was that few if any programs explicitly talked about addressing the street-level impacts of structural racism and other forms of violence, another sign to him that the almost singular focus of those programs on gun homicides and crime offered few possibilities to reframe the narrative about Black and Brown men and truly help heal communities. The Peacemaker Fellowship in Richmond ultimately became the model for the Advance Peace model now being used in Sacramento, Stockton, Fresno, and other cities.

The Peacemaker Fellowship

The Peacemaker Fellowship is designed to first and foremost be about "investing in and developing the full potential of the folks in our community, and through this, reducing gun crime," Boggan would tell me. He was invested in what he called "recycling community assets," or those valuable experts who would form the team of former felons as street-level mentors. Boggan often referred to his work as building a "family culture", and regularly reflected on what his own children and family needed and received as influencing the design of the Peace-maker Fellowship. As he recalled: "We needed a team of highly specialized experts in street engagement and cognitive behavioral therapy. We wanted our fellows, the clients, to see themselves as we saw them; highly intelligent and capable of much more than killing one another. We wanted for our fellows what most want for their own children and family, namely daily, healthy contact and engagement by adults that believed in them and loved them."

Early on in the creation of Richmond's program, Boggan's team identified the thirty or so individuals that law enforcement and others thought were the most influential in the city's current gun activity. He asked his new team of outreach workers to invite that group to city hall to meet with him. His outreach workers laughed it off, telling the seemingly naive Boggan that there was no way these "heavy hitters" would come to city hall, where the police were located, for a meeting. Boggan told his outreach team that if they couldn't convince them to come to city hall, he would need to find another team of outreach workers who could. He told his team if they could get those "in the shadows" to come to city hall, it would be a sign to everyone in the community that his model might work. His team delivered over twenty people to city hall that first year. As Boggan later reflected, "They trusted our street outreach workers who convinced them that we weren't working with the police, that we were genuinely interested in their development, and we weren't going to give up on them, no matter how many times they told us to fuck off."

Credible Messengers

The ability of the outreach team to build trust and get the first group of future Peacemaker Fellows to city hall was a testament to their skills as credible messengers. Credible messengers are people like James, who were once "in the life" of crime, gangs, and gun use; spent time in prison; have worked to improve their lives; and now have unique legitimacy to help others in a similar position.[27] Boggan worked to identify people already in the community and those who might soon be released from prison who were both "street credible" and ready to share their stories, their trauma, and the ways that they were working to improve their lives. He looked for former prisoners that had served long sentences but managed to confront their own traumas, transform themselves inside prison, and clearly articulate that transformation in order to get released. Many NCAs told me that "OGs" ("original gangsters") they were locked up with, whom they often admired on the streets, were the ones that encouraged them to turn their lives around and work on their own healing. Many described joining men's groups, addiction recovery programs, taking classes toward a degree, and talking to troubled youths who came to visit the prison as the kinds of experiences that helped them start to heal. One NCA recalled to me that his addiction recovery program and the Insight Prison Project, which has become a well-known healing-centered program where victims and incarcerated people work together, and also offers a certified violence prevention class, were some of the experiences that prepared him for being effective at street outreach and mentoring.[28] Research suggests that former "lifers" who engage in these types of in-prison programs can make some of the most effective mentors when released.[29,30] One NCA told me, "You need people who have lived the life, but also seen the experiences comin' up that may have drove them to crime and violence. It's not just 'I've repented for some sins' but also, 'I'm aware of the shit I went through, it wasn't my fault, and I'm able to communicate my experiences to a youngster also going through it that they aren't to blame for what it did to them.'"

As Sam described it, "Some of the best rape counselors are victims of a sex crime; some of the best drug counselors are former addicts. The folks who can help you through it are those that know and have traveled the path." In other words, effective credible messengers are also "wounded healers." The wounded healer is someone who has experienced trauma, is often in the process of recovering, and uses those experiences to make them "brothers to others that have been similarly hurt." The wounded healer can both empathize with those similarly hurt and also transform their own past into a source of wisdom to be drawn from while they are acting as a trusted mentor.[31] The oppressed, as Paulo Freire writes in chapter 1 of *Pedagogy of the Oppressed*, "must be their own example in the struggle for their redemption."[32]

In knowing both the street, and the complexities of the root causes of trauma, and being able to communicate them to their mentees, the NCAs needed to have what W.E.B. Du Bois characterized in *The Souls of Black Folks*, as a "double consciousness." Du Bois stated that when Black Americans tried to be accepted in White culture, they had to live "a double life, with double thoughts, double duties, and double social classes." He would say in 1897, "It is a peculiar sensation, this double-consciousness, this sense of always looking at one's self through the eyes of others, of measuring one's soul by the tape of a world that looks on in amused contempt and pity. One feels his two-ness, – an American, a Negro; two souls, two thoughts, two unreconciled strivings; two warring ideals in one dark body, whose dogged strength alone keeps it from being torn asunder."[33] While Du Bois was addressing the burdens of surviving in a White-privileged society and alienation from one's own culture, he was also offering insights into the "gift of second sight," an expanded Black consciousness, and a "multilingualism" that offered African Americans a pathway toward liberation, freedom, and self-realization.[34]

Once hired, Advance Peace credible messengers build their skills by receiving additional training in conflict resolution, cognitive behavioral therapy (CBT), nonviolent communication, and other violence de-escalation skills. CBT is especially valuable in that it has been shown to support individuals and groups to become more aware of and learn how to better control the links between situations, thoughts, emotions, and behaviors. NCAs also learn to navigate systems that likely failed them when they were growing up, including education, housing, health care, and criminal justice.

Identifying Peacemaker Fellows

The Peacemaker Fellowship is reserved for those hard-to-reach people who are the most likely shooters and most likely to be victims of gun violence. It is not open to anyone in the community suffering from the traumas of poverty and inequality. The program is unique from others in that it doesn't focus on changing gang norms, or using threats of sanctions, to convince people to join and stay involved. "What kind of healthy relationship is based on threats?" emphasized Boggan.

The outreach team spends at least 6 months identifying and recruiting these highly influential individuals, before they are invited to enroll in the Peacemaker Fellowship. Even after membership in the program is framed as a prestigious opportunity, most of the people that the program wants to engage are reluctant and skeptical. As one NCA describes it, "It ain't like these people are easy to find, want to be found or are looking for help. The fact that they are still in the streets means they are elusive. And, for good reasons they don't trust nobody. We can't just show up and offer them a fellowship. Most of them are like 'F-you and your F-ing program. Get the F-k out of my face. I don't need that shit.'"

Another NCA told me they focus on the one "tryna prove himself and maybe make a name. There's always a leader or two that's in the bunch, he's making sure that people understand, he's challenging the other guys when they say something that he think is ridiculous so he can get on that other person, and you know just to flex his dominance." The future fellows are initially suspicious of NCAs, often thinking they work with law enforcement, or with a "'useless' nonprofit that may have let them down before." They worry that if they are seen associated with them their street-crew will think they are snitches.

The Peacemaker Fellowship is also unique in that immediately putting down your gun is not a prerequisite for enrolling. Advance Peace recognizes that their fellows live under a constant threat of violence, are often being "hunted," and carrying a gun can offer a sense of security. Very few trust the criminal justice system to deliver justice. DeVone suggested that "if the police really cared and the 'justice' system worked for our communities, we would likely have a very different reality today." One NCA was describing his fellows to me and used the analogy of a multigenerational war, where few know what they are fighting for except to stay alive. "They are like child soldiers, recruited to fight a war they didn't start, but our society don't see them as victims. If this was another country and 14-year-olds were forced to carry weapons, we'd be treating them with compassion," he told me.

The Peacemaker Fellowship has a laser focus on the most influential "soldiers." These are often young people who are alienated from their families, communities, schools, and almost every other institution set up to support them. As Sam told me, "When everyone else has failed them, Advance Peace aims to be there with a caring, consistent, healthy presence." Another NCA described it to me this way: "These youngsters are acting out with guns, it's really just a cry for help. But as a young man in our neighborhood you can't go to someone and say 'I'm hurting.' It's shamed or seen as weak. We have to be genuine. They can see if it's fake. And invest in them when nobody has done that before. Let them know their worth, just for who they are, not anything they do or don't do." The NCAs practice forgiveness, "not as an occasional act," but, as Dr. Martin Luther King Jr. stated, as a "permanent attitude."

According to another NCA, "These youngsters look around and they don't see doctors and lawyers in their communities. They see gangsters and dealers. They are raised by these same people. If that is mostly what you see, it can be what is acceptable and expected of you too. When a youngster is constantly told, 'you are just like your father,' and that father is locked up with a violent past, what is that kid supposed to do?"

Becoming a Fellow

Trust is a foundation of the fellow–mentor relationship and perhaps one of the most important but difficult tasks for the NCA to cultivate. One NCA described to me the process he uses in some depth:

> "Most of the folks we are engaging have been let down by every adult they have encountered their entire lives. They have survived on the street by not trusting anyone. We show up and can't say 'trust us.' They are fearful. We cultivate trust by being consistent in their lives. Everyday. We might just acknowledge them but not really talk. Then they might ask their big homie, 'What's up with dude?' And they start hearing stuff about us, then they hearing your story, and they checking you out. And then they slowly start coming around and even then you don't know when. You can start to see the comfortability starting to happen. Some days just listening and giving

them a ride. Other times its serious conversations. You can't expect them to go from being a cold killa' to bein' a square; you gotta share your journey, how did you get there? That it was a struggle. We show them ourselves now, and make no excuses for it. They feel that and start to show their feelings. We try to get them to see their self-worth, highlight their talents. After a while, he lets his guard down. They start seeing you as that uncle, that father they never had. The majority of them, you get them one on one, they the softest, gentlest people that you could know."

Once a trusting relationship is built between a fellow and their NCA, they are enrolled in the 18-month Peacemaker Fellowship. A first step is for the NCA to work one-on-one with their new fellow to draft what they call a Life Management Action Plan, or LifeMAP. The LifeMAP is tailored to the individual's needs and challenges, and it emerges from ongoing conversations between the fellow and their mentor. The structure for all fellows is the same, but the content is specific to each person's life and experiences. The content is focused on the steps needed for that individual to heal and turn his or her life around. Each plan needs to be based on "where each fellow is in their life and where they can go." The LifeMAP is another feature of Advance Peace that sets it apart from other programs.

Sam emphasized that the LifeMAP sets short-, medium-, and long-term goals for personal safety, safe housing, education, employment, anger management, conflict resolution, creating positive social networks, financial literacy, behavioral/medical health care, substance use disorder support, parenting skills, recreation, and spirituality. Some typical short-term goals might be working on substance abuse or anger management issues; medium-term goals might be improving a relationship with a family member; longer-term goals might be obtaining a GED, a Social Security card, a driver's license, or a job. "You can't expect these guys to jump right into a job or internship, because they aren't ready, and we don't want their first experience with these things to fail," Boggan emphasized. Through the LifeMAP process, the program also ensures that their fellows, and often their families, get to identify the immediate needs they might have, such as food and shelter, and to aim for long-term change. As one fellow described the impact of his LifeMAP, "Now I got a plan for writing and releasing music and getting a driver's license. As soon as I'm up in the morning, my whole day is set up. It's basically put me on a program where I don't have time to be in the streets. They want to see us living and being people, not being a statistic."

The LifeMAP is both a mechanism for ensuring that fellows define their own healing needs (i.e., for them, by them) and a "social contract" with a strong, caring, and consistent adult who is willing to take a risk and believe in them. "We see each one of the fellows as the essential antidote to this urban epidemic of gun violence," one NCA told me. According to Bessel van der Kolk, agency addresses trauma through "the feeling of being in charge of your life, knowing where you stand, knowing that you have a say in what happens to you, knowing that you have some ability to shape your circumstances."[35]

It became clear to me that the Peacemaker Fellowship wasn't an "off-the-shelf" cookbook program, and the fundamental aspect was building trusting, caring, and genuine relationships. The LifeMAP is also a living document because it is updated by the fellow and their mentor every few months to reflect new life goals and the changing relationship between mentor and mentee.

Each fellow commits to joining group learning sessions, or what the program calls life-skills classes. These classes are more like facilitated dialogues, sometimes referred to in the healing literature as circles, where groups of fellows focus on a particular topic over a series of weeks or months, facilitated by a skilled professional. The topics are often dictated by the needs of the fellows, but typically include discussions about what it means to be "a man," group CBT, understanding the forces of structural racism, or how to be a good father/parent.

Once fellows show progress in life-skills classes with other fellows from their own neighborhood, the circle is expanded to include fellows that are rivals from other neighborhoods. Through this process, rival fellows may get to know their "enemy" as just another person, but they also get to work with teams of NCAs in the group setting, both of which can reduce potential conflicts and support healing through empathy. These group sessions, where fellows get to know rivals in safe, facilitated settings, can also reduce retaliatory gun violence in the streets. One NCA described to me a call he recently received from a fellow: "He called me to say that he saw another fellow out of bounds. His brother had just been shot and they suspected it was someone from that rival 'hood. His homies were like, 'let's go.' My fellow's crew rolled up on him, but they'd just had a life-skills class together. Instead of shootin' him, my fellow told them he was cool, sayin' 'that's my sucka partner' and he got outta there smooth."

Knowing Their Limits

The NCAs recognize that their skills only go so far, and many fellows require additional professional supports. Either through the LifeMAP process or just from spending time with a fellow, an NCA will recognize that their fellows could benefit from professional help. An NCA described it to me: "It's what a parent or teacher or coach might recognize, 'this kid needs more than I can give,' but our fellows don't have those attentive, caring adults in their lives." Often the services are for substance abuse or anger management, both frequently linked to unaddressed trauma.

Importantly, in the Peacemaker Fellowship, an NCA will not just refer their fellow to a service, but will also physically take them to the service and even accompany them for the first few sessions. This is often because fellows are initially reluctant to attend any services, since most have been disillusioned by institutions and organizations after being let down by them so many times. According to data gathered by the Advance Peace program in Sacramento and Stockton, none of their fellows were being engaged by any social services or nonprofit programs before they were enrolled in the Peacemaker Fellowship. A related challenge for ensuring that the fellows receive healing services is that many counselors and therapists aren't prepared to handle the population that the Peacemaker Fellowship serves. As Boggan described it to me, "We referred a fellow to a substance abuse counselor and they got high before going in. The first thing the counselor asked was 'are you high?' The fellow says 'Yes, that's why I'm here.' But the counselor sends them away and says come back when you're not high. Same thing with anger management classes. So, we have to accompany the fellow to the service, help them navigate the bureaucracy, support the interaction to ensure they are getting quality and useful professional service."

Since many of the fellows have also been incarcerated, the NCAs regularly ensure that they stay on track with their parole or probation officer, and get quality legal representation.

Milestone Allowance

A controversial aspect of the Peacemaker Fellowship is that when a fellow reaches certain LifeMAP goals, they become eligible for a milestone allowance. Once a fellow is working on their LifeMAP for at least 6 months and achieves 65 percent progress toward a goal (as determined by their NCA mentor), that fellow is eligible for an allowance of up to $1,000 per month. The exact amount of milestone allowance is based on effort and achievements. Importantly, the allowance is just one way to recognize the value of each fellow and signals to them that they are a community asset worth investing in and someone that has real value. The program recognizes that the time the fellows invest in themselves and their communities means something, and the allowance rewards them for this effort.

As one fellow describes the allowance: "It's not about the money, but it's one way they reel you in. It's about setting goals and working on them. But for real, it [allowance] has kept me from doing what I've got to do to eat or support my kid, you feel me? I know I don't got to do some of that shit and risk my future anymore."

Boggan reminded me that the money given to the fellows is a pittance compared with the tax-payer dollars going to police departments, including those in Richmond, Sacramento, and Stockton, on overtime pay responding to shootings. The cost of urban gun violence to the public is hard to calculate, especially since we should never put a price on a human life. However, one estimate is that the US spends about $229 billion annually, or 1.4 percent of GDP, on gun violence.[36] Policing regularly consumes the largest percentage of a city's budget, whether it is Los Angeles, San Francisco, or Richmond, California.[37] The Giffords Law Center estimated in 2019 that the annual cost of gun violence in California was $18 billion, or $479 per resident, which included public expenditures for health care, law enforcement, criminal justice, as well as lost wages and tax dollars.[38] The National Institute for Criminal Justice Reform estimated that in Stockton, California, each fatal shooting costs taxpayers $2.5 million, including crime scene response, criminal justice expenses, incarceration, victim support, and lost tax revenue.[39]

The Peacemaker Fellowship has never spent more than $40,000 per 18-month program, which has at least twenty-five fellows. Boggan tells me that the milestone allowances are closer to $20,000 per cohort. Even if it were $40,000 for 18 months, for twenty-five people, that's about spending $90 per month on each fellow. With an annual budget of about $1.5 million for all staff and expenses, the Peacemaker Fellowship pays for itself by stopping one shooting each year.

Transformative Travel

While much of this book focuses on how cities and programs like Advance Peace in cities can help heal people and places, *leaving* one's familiar place might also help us heal. A key aspect of the Peacemaker Fellowship is what they call transformative travel, or leaving your neighborhood as part of changing your own mindset, your relationship to rivals, and your overall outlook on life. Of course, travel is a privilege for the few who can afford it and have the time away from work, school, or other responsibilities. The psychologist Jeffrey Kottler describes how travel experiences can be as, or more, important than successful therapy sessions, since individuals gain insights from traveling that can transform them in ways office therapy cannot. Kottler states: "People who structure their journeys in particular ways consistently report dramatic gains in self-esteem, confidence, poise, and self-sufficiency. They enjoy greater intimacy as a result of bonds that were forged under magical and sometimes adverse circumstances. They become more fearless risk takers, better problem solvers, and far more adaptable to everchanging circumstances. They become more knowledgeable about the world, its fascinating customs, and its diverse people. Finally, travel teaches you most about yourself—about what you miss when you are gone and what you don't, about what you are capable of doing in strange circumstances, about what you really want that you don't yet have."[40]

Boggan imagined just this personal transformation when building travel into the Peacemaker Fellowship: "Many of our fellows have never left their city, maybe even their neighborhoods. We wanted to blow their minds with experiences only rich kids get, and in the process give them a new outlook that life is worth living, that current ways of behaving and thinking will deny them the opportunities to experience and see the world."

Yet the travel aspect of the Fellowship is not guaranteed. Fellows need to have made progress toward their LifeMAP goals and be participating in life-skills classes, before they are invited to travel. Group excursions can include community service projects, taking college tours, meeting with government officials, and participating in restorative justice dialogues in other communities (Figure 2.3). The fellows are also offered trips across the state, to a professional sporting event, an amusement park, and even international destinations. For example, the ONS program took some fellows to South Africa to learn about apartheid and how South Africans are approaching gun violence.

A critical catch for participating in travel is that a fellow must agree to travel with one of their rivals, who also happens to be a fellow. As described by an NCA: "Once they hear the conditions of the out-of-state/country travel, they are like 'hell no, I ain't traveling with that sucka.' But we make it enticing for both of them. In one case, we got them in the same van, and they didn't talk, or even look at the other one, for like an hour. Then they started to realize, 'this guy likes the same music, sports teams, or whatever, and maybe he ain't so different from me?' We found that after a few days together, they found more about what they had in common and the neighborhood rivalries start to fade. Then you just see them eating, playing, just being like kids again."

Bringing It All Together

A related transformational aspect of the Fellowship is internships, where fellows are matched with a local employer who pays the fellow's

Figure 2.3 Office of Neighborhood Safety Fellows and mentors visit Washington, DC, on a transformative travel excursion. (Source: DeVone Boggan, used with permission)

salary. Most fellows have never held a formal job, so the internships offer them a new experience of what it means to get to work every day, be part of a team, and have deferred gratification. As fellows progress through the program, they also interact with an elder circle or group of "real OGs." This group helps support the fellows through their internship experience, and group members talk with them about how to pursue careers like they themselves have achieved, including the lawyers, doctors, engineers, CEOs, and others, fellows rarely hear about in their communities. The elder circles also act as spaces of healing for long-simmering conflicts and can show the younger fellows that the adults in their lives also need support and healing. The multiple dimensions of the Peacemaker Fellowship are displayed in Figure 2.4.

Keeping the Peace

A key skill of all the NCAs is conflict resolution and "violence interruption." The outreach workers regularly insert themselves between

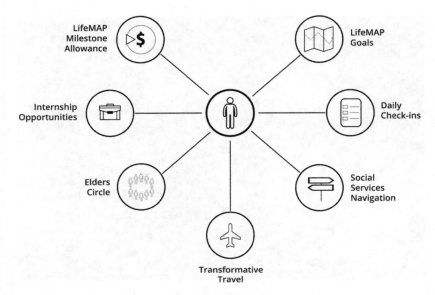

Figure 2.4 Components of the Advance Peace, Peacemaker Fellowship.

"beefs" where guns are drawn and ready. One NCA described how they mediate imminent gun conflicts and confront potential violence before police are called: "Sometimes it's the girlfriend that will call us or another fellow. We might also hear about it from others on the streets or see a social media threat or a music video. We get that call and try to de-escalate the situation. Most critical is having a relationship with them, knowing something about their lives, what and who they care about. In every instance, somebody in the know eventually lets us know that we was the determining factor for the standing down."

Many street gun conflicts that NCAs mediate start as insults on social media, such as Facebook. Sam told me that every day the NCAs are scanning social media to review posts that might be interpreted as insults or lead to potential conflicts. One NCA described how a video posted on social media showed the beating of a well-known, local rapper. After the video went viral, the NCAs feared it was going to trigger a war. One NCA noted, "That had the city in an uproar. Everyone expected a war, since that was what had happened before between those groups. We were on social media, seeing who was posting. We engaged those people in person. We talked to them about other options. We kept talking to both sides. After a year, no retaliation and no deaths. We aggressively get in between every gang social media insult and shooting and made ourselves and our objectives known through our street networks."

In another incident, NCAs intervened when a retaliatory gun conflict was imminent by temporarily moving the conflicting parties out of the city and renting hotel rooms to keep the warring parties "quarantined." Two NCAs stayed with the young people every day and gave them constant positive, life-affirming messages. These types of interventions are part of the repertoire that the NCAs bring to their work, as they intervene to keep heads cool during potentially lethal conflictual situations. Field notes from a weekly report from one NCA described it as follows:

"Keeping close eye on 'P.' Seems like he is looking for a reason to explode in dealing with the murder of his friend at the mall. I informed him to stay off the internet and don't post nothing about the situation. I got him on the phone and let him know we're still in his corner. I am currently trying to get him employed. However he does not see the appeal of the working life when he is finding success in the street life. I just try to stay connected to him and keep the bridge intact as he is an influential player in his gang. He has given me his word to allow me the opportunity to mediate any issues his boys are involved in before escalation on their part. So I speak to him daily."

The NCAs were deemed essential workers in California during COVID-19 and were able to continue their outreach work. They started delivering care packages to families throughout the communities where they were working that included food, hygiene products, and other essentials. They also performed the double duty of trying to educate their fellows and skeptical community members about COVID-19 and managed an increasing number of domestic disputes that arose as people were forced to stay home.[41]

Advance Peace recognizes how hard it is to transition away from the life of gun violence and all your peer influencers. I heard from all the NCAs that their fellows struggle even if they want to leave the street life behind, since they are constantly being pulled back into their old ways, getting attacked and ridiculed for going down a different path. For this and other reasons, the NCAs remain supportive and in contact with their fellows even after the 18-month fellowship, stating that "this isn't just a program for us or them, it's a way of life." Every person who completes the program is considered a lifelong fellow.

Planting the Seeds of Peace

James and Sam acknowledge that although their program in Richmond has been successful in reducing gun homicides, it sometimes feels like "getting clean in a mud puddle," since they aren't able to address all the social and neighborhood inequalities that their fellows regularly confront. All of the NCAs I spoke to acknowledge that they are sometimes just "stopping the bleeding" and their program isn't going to, nor should it be expected to, address the traumas from 400 years of American racism. As one NCA told me bluntly, "Yeah, we know the impacts of slavery, lynchings, Jim Crow, redlining, crack, mass incarceration, killing our leaders, on and on. These ain't going away anytime soon. But, you see, we don't come up knowing about these things. It's like they didn't happen and what we experienced was our fault. We can help our fellows see where some of their anger and pain comes from. We can't address it if we don't name it. Then, we help change the story from, 'it's your fault' or 'what's wrong with you,' to 'I know what happened to you. It happened to me too. It's not your fault.' It's like this gunshot wound. See this scar. This ain't going away. I used to see it as a symbol of pride and how tough I was. I now point to it as a symbol of what generations of neglect and mistreatment have done. It's not going away, but I can heal from that wound and try to move forward and avoid more wounds."

While the work of the Peacemaker Fellowship sometimes seems very individually and locally focused, an underlying thread in the work is to change public safety systems that for too long have limited opportunities for those growing up in underserved communities. All the NCAs were aware of the structural forces working against them, and part of their institutional and policy change is awareness-raising, writing and participating in media events, giving public talks, and engaging in policy advocacy. One NCA described their approach to me this

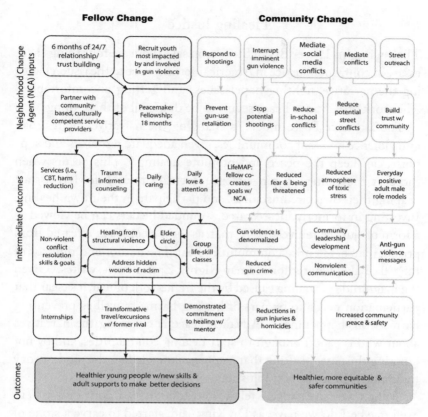

Figure 2.5 The Advance Peace, Transformative Change Model.

way: "We are part of changing the narrative: away from victim blaming; away from more policing and prisons; away from communities don't know or can't do; away from us as being thugs or dangerous. Not only has society, but our fellows have internalized these false narratives. We're changing that story by doing differently, saving lives, and helping point out the policies, laws and systems that need to change for us to continue and have a greater impact. When you combine that with data showing that stopping gun violence saves millions of dollars, maybe we start to see real social change."

The mode of transformative change, of both fellows and communities, put forward by Advance Peace is described in Figure 2.5.

Healing Justice

The civil rights lawyer Bryan Stevenson says there are four things necessary to confront injustice in America: getting close to the issue, changing the narrative, fighting hopelessness and getting uncomfortable.[42] The work of Advance Peace seems to be doing all of these things.

The Advance Peace model is changing the narrative about urban gun violence and that communities, given adequate resources and supports, can keep the peace and promote healing.[43] This occurs when those at the center of gun violence cocreate their LifeMAPs, start shaping their own circumstances, and participate in their own healing. Investing in formerly incarcerated, wounded healers can be viewed as a form of "justice reinvestment" that, as more people are released from prison, may help entire communities heal. The author and director of the Ella Baker Center for Human Rights, Zach Norris, writes, "Given the magnitude of trauma caused by the framework of fear, it's clear that participation needs to be part of healing harms as well as preventing harms from happening."[44] Advance Peace is changing the narratives about who is expert enough to start healing communities, and by not ignoring the past, ensuring that healing acknowledges the modern-day traumatic legacies of past injustices.

"When we can change a fellow's attitude from, I don't give a f-, to 'well maybe I do' we have, as Dr. King said, started to carve a stone of hope out of a mountain of despair," one NCA told me. The Advance Peace model is creating networks of care in communities that are as much personal as political, since they are helping build a political racial consciousness. Moving from fear to care and hope challenges the idea that we are defined by our worst acts. The hope generated by the Peacemaker Fellowship is also transformative: almost all the participants are alive, not incarcerated, and not involved in gun crime; many have steady jobs and families, and some have gone on to, and finished, college. There were no youth homicides in the city of Sacramento for the first two years of the program in that city. The program mediated 108 community conflicts in 2019, ensuring that disputes didn't escalate into gun violence, injury, or death. After the Advance Peace program launched in Stockton, that city experienced a 21 percent decline in gun homicides. A youth-focused community-based organization (CBO) leader reflected on the community impact of the Peacemaker Fellowship: "As the frequency of shootings went down, and our young people could ride the bus or walk home from school without fear, it was like a giant exhale. It's not perfect, but now more teens are riding bikes, using parks, just walking to the store. They just wouldn't do that before."

Another former NCA described the transformative impact of the program this way: "You want to talk about the significant drop in crime? Talk to these young people. They control the flow. So if they're the ones controlling the flow, let's make sure they know that we care about them. The city, the community, we care about you. And the way we show you that we care about you is we're willing to invest in you."[45]

The successes of the Advance Peace model in Richmond and other cities is making some public officials and law enforcement uncomfortable. Lieutenant Arnold Threets of the Richmond Police Department suggested that success where others, particularly law enforcement, have failed can generate envy and resistance, especially when they feel resources might be taken away. A report on the Richmond ONS program also noted how the model threatens ideals of worthiness in American public policy: "Resistance to the ONS method may also reflect a more broadly American stigma against handouts. While the use of tangible incentives such as cash stipends and travel are very much in line with prevailing capitalist values, the very act of giving them away for free—especially to those who may still operate outside of society's lawful boundaries—would seem to conflict with a deep-seated ethos in our culture that opportunity must extend from merit."[46]

Yet, as Boggan powerfully explained, "For the first time in these young men's lives, they have city government seeking them—not with a badge, not with a gun—but seeking them, saying, 'We need your help, we need your partnership, and we want to help you.'"

Healing Cities with Street Love

According to Boggan, the Peacemaker Fellowship is injecting love into public policy: "Our work is an ecosystem of love, healing, affirmation, harm reduction, investment of time, attention, services, opportunities, resources, and personal leadership development tailored to the needs, experiences, and realities of our fellows. It's about fellows taking part in and achieving equitable outcomes, where the product of the engagement is the reduction of gun violence in that community."

The Advance Peace program offers one model for how to acknowledge the traumas of community gun violence and institute practices that help heal and reduce gun crimes. Communities hold a wealth of information and valuable assets that can contribute to both locally and culturally relevant healing strategies. The Advance Peace model suggests that community-driven problem solving can keep locals safe and provide a cascading set of benefits, from direct support to those at the center of violence, to those in their networks, to the entire neighborhood and to the city.

Spreading Urban Healing

Sociologist Patrick Sharkey, in his book *Uneasy Peace*, argues that in each city he studied "every new organization created to confront violence and build stronger neighborhoods led to about a 1% drop in violent crime and murder."[47] This research has also found that the impacts of community-based work are amplified when government (but not necessarily the police) is a partner. This is exactly what is happening in each of the cities adopting the Advance Peace approach, including Richmond, Sacramento, Stockton, and Fresno, California, and Fort Worth, Texas. New York City has moved in the direction of the Advance Peace model with the 2017 creation of the Office to Prevent Gun Violence, which is coordinating a network of community-based organizations to provide intensive street outreach and community engagement to prevent violence. In 2019, the New Jersey legislature passed legislation to create and fund the New Jersey Violence Intervention Program. In California, tens of cities are now participating in the California Violence Intervention and Prevention Program, which is supporting community-based efforts to reduce homicides by focusing on the small segment of the population that is at the highest risk of perpetrating or being victimized by gun crime. Becoming a city for life means inculcating love into public policy.[48]

The healing characteristics of Advance Peace include its focus on participation by those most harmed, relationship building between traumatized young people and "wounded healing" elders, and resources from the city to make this work thrive and survive. These features, plus the power of a community-based organization engaging in the powerful discourse of science, are all features of the healing approach used by residents in the Mukuru informal settlement of Nairobi, described in chapter 3. What is so beautiful about both Richmond and Nairobi is that healing is happening in the most unlikely of urban places and being facilitated by the most unlikely people.

Chapter 3

Slum Scientists Diagnosing Traumas

When COVID-19 was threatening the slums of Nairobi, residents of the Mukuru informal settlement quickly mobilized to protect themselves and their community. Jane Waritu and Doris Bosibori engaged community health workers across the sprawling slum and asked them what the barriers were to keeping people safe. Doris is a long-time community leader who had organized residents to prevent evictions and to demand clean and safe sanitation in Mukuru. Jane is a community mobilizer with Shack/Slum Dwellers International (SDI), and their sister organization, Muungano Wa Wanavijiji, or the Muungano Alliance, which works directly with the urban poor in Kenya. Both women went into action to promote health. Mukuru is one of Nairobi's largest informal settlements, with an estimated 300,000 residents, located just over 4 miles (7 km) from the city's central business district and adjacent to the Makadara industrial zone. The word *Mukuru* means "dump site" in Swahili, reflecting the history of waste dumping that partially defines the area and is a daily reminder to the poor residents as to how they are defined.

Doris is a charismatic leader who operates a hair salon, which is where she heard story after story of her clients experiencing trauma, such as sexual abuse and rape, and the indignity of not having a safe, hygienic, and private toilet or bath. "We were living in daily fear of using a toilet or washing," she explained to me.

Doris started a petition in her shop for women to sign calling on the government of Kenya to deliver their constitutional right to safe sanitation. Word soon spread across the community. Doris partnered with Muungano and SDI to file a legal claim against the owners of the land and the Kenyan government on behalf of over 10,000 women. The case garnered international attention.

"That campaign taught me that us women have power in our collective experiences. In listening to my clients, I also learned that we are more than just what is happening to us. We are able to solve the challenges we face because we are already doing it. We just need the resources and power to reach everyone."

Now, Doris and Jane are addressing a similar fear, generated by COVID-19. "It was a little different with the unknown fear of COVID, but the lack of basic services was still the main issue," Jane told me. "We asked the health workers what the community needed to stay healthy, and water, toilets, and food were the main issues."

Jane and Doris tapped into the hundreds of Muungano Alliance members across Mukuru. The Muungano Alliance has been organizing slum dwellers across Kenya, and particularly in Nairobi, for decades. They have primarily focused on building social and financial capital with the poor and leading action research with residents. Much of this research highlights the gross inequities slum dwellers face in terms of living conditions. Muungano uses these data as an advocacy tool, pressuring government and international organizations to direct their investments into lifesaving drinking water, sanitation and energy infrastructure, new housing, education and youth programs, and other initiatives for the urban poor.

Jane, Doris, and the Muungano Alliance had already gathered preliminary data with resident "street scientists" in Mukuru to help convince the Nairobi city and county governments to declare Mukuru a Special Planning Area (SPA). This was the first time that a slum in Nairobi had received this designation, and it was both practically and symbolically important. Practically, the SPA designation stopped illegal development in the community and legally empowered Muungano to co-lead a research-to-action process that generated a new community development plan. It recognized that the informal settlement of Mukuru was a community (something governments often want to ignore) and that the area had significant challenges that threatened the health of residents and the entire city. It was also an acknowledgment by government that the lives of the poor mattered, they deserved attention, and that after years of resident-led research their evidence was worthy of action.

In their COVID response, Doris and Jane used their health and mapping data to strategically locate where new temporary toilets and water points should be located to ensure safe sanitation and handwashing. Jane told me, "We knew which schools didn't have toilets or water. Which group of structures didn't have functioning yard taps. Where street vendors, who were feeding hundreds, were concentrated." Within days Muungano brought in hundreds of temporary water jugs for handwashing stations (Figure 3.1). The health volunteers provided soap.

Doris described to me what would likely have happened if the COVID response had been left entirely to public health experts: "If it was the Ministry of Health coming in here or some global NGO that had lots of money but didn't know this community, they would have missed all the vulnerable locations. We knew from years of mapping and data collection. In a day these places had clean water."

Muungano also helped provide electronic thermometers to the over 500 community health workers so they could take temperatures to screen people who might be infected. The health workers took temperatures when they delivered free food to households, another emergency measure put in place by Muungano. Food was also distributed at central locations, but only after residents identified places where this could be done in a socially distanced way. Resident volunteers who had helped map the entire community were now enrolled to identify particularly vulnerable households, such as where a woman lived alone or was pregnant. Locals also quickly turned to their sewing skills for making cloth masks. Muungano and their network of citizen scientists distributed the masks for free to as many residents as possible. The community surveyors also helped identify areas in the community that

Figure 3.1 Water access in Mukuru, Nairobi.

could act as isolation areas for infected residents. It is often a challenge in slums for residents to get care, and there is a reluctance to remain in a hospital for treatment due to fear of the costs.

These early measures helped prevent widespread deprivation in Mukuru, especially as the economy ground to a halt and an evening curfew was harshly enforced by the government. Within days, the Kenyan government invited Muungano and some resident experts to join the newly created National Ministry of Health, COVID-19 Taskforce. The task force would guide efforts to prevent a widespread outbreak of SARs-CoV-2, particularly in the densely packed informal settlements in Kenya's largest cities of Nairobi, Mombasa, and Kisumu.

While the task force worked to deliver rapid disease prevention to the slums and the entire population, the rates of COVID-19 infections and deaths did not spike in Nairobi or Kenya. This was a surprise to many because in Nairobi, particularly among the urban poor, thousands are HIV-positive and manage their infection daily using antiretroviral drugs. Those fighting HIV by definition have compromised immune systems, so the hypothesis was that COVID-19 would tear through Kenya's informal settlements like AIDS had done or Ebola did in Guinea, Liberia, and Sierra Leone in 2014. Nairobi also has a high incidence of tuberculosis, with an increasing number of undetected cases, also leading epidemiologists to claim that, as an airborne disease, COVID-19 would create a heavy disease and death burden for those living in urban slums. In Mukuru and similar slums like Kibera, Mathare, and Korogocho, close to one-third of the children have stunted growth due largely to malnutrition. The cause of malnutrition in the slums is multifactorial but includes high food prices, widespread food contamination, chronic diarrhea, and frequent parasitic infections, all of which compromise nutrient absorption and limit growth. These same factors can also compromise the immune system, so again the thought was that a COVID-19 outbreak would ravage children in the slums. Additionally, chronic illnesses, such as diabetes, hypertension, and rheumatic heart disease, are increasingly common in Nairobi's slums and are the same preexisting conditions and comorbidities tied to COVID-19 infections and deaths burdening Black, Indigenous, and People of Color in rich countries.

Yet, as of December 2020, in Kenya, a country of over 50 million people, there were just over 90,000 cases nationwide and 1,500 deaths. At the same time in California, a state with about 40 million people, there were over 1.65 million cases, and over 21,000 deaths. In Nairobi, 90 percent of those testing positive have been asymptomatic. Few epidemiologists agree on why this is the case; some suggest the Kenyan population is younger than others around the world. Others speculate that Kenyans spend more time outside, avoiding indoor exposures. Still others suggest that East Africans may have immunity to coronaviruses from previous exposures.[1] While a definitive answer may take some time, the rapid response by resident scientists may have helped stave off widespread suffering. It also contributed to a new power and legitimacy for slum communities who had been dumped on and ignored for decades.

According to Patrick Njoroge, a community organizer with Muungano, "We used the COVID-19 crisis to show we were prepared and didn't need outsiders telling us what to do or what we needed to protect ourselves. We used this legitimacy with government to push for more systemic change. We brought in youth leaders and helped create what became the National Hygiene Program,[2] called Kazi Mtaani (jobs in our 'hood). We knew the first thing the community wanted was an opportunity to earn, to have the resources to make healthy choices."

As the COVID crisis hit other countries, the Kenyan government adopted Kazi Mtaani, and employed thousands of youth to clean up the slums by unclogging drains, collecting waste, and helping to prepare dirt roads and paths to be paved. The program also employed youth to plant thousands of trees and start building bridges for safer river crossings. Young people were also employed to help repair and paint government facilities in and around the slums and to start a large-scale urban agriculture initiative in over 173 informal settlements.[3] The program pays youth slum dwellers up to $5 per day for this work. Payments are made to youth through the cell phone–based payment system called M-Pesa.

Joseph Kimani, another organizer with Muungano told me, "The jobs have helped change the opportunities for youth, but also have begun to really change the communities. Seeing slums with newly paved roads and youth getting paid by government to collect waste was something very new. Kazi Mtaani has us seeing how we can repair our communities in new ways."

Citizens as Health Scientists

Community scientists help promote healing by defining the hazards they face. This helps build new relationships within the community and with supportive outsiders (such as academic researchers), and contributes to the cocreation of solutions where residents can "see themselves" in the data underwriting interventions.

Mukuru is one of the poorest and environmentally hazardous urban areas in all of Nairobi and possibly in East Africa. Its residents face multiple, overlapping hazards and traumas, and its poverty and political vulnerability make it an unlikely site for healing. There are millions of people today living in urban informal settlements, and the numbers are only expected to grow. The community science processes in Mukuru demonstrate that those suffering the most can and must be viewed as experts in diagnosing the traumas they are experiencing and be active agents in designing solutions for healing.

Unfortunately, it is common for professional scientists, many in the fields of public health, medicine, and environmental protection, to ignore the knowledge of those in cities living with toxic exposures and disease. In my 2005 book, *Street Science*, I wrote about the importance of local knowledge in technical scientific issues. I built upon longstanding ideas in public health and medicine focused on community-based participatory action research (CBPAR), which emphasizes that good science in complex, hard-to-reach places demands participation of local people.[4] The participation of local people in researching the risks they face and also in remediating those risks, has come to be called coproduction.[5]

Coproduction is an important aspect of urban health and healing because it involves the identification of stressors or hazards by the person experiencing them instead of someone from the outside, such as a professional scientist, defining them. Imagine the process of walking into your physician's office with a pain or concern about your body. You know more than your clinician about how you are feeling, where in your body the ache is, what you have been doing in the last day or so, what you might have eaten or been exposed to, and other things about your body and the context of your pain. This is critical information to correctly diagnose what might be causing your pain or illness. As the conversation with your clinician proceeds (and hopefully it does for more than a few seconds), a well-trained doctor will start to ask probing questions and will follow up with statements or descriptions about events that you provide. The clinician should use their training to listen for certain clues that might lead them to recommend further diagnostic tests. This process of dialogue, listening, diagnosis, and hypothesis testing utilizing multiple forms of expertise—those of the patient and physician in this case, is the process of the coproduction of expertise. As Sheila Jasanoff of Harvard University has reminded us in her work on expertise in complex scientific problem solving, depending on the questions asked, the layperson or professional may be equally expert. This doesn't make expertise or science entirely relative, but it demands that the context always be taken into consideration and the process of inquiry given equal weight as the products, or the outcomes, of that process.

CBPAR may be familiar to those in the field of public health. CB-PAR combines professional techniques with community insights to define problems and research questions, gather and analyze data, direct action, and evaluate the efficacy of interventions. This method, building from traditions of participatory action research (PAR), aims to make research more democratic, ensure that poor people and People of Color are active participants in decisions that impact their lives, and incorporate local knowledge and lived experience into research and action. In these ways, CBPAR can enable street science processes to open up how authoritative technical knowledge is produced and becomes stabilized or institutionalized over time, so that it becomes a "given" or "taken for granted truth." Like CBPAR, street science aims to problematize the origins and substance of the meanings of policy issues, who was included or left out of generating these meanings, and, builds on constructivist work in the social sciences highlighting that scientific legitimacy is simultaneously a social, political, and material phenomenon, none of which can be disentangled from the others. *Street science* aims to respond to those critics of CBPAR by suggesting that science and technology are not "contaminated" by society, but rather embed and are embedded in "social practices, identities, norms, conventions, discourses, instruments, and institutions—in short, in all the building blocks of what we term the social."[6]

Street science can help reveal the complex, often overlapping factors that influence health in cities, especially those traumas and toxic stressors identified in chapter 1. Importantly, street science can help emphasize that cities are always doubly constructed; first, through the material and built environment (i.e., the buildings, streets, parks, etc.), and second, through the assigning of meanings, interpretations, narratives, perceptions, feelings, and imaginations to those urban spaces. The assignment of meaning, such as "that is a safe place" or "that is a nice neighborhood," is constructed by both local people and interested institutions. For example, a real estate company might give a neighborhood a new name to make it attractive for marketing purposes and to avoid a label or stigma from the past. This was the case when private developers attempted to rename part of Harlem in New York City "SoHa" (similar to a wealthy White area in New York called SoHo), which was criticized by residents as an attempt to erase the community's identification as a home of Black culture.[7] Street science is always a contested process, as meanings are made, remade, challenged, and redefined.

The attention to process and participation is a central tension within the street science process. Elinor Ostrom, the Nobel Prize–winning economist, studied how local people who were "outside" the organizations or institutions of service delivery, could be essential in the effective delivery of that service. In one case, she documented how local residents worked with public officials in urban Brazil to build and manage infrastructure.[8] By "insiders" she meant the government agencies and civil servants that tend to produce and deliver education, health, or infrastructure. According to Ostrom, the residents or "clients" of these services should be viewed as active, not passive, agents from the outset in the planning, design, construction, and delivery of essential services. In the Brazil example offered by Ostrom, municipal government officials in Recife actively encouraged local citizens to codesign a condominial sewer system. Residents decided on the layout and location of the pipe and whose property would be impacted. They also engaged in discussions over the trade-offs of different decision options and ultimately how the system would be maintained and managed. In many ways, Ostrom's work identified the key aspects of street science, since she aimed to ensure that local communities had ownership over the process and outcomes (in this case a sewer system), which would be more efficient in the long run since it could avoid typical challenges of delivering services to low-resourced urban areas, such as the lack of maintenance or ensuring affordability for all. As Ostrom points out, coproduction demands not just reenvisioning the ways publics or residents participate in science and municipal service delivery, but a wholesale reimagining of the institutions of the state and changing the mindset of civil servants to be active participants rather than technocrats.

Beyond Citizen Science: Street Science as a
Step toward Healing

As defined by US government agencies, citizen science is primarily either a way to capture hard-to-reach information using volunteers or an attempt to ensure that lay publics understand, appreciate, and see the rationale behind the findings from professional scientists.[9] Yet there is almost no discussion of how citizen science might support health and healing, despite decades of knowledge that when we are more involved in understanding what harms us and how, we tend to take more proactive and preventive measures.[10] There is also very little engagement with whom the citizens in participatory science are or should be. Street science aims to make explicit that those who are already suffering and harmed by science, technology, and medicine, such as Black, Indigenous, People of Color (BIPOC), women, those with disabilities, and others, must be at the center of the process.

The volunteers in citizen science rarely, if ever, benefit economically from professional scientific findings or processes. Scientists frequently gain financially from their discoveries, publications, and patents. Street science recognizes that a key aspect of healing must be that those whose bodies and communities have been exploited, dehumanized, and extracted from must share in the economic *and* human health benefits of the science they coproduce.

The author Anand Giridharadas eloquently pointed out in his 2018 book, *Winners Take All: The Elite Charade of Changing the World*, that wealthy philanthropists are often behind the setting of scientific research agendas that have a large influence over universities and international institutions but are entirely divorced from democratic accountability.[11]

Giridharadas cogently argues that the world needs to stop outsourcing the changes needed to heal and address global challenges to "plutocratic elites," or the unaccountable billionaires setting the global health agenda, such as Bill Gates, Michael Bloomberg, Mark Zuckerberg, the Sackler family, and their related philanthropies. These "recently enlightened" billionaires now willing to give away their money, got rich on the backs of low-wage workers by not paying their fair share of taxes, and fighting to retain their monopolies, according to Giridhara-das. The origins of their wealth are often through means that starved the public sector of the resources to do good.

Giridharadas delves deeper into why these elites are bad for democratically setting the health and healing agenda, stating that these people and their organizations "mostly aren't democratic, nor do they reflect collective problem-solving or universal solutions. Rather, they favor the use of the private sector and its charitable spoils, the market way of looking at things, and the bypassing of government. They reflect a highly influential view that the winners of an unjust status quo—and the tools and mentalities and values that helped them win—are the secret to redressing the injustices."[12] He argues that these elites have "captured" so many nonprofit organizations, nongovernmental organizations, university research centers, and even international agencies (such as the World Health Organization), that it is often hard to identify what a true people's scientific and policy agenda might look like.

Giridharadas suggests that the legacy of settler colonialism is still with us today, lodged inside wealthy foundations and "do-gooder" philanthropies. The lack of representation of leaders and ideas from the South, particularly communities like Mukuru, remains the reality in global health. This form of "health colonialism" can, for instance, result in global health resources going to address rare diseases while millions die each year from easily preventable diseases like diarrhea. According to Dr. Madhukar Pai, director of McGill University's Global Health Program, along with coauthors, "Global health organizations, for example, are still primarily located in the global North, are mostly run by leaders who come from high-income countries, and have taken a long time to accept civil society or patient community representation on their boards. Even when organizations do have such representation, most of those appointed still do not hold decision-making powers. Women as well as experts from low- and middle-income countries are still strongly underrepresented in global health leadership positions across health sectors. Researchers, funders and universities from high-income countries continue to dominate global health research."[13]

Of course, who gets to even raise these issues and lead decolonization discussions—even how and when this term is used—is contested.

I am not suggesting that there is one strategy or force for decoloniz-
ing health agendas and action, but that ideas and interventions too
often ignore those at the center of the health and healing needs, such
as those in Mukuru. Street science may be one way to ensure that the
healing agenda is made by, not for, the urban poor.

Street Science for Health and Resilience in
Mukuru, Nairobi

The Mukuru informal settlement comprises three communities, Mukuru Kwa Njenga, Mukuru Kwa Reuben, and Viwandani, and thirty-
one villages or neighborhoods. The community is located in the eastern
industrial belt of Nairobi, bisected west–east by the Ngong River. In
the 1980s the Kenyan government issued 99-year leases to private investors for the land that is now Mukuru. The lease agreement was
for grantees to established industries as well as redevelopment plans
within 6 months. The plans were never drafted. Instead the leasehold-
ers "sold" parcels for third parties to build basic rental housing. These
structure owners are the community's "slum landlords." (See Box 3 for
more on Nairobi and Mukuru.)

Like many informal settlements in Nairobi, Mukuru's built environment is characterized by a series of densely constructed, nearly 10- ×
10-foot (3- × 3-meter) informal structures made of corrugated sheet
metal and wood, many having dirt floors. Almost all the residents are
renters. The tenants pay close to 4,000 Kenyan shillings a month, over
a third of their income, for poor-quality housing and then pay extra for
water, electricity, and each toilet use. This is what we call the poverty
penalty—the poor paying high costs for low-quality living. However,
residents of Mukuru pay and stay because the settlement is located
near informal, day-labor jobs, they are often close to family and social
supports, and they just don't have many other choices in Nairobi.

In some villages within Mukuru, the sheet metal homes are stacked
on top of one another to create a second floor. They are almost all
organized in a haphazard way, since some areas were built very rapidly
as former squatters built structures. This makes the area surrounding
the structures hard to navigate. Moving around the community, one

Figure 3.2 Street in Mukuru, Nairobi.

has to navigate narrow dirt paths, traverse large ditches where water or waste is allowed to gather, and then reach wider dirt roads where the occasional vehicle will pass and connect the community to the rest of the city (Figure 3.2).

I have spent many weeks over the past 6 years in Mukuru, attending community workshops, working with residents and NGO partners on collaborative research, and interviewing tens of youth, health care workers, teachers, street vendors, and many others. My time there was always as a partner with Muungano and SDI. My team of researchers was asked to join their consortium to help prepare for and then cocreate the SPA analysis and recommendations. I had spent the 5 or so years before we started in Mukuru, working with residents and community groups in the Mathare informal settlement, another sprawling, self-built slum to the north of Mukuru. Both Mukuru and Mathare had once been sites for colonialist and postcolonial elites to extract resources from the earth for profit. Both places had large rock quarries that served the growth of Nairobi and East Africa. Today, both

Mathare and Mukuru have been left bare; the once fertile soil was scraped down to the bedrock and clay, so that rain and river waters pool on the surface. Like most informal urban communities around the world, Mukuru's residents are typically from outside the city and frequently expect that this is a temporary stop in a journey toward greater economic and residential mobility. However, as is evident from the thousands of families, middle-aged residents, and elderly residents in Mukuru, the place has more often been a final destination. The long tenure of many of the residents in Mukuru means that generations of Kenyans have been unfairly exposed to the structural violence that exists in this and other informal settlements—stigma, lack of basic infrastructure, daily threats of violence, gangs and cartels controlling most services and monitoring movement—and an absence of the state. The urban poor in Nairobi's slums have been left to survive and navigate the daily risks that they face on their own.

Mukuru has a set of risks and traumas related to its built environment and location that other slums in Nairobi do not face. First, it is close to Nairobi's industrial area, where gated buildings spew smoke and release colored effluent from pipes that poke out at random from their fence-line facilities. Many of the buildings are noisy day and night, and few of the industries employ local residents. A railway that serves the industries runs through the residential area of Mukuru. The rail tracks and an ever widening buffer zone between the tracks and the community act as a spine that splits two of Mukuru's settlements, Kwa Njenga and Kwa Reuben. The railway tracks make for a common travel route, many times a dangerous one, as well as a dumping ground. There is no municipal waste collection in Mukuru, so residents must find their own ways to dispose of household and human waste. Garbage, like in most cities, is a lucrative business, so groups of youth "cartels" have moved in to control its collection, recycling, and disposal. International NGOs have found human waste a valuable commodity in Mukuru, as it is the home of a company called Sanergy, which installs portable toilets. These toilets are leased to a resident who charges other residents per use, keeps the toilet clean, and provides the waste back to Sanergy, which they sell as fertilizer. While this sounds like an environmentalist's dream, portable toilets are inadequate for managing the waste of a community of over 300,000 people, and they fail to address the stressors and risks that women face around toilets, namely stigma and sexual violence.

Mukuru faces unique risks from Nairobi's largest petroleum pipeline, which traverses one side of the community. A village in Mukuru, called Pipeline, was the site of one of Nairobi's worst pipeline-related fires, which killed at least seventy-five people and severely burned hundreds. According to news and resident reports, the pipeline had a large leak, and Mukuru residents came to capture some of the oil for their personal use. The UK *Guardian* news report on the explosion and fire capture the conditions in Mukuru at the time:

> "The fire that consumed the slum highlighted the squalid living conditions for many in that settlement, which sprang up to serve the city's industrial area. Rescue workers had to dodge hanging wires that bring illegal power to the tin shacks. Residents cannot afford electricity, but most have a television aerial jutting above their homes, powered by the thriving underground economy. Many interviewed said the disaster could have been averted if government agencies had not all but abandoned the area. 'Here it is every man for himself,' said Washington Ouma, a 23-year-old casual worker. 'If police on patrol ventured here, they would have noticed that people had been scooping oil for nearly 12 hours and would have stopped it.'"[14]

In spite of these and other risks, Mukuru residents came together to push back against an absentee government and exploitation by industry. Organized by Muungano, they began to document their living conditions, from dangerous toilets to polluted air and water to frequent floods. They used evidence and data to set the redevelopment agenda on their terms.

Women's Safety, Sexual Violence, and Sanitation

In urban Kenya, inadequate sanitation is one of the leading causes of illness and loss of life for women aged 15–49.[15] Both Amnesty International and the African Population and Health Research Center,[16] one of the most experienced research groups studying health in urban informal settlements, note that inadequate and unsafe sanitation in

Nairobi's informal settlements forces girls and women to be unnecessarily exposed to pathogens, urinary tract infections, physical violence from rape, and the stress of not having secure and dignified places to change sanitary napkins, wash, and relieve themselves, especially at night.[17,18]

The slums of Nairobi are infamous for the plastic bags full of human excrement that "fly" through the community due to the absence of adequate sanitation. With the help of Muungano, the women mobilized—over 10,000 marched to city hall and filed one of the first ever class-action lawsuits against the Kenyan government for the right to safe toilets.[19,20] They demanded their constitutional right to safe sanitation, as defined in Kenya's 2010 Constitution. In order to support their claims, the women codesigned a data-gathering process with my research team.

The women were trained to spatially map every toilet location in Mukuru, describe the type of toilet and any other features, such as cost, if it had a lock, lighting, security, or whether it connected to a sewer pipe or drained into the open street (Figure 3.3). They found that there were 1,356 toilets in Mukuru, which meant that, on average, about 220 people shared one toilet. In some cases, we found that up to 547 households, or about 1,500 people, shared one toilet. Consider that the Sphere Humanitarian Standards, the international guidelines for emergency response, such as establishing a camp for displaced persons during war or after an earthquake or other disaster, recommends no more than 50 people per toilet.[21]

Of the thousand or so toilets that did exist, over 75 percent were pit latrines with no locks or security. Less than 2 percent of households had access to a private, in-home toilet. Everyone else had to pay for each use, "pay per wipe" as they described it to me, which cost about five Kenyan shillings. Considering that the average household monthly income in Mukuru was 12,000 shillings, we estimated that toilet use was costing a household between 7 and 12 percent of its monthly income.

The women who conducted the community mapping also found that fewer than half of Mukuru's 300,000 residents lived within 50 meters of a toilet. This was largely because the toilets were concentrated in certain areas of the settlement. For instance, the Sanergy toilets

Figure 3.3 Typical toilet in Mukuru, Nairobi.

(glorified porta potties), often called Fresh Life, are concentrated along streets with lots of pedestrian traffic and activity to ensure that they get a good return on investment. What this spatial unevenness meant for many women and girls was that at night they were either forced into open defecation, using a bucket inside their structure as a toilet, or in some cases, they told us they stopped drinking any liquids after 5:00 or 6:00 p.m. to avoid having to use the toilet after dark. The impacts, according to interviews and focus groups about these findings, were devastating for the mental and physical health of girls and women.

The women went beyond the quantitative spatial and survey data and had the idea to give voice to the experiences of young women and adolescents. Along with the Muungano organizers, they asked teachers from schools in Mukuru to offer girls the opportunity to tell their stories through an assignment. After learning about the health and ecological impacts of inadequate sanitation they were asked to tell their own stories about their experiences using community toilets. There were over fifty essays, and each had a unique and tragic component to it. They recalled the regular fear of using the toilet and frequently witnessing or experiencing sexual violence and rape. They described the raw indignity of having to defecate in the open and not having a place to change and dispose of menstrual pads, and of being forced to witness family members washing naked in the open or using a bucket as a toilet. Some of the young women described having frequent flashbacks after being sexually assaulted while washing or using a toilet. Still others mentioned the stigma and discrimination they faced after getting pregnant after being raped and now being HIV positive.

Edith Kalela, who was working with Muungano Alliance and the women to organize their data and advocacy efforts, noted, "Telling their stories was both empowering and healing. It was their voices and their experiences. The stories also pointed out that this wasn't a woman or girls' issue. The men, the community, the government, the institutions supposed to protect, were all put on notice. The women's work made this a city and national issue, and a global human rights issue." With permissions, I've reproduced some of these powerful stories that the young women wrote (Figure 3.4).

Street Science as Resistance and Power

While we were processing the quantitative and qualitative data from the women's street science project, a number of us were invited to a workshop in Nairobi sponsored by the Bill and Melinda Gates Foundation. Gates was supporting some related data collection work by SDI, which acts as the global network convener and secretariat for Muungano. One workshop session explored how our ongoing Mukuru work might inform the Gates's "Reinvent the Toilet Challenge."[22,23] As part of this initiative, the Gates Foundation was funding consortia of universities, industries, governments, and development banks to come up with innovative solutions to the lack of safe, sanitary, and sustainable toilets. As they described the toilet challenge during the workshop, I was struck by how the community members living with the toilets were not part of the conversation, initiative, or resources Gates was offering. The Gates Initiative sought out scientists to design

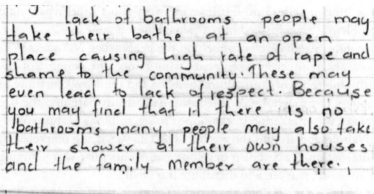

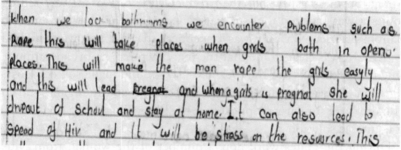

Figure 3.4 Essays about toilets and indignity by girls in Mukuru.

a decentralized, environmentally sustainable, profitable, twenty-first-century toilet. They presented findings during the workshop from a Boston Consulting Group study which estimated that the sanitation market in developing countries was an untapped $6 billion and was ripe for "disruptive technologies."[24] The World Bank president, Jim Yong Kim, stated at another event, called the Gates Toilet Expo, that the Bank was partnering with Gates to "help catalyze a new generation of solutions that can bring safe sanitation to everyone, everywhere on earth."[25]

One of the innovative "solutions" discussed at the workshop was the "pee-poo bag."[26] The Peepoo bag promised to be a hygienic way to relieve oneself into a compostable bag that would sanitize the waste and then decompose, providing "triple benefits" for the slum, according to its inventors: safe toilet, hygienic disposal, and enriched soil for gardens. The manufacturers of the Peepoo bag claimed that by "turning human waste into fertilizer in a very short time, what could be a problem is transformed into a valuable resource,"

The white, Swedish scientist behind the Peepoo bag is Anders Wilhelmson, an architect and professor, who gained the support of the Swedish University of Agricultural Science and the Royal Institute of Technology in Stockholm. Wilhelmson had already patented the bag technology, was marketing it, and hoped to sell millions to slum dwellers in Nairobi and around the world.[27] The bag was being marketed by IAS International, a Swedish development agency that was planning to manufacture, market, and distribute it globally.[28]

The business aspects of the product were one of its key selling points. I was shocked that such a product was making the rounds in Nairobi's slums. Not only was I skeptical that the bag was safe and hygienic, it was clear to me that the manufacturers hadn't spent much time in Mukuru, where the rock and clay ground made soil composting more a dream than a reality. My partners at Muungano and in Mukuru were similarly skeptical that the Peepoo bag was a sustainable or equitable solution.

During the Gates workshop, a number of the women from Mukuru in the room were asked to share some of their research findings. They described the indignity of not having a safe, in-home toilet. They questioned technical innovations that Gates was supporting, like the Peepoo bag, and whether they were an actual solution or a distraction from what they really wanted and deserved. Doris from Mukuru spoke out and challenged the Gates team's emphasis on technological solutions like the Peepoo bag as a way to achieve the twenty-first-century toilet: "We understand that you will likely go back today to your hotel or home and have a toilet that can flush, water for washing, and even a lock on your door for privacy. I wonder if you would agree that the twentieth-century toilet is doing just fine for you? The technology is already here to give us slum dwellers that. I don't see why your science should focus on a future toilet that you yourselves won't use but you expect the poor to graciously accept. Maybe the Gates-funded scientists would like to use the Peepoo bag for a week and stay in Mukuru, while us women can use their hotel? After which we can debate the way forward." It was clear that the Gates people and researchers were numb to the human conditions in Mukuru. The Mukuru women, in part empowered by their lived experience and their street science documentation, were not going to settle for "putting lipstick on a pig." They expressed with no reservations that the technologically advanced Peepoo bag was an insult. The meeting only galvanized the women and Muungano to further their efforts for what residents believed were more equitable, democratically derived, and healthy interventions.

From Boutique Project to Integrated Planning

We used the mapping, survey, and narrative data generated with Mukuru residents to support the SPA upgrading plan. As Jack Makau, the director of SDI-Kenya would tell me as we walked together through Mukuru, "The SPA was important to give voice to what residents in Mukuru already experienced every day. It was important to capture not just risks but also identify the ways residents were coping with different health issues. The SPA process put in motion a process that looked at other, related issues, such as education, environmental pollution, economic development and land rights."

As Makau so insightfully suggests, making your own suffering visible to yourself and others is a key aspect of healing. When cities fail to acknowledge "suffering in plain sight" it further marginalizes communities and allows the structural violence to continue. The suffering in Mukuru would be silent no more, and residents continued to mobilize and engage in science to demand healthy improvements.

Documenting Air Pollution

A key challenge for the SPA was to gather evidence to either confirm or question the perceptions of residents that their reports of black smoke and smells in the air were damaging to their health. According to the World Health Organization, air pollution in cities is causing more death and disease than tobacco, malaria, and HIV combined. However, the community didn't have the same type of data about air pollution that they had about toilets. A first step was to mobilize young people who were already making music videos to tell their stories. Muungano enrolled youth to make a documentary about the reasons they thought they regularly experienced odors, itchy eyes, skin rashes, and running noses. In one video, "The Unchecked Injustice," the youth asked other young people to describe what they experienced in their daily activities.[29] The video shows dark clouds of smoke emanating from the neighboring industries and the oily liquid that was released from the industries and flooded the open drains across the community. The youth noted that local air pollution also came from burning garbage and tires, but this was largely because there was no waste collection, and the piles continued to grow larger. The videos helped mobilize a number of youths to work with the Stockholm Environment Institute (SEI)-Africa to be trained as air pollution citizen scientists.

As Philip Osano, director of SEI-Africa, describes it, "We mobilized the youth, who were already expert in knowing where pollution was coming from and the impacts on families. We knew that a recent study of matatu (private minibuses used for public transit) drivers showed how bad the air on-the-ground could be, especially for the urban poor. But, no one really had good data from inside a slum. It was important to have youth be leaders in the process."

A team of youth citizen scientists were recruited, and they first helped my university team map the locations and activities of all the industries surrounding Mukuru. We added research on the kinds of production practices, the types of chemicals that might be used, and the typical waste products from the industries the youth identified.

The field survey found 1,151 industrial sites in the area surrounding Mukuru, 718 of which were suspected of using unregulated, toxic production processes (Figure 3.5). The youth scientists documented when they observed dark smoke and blackish water coming from pipes sticking out of the fences and rooftops of the industries. At least ten different waste-burning sites were identified and mapped by the youth researchers. One facility, called Usafi Waste Disposal Plant, was found to be burning medical waste without any emissions controls.

Six youth were then trained to carry a low-cost air pollution monitor in their backpack and walk the community using frequently traveled pathways and roads that they selected. They did this for at least 5 hours a day for 2 weeks. The monitors captured small particulate matter (PM)

Figure 3.5 Polluting industries surrounding Mukuru.

pollution, called PM 2.5. The youth shadowed residents in Mukuru as they conducted their daily business, whether it was street vendors, a community health worker doing home visits, a primary school teacher, a secondhand clothes hawker, and other youth who were doing manual day labor, such as waste picking and recycling. They shadowed the workers as well. The point was to ensure that the science reflected the lived reality of the community, not the air measured on the rooftop of a building, which is typical in urban environmental sampling. All the movements of the youth scientists were tracked using GPS, and they kept a diary or log detailing where they went and what they witnessed.

What the youth scientists found only confirmed their suspicions and those of many in Mukuru. The monitors returned PM 2.5 readings with a mean between 22 and 40 $\mu g/m^3$, with daily peaks between 100 and 350 $\mu g/m^3$. These values far exceeded the World Health Organization's safe annual exposure average of 10 $\mu g/m^3$. A map was generated based on the youth citizen scientists walking routes and included air pollution concentrations at select intervals. The map displayed the different walking routes citizen scientists took and the measured concentrations of pollutants along those pathways. The industrial and other community activities identified earlier were included in the map to suggest potential pollution sources.

According to one youth street scientist, "I learned a lot during the project but more important, we are showing that the disease and illness is not our fault of just cooking or waste burning. The highest pollution was in the areas near the industries where we often saw them polluting."

Another researcher told me, "There is a place over in Rurie (one of the neighborhoods) where they take apart batteries and burn them and another where they are doing something with steel, I think. Over there we are always sneezing, and we weren't sure if it was because of us or the air pollution. Now we have more evidence about what is making us sick."

We also held workshops so other community members could discuss the findings, possible sources of toxic air pollution, and the health impacts, and begin to generate ideas for interventions. Workshops also included national and county government officials, representatives from over forty civil society organizations, and academic and health professionals. The research process aimed to be transparent and democratic from the outset, value the knowledge and skills of young people, and let the government know information was forthcoming that they would likely need to respond to. In the workshops we continued to share preliminary results and enroll residents in helping to draft policy and practice responses to the findings.[30]

Armed with their findings, the youth and research partners met with air pollution regulators from the Kenyan National Environmental Management Agency. The government regulators told them it was difficult for them to set and enforce pollution standards for so many small industries. As the negotiations continued, SEI created the Kenya Air Quality Network, consisting of community members, policy makers, and scientists, to further investigate the ways to reduce pollution in Mukuru and all impacted communities across Kenya.

Another group of youth scientists were trained to take soil samples, since many also suspected that the ground was full of contaminants from the industries. They collected soil samples across the entire community and had the results analyzed in a university lab. The soil sampling data found the presence of arsenic, lead, nickel, cadmium, and zinc, all of which can be serious health hazards if humans are exposed for prolonged periods at high levels. However, there is no safe exposure to lead, and it is especially damaging to the developing child's brain. The youth scientists documented that there were at least four informal, used lead-acid battery (ULAB) and electronic waste recycling operations in Mukuru. They observed that Mukuru ULAB recyclers tended to break up used batteries, remove the lead plates, and use open burn pits to melt down the materials, all creating lead-containing fumes and releasing dust and uncaptured waste into the surrounding soils.

Flooded Streets in Mukuru, Nairobi

Flooding and frequent cholera outbreaks are other concerning risks facing Mukuru residents. In the survey mentioned earlier, 17 percent of all households reported experiencing flooding in their homes at least once in the last 6 months. The frequency of flooding varied by settlement, with 34 percent of households reporting flooding in the past 6 months in Mukuru Kwa Reuben, compared to 21 percent in Viwandani. Forty-two percent of respondents noted that flooding had impacted their health in the last year (Figure 3.6).

To document who was most at risk and identify potential solutions, youth researchers working with our team and Muungano reviewed elevation maps of the community provided by the Nairobi Water and Sewer Company. We found that certain villages in Mukuru were almost 40 meters lower in elevation than other villages. Using handheld GPS devices, the community researchers walked these areas to document visible signs of severe flooding, like water stains on building walls. They also interviewed residents asking about flooding, particularly in areas where there were reports of cholera cases. Using this mixed set of methods, the researchers drafted the first ever flooding map of the community that included the local knowledge of those who experienced these risks. Importantly, the map highlights the relationships between frequent flooding and toilets, mostly pit latrines that were also impacted during these events. The researchers also created easy-to-understand graphics documenting the related, often overlapping,

Figure 3.6 Flooded street in Mukuru.

traumas from frequent flooding. These data were used to generate risk-reduction ideas in follow-up community-wide planning meetings. As part of their commitment to move from research to action, Muungano organized community consultations to discuss flood mitigation and how to eliminate risks. My team from UC Berkeley participated and helped turn their ideas into a specific riparian plan that was integrated into the overall set of healthy redevelopment proposals for what became the Mukuru Integrated Development Plan (MIDP).

The street science findings became the central focus of a Muungano-facilitated community planning process to further draft the MIDP. To ensure robust participation across Mukuru's sizable population, Muungano launched Baraza Ndogo (neighborhood forums) where at least 100 households sent representatives to engage in the planning process, called Tujuane Tujengane (Swahili for, Let's know each other, so we build each other). Women and youth were made leaders of the process. According to Patrick of Muungano, "The women were knowledgeable and respected, since some were the leaders of the health workers. They also were leaders of the fight for safe toilets and were often the first people in a household that cared for or treated someone that might be ill. They were the healers. It was important to have them lead the planning for how to improve the community."

After over 130 meetings spanning two and a half years, the street science data from the women and others were integrated into MIDP, which was completed at the end of 2020. The evidence gathered by the street scientists didn't just influence a plan, it contributed to new projects that are already having a positive impact on the lives of Mukuru residents.

Healing Infrastructure: The Mukuru Special Planning Area

By the time COVID-19 had emerged in Kenya, the Mukuru community and the Muungano Alliance had successfully drafted an integrated upgrade plan for the informal settlement. Specific sector plans were being consolidated to link new roads and drainage with water and sewer systems. A plan for new schools, health clinics, and markets was agreed upon, as was a strategy for waste collection and flood protection. The MIDP also linked the settlement to the fabric of the entire city, ensuring that residents could have not only physical mobility through new transit access but also social access through connections with institutions outside the community.

In part as a response to the emerging global COVID-19 crisis, the Kenyan government stepped in to quickly deliver services and supplies to informal settlements. The Nairobi Metropolitan Services Agency was given the leadership role to deliver infrastructure to the slums, and a military leader, General Mohammed Badi, was put in charge. During one of General Badi's first visits to Mukuru, he announced to the community, "Since Mukuru was declared a Special Planning Area, the community and NGOs had agreed on which areas to clear and which not. . . . I wish to report that Mukuru Informal Settlement Renewal Programme is well underway and we have extended the Special Planning Area Framework for the area for a further two-year period." Three sector plans—water and sanitation, roads and drainage and electrification were finalized and implementation commenced in May 2020.[31]

The Nairobi Metropolitan Services (NMS) agency had adopted the community's plan, and began implementing its recommendations. According to Patrick of Muungano, "Maybe COVID was a blessing in disguise for us. I was scared of what the NMS and their military approach was going to do, or not do. Our resident-led research had helped create a plan for action, and we were ready when they approached the community. We could show them where the community agreed the roads and bridges should go. We could show them how many households needed water and toilets. We showed them where waste collection and pollution clean-up were needed. Without that plan, who knows what they would have done, how many would have been displaced and whether we would even have a Mukuru community still standing."

Thus the street science that informed the SPA process resulted in a plan in which residents told government where and which infrastructure needed improvement. The street science placed the concerns of residents, namely women and youth, at the center of the process. These same women and youth were trained with new skills and received financial support for their efforts.

By the middle of 2020, even with the concerns of COVID-19 still present, the Nairobi Metropolitan Services had followed the community's plan and installed new drains for Mukuru's arterial roads, and, for the first time ever, roads in Mukuru were tarmacked (Figure 3.7). The Kazi Mtaani (hygiene) program had hired, trained, and employed thousands of Mukuru youth that might have left school or been victims of violence.[32] By September 2020, over 17 kilometers of roads in Mukuru had been regraded, drainage was installed, and the roads were paved, most including sidewalks and bicycle lanes.[33] By August 2020, at least six new boreholes had been completed, and a new trunk sewer pipe was installed to connect the community to the municipal sewer system. The sewer was paid for by the World Bank, which, for the first time, prioritized Mukuru as part of its Kenya Informal Settlement Improvement Program. Resources were arriving in Mukuru providing needed life-supporting infrastructure and jobs. As Dorris told me, "We

Figure 3.7 Newly paved road in Mukuru. (Source: Jane Wairitu, used with permission)

can now start installing twentieth-century flush toilets, since we have the water and sewer connections."

Also at the request of the street scientists who worked with the community health workers, local clinic improvements, commissioned by the government of Kenya, started in Mukuru Kwa Reuben, and a new hospital began construction in the Viwandani community of Mukuru.[34,35] The president of Kenya, Uhuru Kenyatta, stated while speaking from Mukuru, "The idea is to take health services as close to the people as possible and with the completion of the 24 new hospitals we will increase the bed capacity in Nairobi's informal settlements."[36] Finally, a new social housing development for Mukuru residents, on a 56-acre parcel adjacent to the community that was illegally used for industry, was launched in August 2020.[37]

According to Jane Weru, director of Akiba Mashinani Trust, an NGO that advocates for housing with the urban poor in Kenya, "The Mukuru SPA process expresses our value that community knowledge and experience should drive redevelopment. In Mukuru, public health was a priority, especially for women and youth, and their research has resulted in real improvements. There is still a long way to go, but what had happened in Mukuru is unprecedented. We may be seeing the most significant steps in an African city for dignified redevelopment."

Chapter 4

Cocreating Places for Urban Health and Healing

onie and Carmen are sisters who grew up in the same house in the Iron Triangle neighborhood of Richmond, California. Now middle aged, they have watched their neighborhood change over the years, some Black residents left, Latinx families moved in, gun violence subsided, and jobs have come and gone, but one thing they could always count on was that their next-door neighbor was Elm Playlot. Elm Playlot was a typical neighborhood park in a rough, inner-city neighborhood; a little green space with playground equipment that was a decade or two old. As Tonie described it to me, "This wasn't the place people just left their kids to run around. It was mostly just a dirt patch, a few big old trees, a tire swing. You had all kinds of other things happening too. Dice games, abandoned dogs runnin' wild, men drinkin' and shooting guns at night. There might have been more needles on the ground in the '80s than blades of grass."

Eddie Doss, who lives across the street from Elm Playlot, agreed with Tonie, telling me "people used to party all night here and the neighbors didn't like it." The Iron Triangle neighborhood, which gets its name from three sets of railroad tracks that used to define its boundaries, was once one of America's most violent and unhealthy neighborhoods. The Iron Triangle and the city of Richmond have experienced a radical, mostly positive transformation (see chapters 2 and 6). In 2000, the Iron Triangle had the lowest life expectancies of any zip code across the nine-county San Francisco Bay Area. While just across the Bay from Silicon Valley and the riches of San Francisco and Marin County, the Iron Triangle had a median household income of just over $28,000 in 2010. Yet, by 2019, life expectancy in the neighborhood had increased by 5 years, the number of shootings had been reduced by over 30 percent, median household income had reached almost $40,000, and almost 60 percent of residents were rating their health as good or excellent. The work of Tonie and Carmen and how they helped transform Elm Playlot has had a lot to do with these positive changes.

As I walk through the gate of Elm Playlot on a sunny January day, the park looks nothing like the neighbors' descriptions of what it was only a decade or so earlier. There is a line of kids waiting to use the park's zip line. Another group of preteens are huddled around a large open window of what was once a house adjacent to the park, but now acts as an office for Pogo Park, the community group that redesigned Elm and now manages its day-to-day activities. The building has an industrial kitchen and meeting space, and the kids at the window are getting a free afternoon snack. A few feet from them are some rabbits and other small farm animals, and kids can pet them and learn about their habitats. Across a winding path and beyond an herb garden is a small waterfall and rock garden. Brandon Harris, a lifelong neighborhood resident and Pogo Park employee, tells me this area is the meditation space, complete with small benches and flowers. In one corner of the park is a large open space that Rosa, who is also a local resident and employee of the park, tells me in Spanish is where Zumba class is held and movies are shown. Just beyond the exercise space are a few 55-gallon drums that have been cut in half and mounted on posts, and are, according to Brandon's brother Tracy, "the best BBQs you'll find outside of Texas."

Elm Playlot has been transformed, but not by architects or planners with a commitment to green cities. The changes have come at the hands of local residents of the Iron Triangle neighborhood, who decided in 2006 to take back their park and the well-being of their neighborhood. It started when Tonie and Carmen met Toody Maher, who was a recent transplant to Richmond looking to partner with residents to create a beautiful and safe place for kids and families to be together and play. Toody was a White newcomer to a largely Black neighborhood. Tonie and Carmen, along with another woman called Ms. Mason, were the "Black Matriarchs" of the streets surrounding Elm. They struggled to agree on a way forward, but they agreed to form the Elm Playlot Action Committee in order to recruit more residents to join them. Brandon, his brother Tracy, and other young people in the neighborhood got involved. "Most of the organizing by Black people in this neighborhood that I remember was always against somethin'. This was about a vision for what we wanted," Brandon reflected. Together they enrolled young people to take pictures to define what they saw and what they wanted their neighborhood to look like. The committee worked with Toody to craft a process where residents codesigned the park. As part of the process, residents would build a temporary park, a pop-up, and watch how people used it. "If the kids came and used it, we knew it was a keeper; if nobody used it, we scrapped the idea and started over," said Tonie. After a year or more of iterations, the final design was ready, and residents were trained and employed to build the fences, benches, and play structures.

Today, these same residents, and often their children and other locals, continue to run the programs at the park, build and maintain equipment, and keep it green and clean (Figure 4.1). The original committee turned into a nonprofit group called Pogo Park, and they are now building a network of neighborhood parks and safe streets, what they are calling the "yellow brick road." Elm Playlot has become, as Brandon told me, a place where residents can come to "escape the stress of their lives and let their hair down" (as he released his long dreadlocks).

Urban places, even an urban park in the heart of one of America's most violent neighborhoods, can help communities heal from the injustices of violence, racial segregation, and environmental injustice. The story of Pogo Park reveals how communities can turn urban places

Figure 4.1 Elm Playlot in the Iron Triangle neighborhood, Richmond, California, in 2020. (Source: Pogo Park, used with permission)

that are synonymous with deprivation, divestment, and despair into sites for health, healing, and hope.

In addition to my experience working with Pogo Park in the Iron Triangle of Richmond, California, I spent time with a similar community in Medellín, Colombia, called San Javier or Comuna 13. San Javier was the site of Colombian military occupation, drug gangs, and other forms of violence until the early 2000s. It was then that San Javier's residents were embraced by a new mayor in Medellín, named Sergio Fajardo, and together the city and community began a process of transformation and healing. Over the course of 15 or so years, a series of projects and programs were initiated in San Javier with the explicit aim of helping residents reconnect to one another and the resources and opportunities offered by connecting to the rest of the city. As in Richmond's Iron Triangle, the residents of San Javier help codesign the projects, and today they are employed at the new community centers, schools, parks, and other facilities in the neighborhood.

Parks, Place, and Urban Healing

The notion that places can heal is not a new idea in medicine or urbanization. Hippocrates in *Airs Waters and Places* in 370 BC, said that the "the constitutions and habits of a people follow the nature of the land where they live." The healthy places for Hippocrates were the sunny, breezy hillsides, where sunlight could act as a "disinfectant."

The Aztecs, Mayans, and Incas all built communities that utilized natural capital through design and engineering, such as building elaborate aqueducts to transport water, or utilizing nature to protect themselves and support the well-being of the population. The Aztec city of Tenochtitlán. Tenochtitlán, what became modern day Mexico City, was thought to be one of the most orderly and clean cities in the hemisphere at the time, with a waste-collection system, baths, and floating urban gardens to grow food. The Incan empire in the fifteenth and sixteenth centuries extended throughout the Andes Mountains from modern day Colombia to Chile, with cities built to be oriented toward the sun, terraces for growing food, and a network of roads.

The Spanish conquistadores killed off these civilizations and created their own colonialist design guidelines, part of the Laws of the Indies, to direct healthy town planning. These designs included a lattice or grid street pattern and a central plaza, and they specified where noxious activities, such as slaughterhouses and tanneries, were to be located, so no "harmful wind blowing through may cause harm to the rest of the town" (Ordinance 121).

In the modern era, planners, activists, and artists continued to emphasize the healing power of places, particularly green spaces. Westward settler-colonialism in America created the National Park System. John Muir, the conservationist and slave owner, would call the Sierra Mountains of California his "temples" and "where nature may heal and cheer and give strength to body and soul alike."[1]

Frederick Law Olmsted, the designer of New York City's Central Park in 1858, would call urban parks "the lungs of the city" and supportive of the "health and vigor of men."[2] Olmsted wrote in 1882 an essay that appeared in the publication *The Sanitarian*, called "Trees in Streets and in Parks": "Parks are now as much a part of the sanitary apparatus of a large town as aqueducts and sewers."[3] In arguing for the creation of a park to preserve Yosemite in 1865, Olmsted wrote that natural scenery in parks offers "relief from ordinary cares" and "the means of securing happiness."[4] Olmsted may have been echoing the sentiments of Henry David Thoreau, whose 1845 *Walden* suggested that "nature is but another name for health." Of course, Thoreau was part of the "Transcendentalist Movement," which believed that nature could help "return humanity to reason" and was a harsh critic of government treatment of Native Americans, the war with Mexico, and slavery.

Today, there is an ongoing belief and increasingly convincing scientific evidence that urban nature can help us heal from trauma and support health more generally.[5]

Parks and Greening as the Antidote?

Some in the design fields have embraced what is called biophilic design, building on Edward O. Wilson's notion of *Biophilia*, published in 1986, which argued that human affinity for contact with nature helps us connect to all other living species and that connection can help us heal.[6,7,8] Biophilic cities are urban environments with lots of exposure to quality green spaces, and this is thought to provide cognitive, affective, and psychophysiological benefits that reduce stress. Biophilia and related ideas suggest that when we are in, nearby, or even have a nice view of green space, it can help our mental health, restore our fatigued brains, enhance recovery from stress, and even increase our sense of hope.[9,10]

Cities around the world are taking these ideas seriously and trying to provide healing green space within their borders or providing residents the opportunities to access nature nearby. For instance, South Korea created Health Improvement Camps in 2009, where they bring families and children to national parks to address stress-related autoimmune diseases, such as eczema and asthma.[11] In Japan, researchers have been studying the mental and physical health impacts of "forest bathing" or known in Japanese as Shinrin-yoku. While not a new idea or practice, forest bathing typically involves leaving a dense urban area and going for a meditative walk through nature for at least 15 minutes. After forest bathing, practitioners have been shown to have decreased their heart rate, their levels of cortisol—a key stress hormone, and their blood pressure.[12]

The health benefits of being in nature may be the result, at least in part, of what researchers call attention restoration theory (ART). ART is what happens when our directed attention, what we use constantly to focus and problem solve, is turned down and we allow our brains to recover. This process of "turning off" from constant focus on external challenges restores our tired and depleted brains.[13] When in nature, walking or just sitting, ART research suggests we are more likely to let our brains "chill out" (not the technical term), which can improve our mood, self-esteem, ability to pay attention later, and imagination.[14,15]

All this reminds me of the Buddhist monk Thich Nhat Hanh's powerful notion of "walking meditation," which he describes in the work *Peace Is Every Step*: "Walking meditation is first and foremost a practice to bring body and mind together peacefully. No matter what we do, the place to start is to calm down, because when our mind and our body have calmed down, we see more clearly. When we see our anger or sadness clearly, it dissipates. We begin to feel more compassion for ourselves and others. . . . With each step the earth heals us, and with each step we heal the earth."[16]

The restoration of the imagination through access to urban nature may be significant for healing. For instance, psychologists have known that imagination is a key pathway through which a child can transform, however temporarily, fear, anxiety, trauma, and suffering. Imagination can allow our brain to be curious and playful and to explore safely who we are and what matters to us. When children are traumatized at an early age, their brain goes into survival and hypervigilance mode, where situations that might seem like opportunities for imaginative play are interpreted as threats.[17] As Bessel van der Kolk writes in *The Body Keeps the Score*, "Imagination gives us the opportunity to envision new possibilities—it is an essential launchpad for making our hopes come true. It fires our creativity, relieves our boredom, alleviates our pain, enhances our pleasure, and enriches our most intimate relationships" (17).

In the 1980s, researchers suggested that hospitalized patients re-covered more quickly from surgery when they could view nature from their window.[18] Roger Ulrich, a psychologist, discovered that for gall-bladder surgery patients, with everything else being equal, those whose beds looked out to trees healed at least a day faster, required less pain medication, and had fewer complications than those whose windows looked at brick buildings. The findings mirrored those intuited in 1863 by Florence Nightingale, the nurse and public health reformer, who wrote, "Among kindred effects of light I may mention, from experi-ence, as quite perceptible in promoting recovery, the being able to see out of a window, instead of looking against a dead wall; the bright co-lours of flowers; the being able to read in bed by the light of a window close to the bed head. It is generally said that the effect is upon the mind. Perhaps so, but it is no less so upon the body on that account."[19]

Perhaps a view of nature isn't going to cure cancer, but it may help improve one's attitude, and hope can help us heal.[20] Greening vacant lots was found in Philadelphia to reduce psychological distress of adults living nearby.[21] In Wisconsin, mental health outcomes were improved the greater the access residents had to green space.[22] In Holland, prox-imity to green space seemed to improve self-rated health and lowered the risk of physician-diagnosed diseases.[23]

Even Western hospitals are increasingly being designed with heal-ing gardens and views of nature. At my own institution of UC Berke-ley, architects, public health, and medical professionals worked in the 1980s to reinvigorate gardens and nature into Western health care, where hospital construction had turned toward making buildings to be as sterile as labs. According to Clare Cooper Marcus and Marni Barnes, who wrote *Gardens in Healthcare Facilities*, people like the ar-chitect Roslyn Lindheim and epidemiologist Len Syme began teach-ing and working together at UC Berkeley in the 1970s to link design and health. Marcus noted that she and others began to recognize that "when you asked someone to imagine a healing environment, almost everyone made some reference to nature, yet when seeking medical care we find ourselves in environments virtually devoid of nature or ac-cess to it."[24] The professors redesigned courtyards, entrances, and park-ing lots at hospitals in Berkeley, San Francisco, and across Northern

California. One of the most well-known was the Planetree Model, whose first design was in 1985 on a surgical floor at Pacific Medical Center in San Francisco.

The Planetree model emphasized the human experience, including social relationships and participating in one's own healing, over technological efficiency.[25] What this meant was that the physical and social function of the ward were altered. The nursing station was redesigned to no longer have high counters and barriers to information, and instead a small library was created where charts were available to patients and families as well as medical books and journals. A lounge was designed adjacent to patient beds to "deinstitutionalize" the environment. Bedrooms for visitors were created. Patient rooms and the entire ward were redesigned to include natural wood and skylights, plants and fountains, and patios and balconies to provide access to nature. A kitchen was built so patients could have "homecooked meals" and eat together with visitors on their own schedules. The Planetree Model is now used around the world, and evaluations suggest it contributes to higher worker and patient satisfaction and improved health outcomes for some.[26]

An important but underemphasized aspect of the Planetree Model is that the physical design changes and access to nature are supposed to increase patient and family participation in the healing process. The new designs center the patient *not* the medical technology. For urban nature and green spaces, centering the users and helping to foster social interaction should also be a focus. The World Health Organization's 2017 report, "Urban Green Space Interventions and Health," states that "urban green space interventions seem to be most effective when a physical improvement to the green space is coupled with a social engagement/participation element that promotes the green space and reaches out to new target groups."[27] The process of codesign brings people together, and these lasting connections may be more beneficial for health and healing than the green space itself.[28]

In most cities, access to large swaths of nature or forests may not be possible for everyone. In Oakland, California, pediatricians are writing "park prescriptions" to encourage social interactions and facilitate healing through nature for their young Black and Latinx patients and their families.[29] In this program, most patients come from neighborhoods where poverty, lack of quality schools, and gun violence are frequent sources of stress for young people. While the prescriptions aren't intended to ignore the structural causes of these inequities, they entitle the patient and their family to join a group trip to a regional park. The park trip is led by a naturalist and a physician, and includes unstructured play, physical activity, and a group picnic. According to the park prescription research led by Dr. Nooshin Razani, of the University of California San Francisco Benioff Children's Hospital in Oakland, it is critical that the prescription be as culturally competent as we would expect the clinician to be. By this she means ensuring that the park experience isn't designed around what White, wealthy people might do. Dr. Razani's research reveals that when nature access is culturally appropriate, cocreated with patients and their families, and frequent (just like taking one's prescribed medication), stress—measured by both perceived stress and cortisol levels—can be reduced. In this case the health advantages of access to an urban park extend beyond increased exercise and the health benefits of physical activity.[30]

Pogo Park's Story

How Elm Playlot and the larger organization that created it, Pogo Park, became a site of healing reflects the ideals expressed in the research that healing is equally about process, participation, and place making.[31]

As Tonie, Carmen, and Toody organized residents into the Elm Playlot Action Committee in 2008, the City of Richmond was required by law to update its General Plan.[32] The General Plan is like the land-use constitution for a city and includes a vision and specific objectives for development over the next 30 years. Tens of community meetings in the Iron Triangle neighborhood about the General Plan update had been held. One of the major concerns voiced by residents was gun violence and the lack of safe places for children to play. The General Plan had identified Elm Playlot as one of a number of underused playgrounds, and the proactive city manager at the time, Bill Lindsey, had an idea. He told me, "We were meeting about the future of the city, but

the urgent needs were apparent. Richard [Mitchell, the former Director of Planning], had a list of small parks that could use a facelift. Elm
was there and we approved some standard play equipment."

The equipment upgrade for Elm included a prefabricated play
structure that cost the city about $150,000. It arrived by truck in March
2008. The City of Richmond's Parks Department installed the equipment. "It looked beautiful," Brandon Harris who was a teenager at the
time told me, "but within a few days the abandoned dogs were back,
the graffiti covered it, and most of it was burned down."

Toody, Tonie, and Carmen took another approach. First, they used
their own money to buy a 3-foot-high fence and wrapped it around
the edge of Elm Playlot. "We were reclaiming the space for the community," says Carmen. Next, they cleaned the lot, brought in a porta
potty bathroom, and planted beautiful flowers and plants around the
run-down space. Third, they connected with Joe Griffin, a Richmond
resident and UC Berkeley public health student, who was interested in
a participatory process that engaged young people to document neighborhood life around the park. Together with Brandon, Joe organized a
team of residents and youth to use a process called Photovoice where
they would take pictures of the neighborhood and then write or record
a short description of what that picture meant to them. The objective
was to create a youth vision of the neighborhood and how Elm Playlot
might fit in that future.

Toody convinced a nearby artist who owned a warehouse in the
neighborhood, called Scientific Arts Studio, to lend a helping hand.
The studio had professional fabricators who made large sculptures,
like the giant baseball glove at the San Francisco Giants' stadium. They
agreed to train members of the committee in design and construction,
including carpentry and welding.[33]

While the training was ongoing, Toody and the committee used
the assistance of the architects and planners leading the City's General
Plan update, a consulting firm called Moore, Iacofano and Goltsman
(MIG), to help them create maps, 3-D designs, and cardboard models
of the Elm Playlot. They recruited another nonprofit, Urban Ecology,
to help them, and hundreds of residents were brought in to participate
in the codesign process. "We received a grant for about $40K from the

City to do this redesign, but they had already spent over $150,000 on wasted equipment," Maher proclaimed. The traditional participatory design process wasn't resonating with residents. "We needed to see and feel what it might be like," James Anderson, who leads the construction team at Pogo Park, told me. "We built temporary equipment and used it before finishing the design."

This temporary, or "pop-up" design process isn't easy or cheap, but it was essential to ensure that the future park was going to reflect the community's vision. "If people wanted to put a tree somewhere, we just went out and got a tree in a five-gallon bucket and put it there, so people could actually see and feel it," explained Maher.

All the new action around Elm Playlot caught the attention of researchers from Children's Hospital in Oakland, who approached Toody about surveying residents to document their current use of the existing park, how well they knew their neighbors, and how often their children were physically active. According to a grant for this research written by the principal investigators, Dr. June Tester, a physician, and Irene Yen, an epidemiologist, both at UC San Francisco, the objectives were to document existing childhood use of Elm Playlot and examine neighborhood social cohesion and satisfaction around two Richmond parks, Elm Playlot and Virginia Playlot. The goal was to gather baseline data before Elm was reconstructed to enable a second wave of the survey to determine if the codesign and reconstruction of the park had an impact on children's park activity, neighborhood social connections, and overall community well-being.

Carmen was quoted in 2009: "Hopefully the park will change things at least a little bit. There are a lot of people in the neighborhood I don't know, and I have neighbors I should know. There's a lot of separation around here, too much negativity. Maybe this park will be a place where we can get together."[34]

Tonie and Carmen were trained to go door-to-door to survey their neighbors, children in the park were asked to wear accelerometers, and a team from the neighborhood kept observational notes and documented activities in and around the park. "It was a long survey but we must have knocked on a few hundred doors in a couple of months," Carmen remembered.

In fact, the resident researchers reached 198 households, 58 percent of which were around Elm Playlot, and the others were in the neighborhood of Virginia Playlot. While the research proceeded, Pogo Park became an official nonprofit organization and started raising money to support staff and the pop-up park. A shipping container was donated and delivered to the park to act as an office and storage shed. "One powerful message from the youth Photovoice project at that time was that housing, garbage, and safety were their primary concerns," Joe Griffin told me. There were empty properties with boarded-up windows around the park. One small house adjacent to the park was also abandoned, and Toody and the team agreed that they should try to make that their office and a community meeting space. They raised $50,000 from donations and bought the house, and then began renovating it. In a few months, volunteer community labor, materials, and "sweat equity" had turned the old abandoned house into a new meeting space, with offices, an industrial kitchen, and two high-quality, wheelchair-accessible permanent bathrooms. "The number-one amenity people wanted in a new Elm Playlot was a safe bathroom," Toody noted. Just like the women activists in Nairobi, the Richmond activists knew that a foundation of community health is not having to worry when nature calls.

The purchase of the house was a turning point in the redevelopment of Elm Playlot and the emergence of Pogo Park as a community development organization, not just a park designer. They began negotiating with the City of Richmond for a joint-use agreement, in which the City holds the land and liability insurance, but the community manages the programs, and in this case builds the space. The community surrounding the park also needed support since many of the homes were abandoned at the time. Pogo Park worked with the City's housing director and convinced him to use a federal grant to purchase and remodel multifamily housing in the neighborhood and to keep the homes extremely affordable. The City used the federal government's Neighborhood Stabilization Program (NSP) to "purchase and rehab blighted, foreclosed, and abandoned properties and demolish blighted structures all in order to stabilize our most economically challenged neighborhoods" the City of Richmond stated in its project application.

Pogo Park remained closely involved in this process to ensure that residents were not displaced and that rehabilitated homes were affordable to local residents.

As the housing and land stabilized around the park, the community completed its design process, and, along with its nonprofit partners, presented it to the City (Figure 4.2). According to the city manager, Bill Lindsey, "It was a beautiful design, but more importantly it was the residents' vision. The zip line, the play spaces, the round benches, the office and bathrooms. All of it made it a unique, multiuse community space, not just a playground."

With the approvals to move ahead, residents began to construct different pieces and areas of the park; the play equipment, fences, benches, pathways, and gardens (Figure 4.3). However, the construction, like the design, was also an iterative process. As James described it to me, "It would have been nice to complete the whole things in a few months, but we wanted to build it ourselves. I could pour concrete but didn't know how to weld. So it took time." When some equipment and landscaping were completed, the residents were trained to build a different area of the park.

In 2013, Pogo Park acquired a second park a few blocks away, called Harbour 8, and they began dreaming about how to connect the two neighborhood assets. This slowed the construction of Elm. By 2015 Elm was staffed by residents who were staff of Pogo Park. They oversaw everyday maintenance and programming for kids and adults, and they distributed over 9,000 free meals each year. Over 15,000 children visit Elm Playlot each year, with about twice as many adults as either chaperones or visitors themselves. Tonie told me that parents started just "dropping their kids off at the park since they trusted us so much to take care of them. That was unheard of before we did all this." By 2016, the team was so skilled in construction that they won a Google Challenge grant to create a spin-off company called Pogo Park Products, where they are now codesigning and building equipment for other community park projects. The social enterprise is aiming, according to Toody, "to be an engine of economic development in the Iron Triangle."

By partnering with the City of Richmond, Pogo Park was awarded a State of California grant for $2 million, intended to rebuild parks in

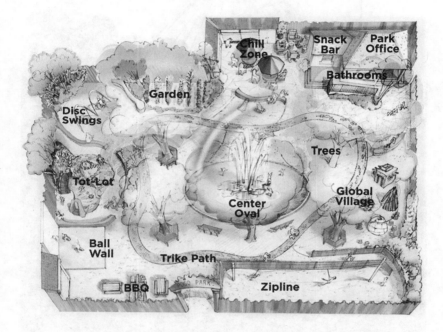

Residents of Richmond, California's Iron Triangle neighborhood worked for four years to create a design and layout for Elm Playlot, a .5 acre "pocket park" that lies in the middle of their neighborhood. Their vision for transforming Elm Playlot into a vibrant community hub is contained in this book, brought to life by Maren Van Duyn's magical drawings.

Figure 4.2 Elm Playlot Community Vision. (Source: Pogo Park & Scientific Arts Studio)

distressed urban neighborhoods. By 2018, a codesigned process for the Harbour 8 park was completed by residents, as was the new safe-streets design, the Yellow Brick Road, which used design strategies to make streets and sidewalks in the Iron Triangle safer by slowing down vehicles and providing clear and safe pedestrian travel to important destinations in the neighborhood, including parks, public housing, schools,

Figure 4.3 Pogo Park employees build the play equipment for Elm Playlot.

train/BART stations, retail shops, and community centers (Figure 4.4).
Due to the success of Elm Playlot and Pogo Park, the City agreed to
purchase the land adjacent to Harbour 8 to allow the park to expand
and include a community center building, restrooms, new play areas,
and stalls for small businesses. Pogo Park applied for additional resources for Harbour 8 from the State of California Department of
Parks and Recreation, and received $8.5 million under a grant program

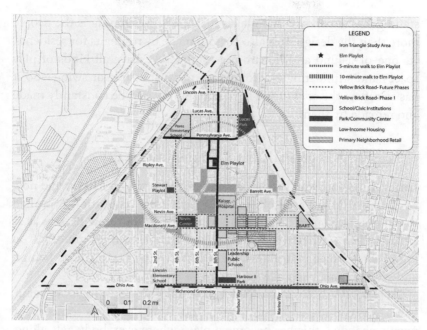

LEGEND

- – –   Iron Triangle Study Area
★   Elm Playlot
IIIIIIIIIIII   5-minute walk to Elm Playlot
IIIIIIIIIII   10-minute walk to Elm Playlot
· · · · · · ·   Yellow Brick Road- Future Phases
———   Yellow Brick Road- Phase 1
▢   School/Civic Institutions
▢   Park/Community Center
▢   Low-Income Housing
▢   Primary Neighborhood Retail

Figure 4.4 Map of Iron Triangle, Elm Playlot, and select community features.

called Proposition 68, which expanded the State's Sustainable Communities and Climate Change Reduction program.[35]

As Maher told me, "The next phase of our work is about continuing our commitment to sustainable and healthy community development. This means having residents build the most beautiful spaces in their own neighborhood, and ensure they benefit socially, economically, and health-wise."

The coconstruction of Elm Playlot and the beginning of Harbour 8 park created tens of new permanent jobs for local residents, and Pogo Park had employed about 120 residents for some period of time between 2009 and 2019. The full-time staff consists of about ten people who make over $20/hour with full health and other benefits. According to Maher, Pogo Park had paid out over $1.5 million in wages and small contracts, all to community residents between 2009 and 2019.

As Maher reflected about the keys to the success of Pogo Park, she emphasized, "It's the people. Not just in design but in the everyday staffing of the parks. What makes it safe and welcoming is the people more than the design. It is also custom made by residents for residents. Its one-of-a-kind and not from a catalog. We have all kinds of play spaces and stimulating environments, not just a slide or swings. So it has to reflect the soul of the local community and be constantly made and remade by them."

Pogo Park and Community Health

James Anderson, who lives across the street from Elm Playlot and now works with Pogo Park, told me that before the renovation, "you had to be a pretty tough cat to come to this park," but now he sees it as a place where, "when a kid comes here, it changes their mindset, you know what I mean? It allows them to leave the crazy streets behind and gives them a big smile."

"It [Pogo Park and Elm Playlot] has brought people together again, like it was coming up around here," said Tonie. "Even as some of the people changed, this has become a place where everybody gets along, we look out for one another, and people can trust it'll be safe."

My team of UC Berkeley researchers set out to ask residents just those questions, namely whether they knew, trusted, and were willing to work with their neighbors. In 2019, we designed a study to return to all the same households and respondents that had been surveyed in 2009, and ask them the same questions. We wanted to test whether Elm Playlot and the work of Pogo Park were having an effect on those living around the park and the entire neighborhood. We managed to return to 145 of the 198 respondents, 65 percent of which were within the Iron Triangle, and 35 percent were outside the neighborhood. In order to ask about the strength of social connections and trust in the neighborhood, we asked people (in either English or Spanish) to rate whether they strongly agreed, agreed, disagreed, strongly disagreed, or neither agreed nor disagreed, with the following statements:

The friendships and associations I have with other people in my neighborhood mean a lot to me.

If I need advice about something, I could go to someone in my
   neighborhood.
I borrow things and exchange favors with my neighbors.
I would be willing to work together with others on something to
   improve my neighborhood.
I regularly stop and talk to people in my neighborhood.

What we found was that in 2019, within the Iron Triangle there was
a 43–102 percent increase in strongly agreed or agreed responses for
statements 1–3, compared to 2009. For those outside the Iron Triangle,
there was a 13–23 percent increase. We also found that the percentage
change within the Iron Triangle was statistically significant, with 99.9
percent confidence, meaning that there was a 0.1 percent chance that
this was random (Table 4.1). It appears that Elm Playlot and the work
of Pogo Park are having a significant impact on social connections in
the Iron Triangle.

   This is critically important for health and healing, since we know
that social connections between neighborhoods and friendships can
modify the adverse health impacts from experiences with racism, discrimination, and poverty.[36] Social cohesion can do this by lowering the
levels of C-reactive protein (CRP), and high levels of CRP in your
blood are associated with increased risk of heart attack and stroke.
Strong social connections in your neighborhood have also been associated with lowering levels of interleukin-6 (IL-6), which is often
generated by stress, and too much IL-6 contributes to internal inflammation, a weakening of the autoimmune response, decreased levels of
zinc and iron, and greater susceptibility to viral infections, including
influenza, hepatitis C, and HIV.[37] Neighborhood social cohesion is also
associated with moderating blood pressure, improving cognitive development, improving sleep, and limiting the accumulation of visceral
fat—the type of fat that surrounds your internal organs, which is not
always visible externally and raises your risk of heart disease, type 2
diabetes, and stroke.[38,39,40]

   We also looked at data in Richmond starting from 2007 collected
every 2 years as part of the National Community Survey administered

Table 4.1 Results of the Iron Triangle Household Survey, 2009 and 2019.

Survey Item	% Responding strongly agree or agree inside Iron Triangle		% Change 2009 to 2019	% Responding strongly agree or agree outside Iron Triangle		% Change 2009 to 20019
	2009	2019		2009	2019	
The friendships and associations I have with other people in my neighborhood mean a lot to me.	64	94	+45*	73	88	20*
If I need advice about something, I could go to someone in my neighborhood.	62	88	+43*	75	84	13
I borrow things and exchange favors with my neighbors.	30	60	+102*	49	61	23
I would be willing to work together with others on something to improve my neighborhood.	90	96	+6	96	99	3
I regularly stop and talk to people in my neighborhood.	67	77	+14	76	76	0

*p < .001 or statistically significant with 99.9% confidence.

by the International City Management Association. This survey asks similar questions in cities across the country. The data are compiled into Richmond's Community Survey, which typically has between 4,000 and 5,000 responses from all areas of the city. When we looked at specific questions related to the quality of one's neighborhood, recreational opportunities, the ease of walking, and quality of life, we found that a significant number of respondents from the Iron Triangle reported that their place was excellent or good. For example, between 2009 and 2019, there was a 157% increase in the number of Iron Triangle respondents reporting that their neighborhood was an excellent or good "place to live" and a 143% increase in the number reporting that recreational opportunities were excellent or good. Across the same time period, there was a 33% increase in the respondents from the Iron Triangle reporting that their quality of life was excellent or good and a 78% increase reporting that the reputation of Richmond was excellent or good.

Those working in Richmond but living outside the Iron Triangle also reflected on the radical changes in the neighborhood. Former chief of police, Chris Magnus, stated, "As Pogo Park staff worked on the redesign and renovation of the park, the character of the neighborhood changed significantly. The presence of responsible adults at the park made local parents feel comfortable in bringing their children to the park to play and exercise. Pogo Park staff maintained regular communication with the Richmond Police so that residents could report suspicious activity to park workers, knowing the police would be informed. As a result, the reduction in incidents of violent crime, drug dealing, and vandalism in the immediate neighborhood of Elm Playlot has been dramatic."[41]

The former city manager of Richmond, Bill Lindsey, reflected: "We had no idea that the transformation of that little park in the Iron Triangle could lead to such a big change there and across the city. We had more parents from there coming to meetings, more people demanding policy changes. Young people from there went on to be leaders. People from around the region, even the country, come to see Pogo Park now, because the transformation of the place and people has been nothing short of remarkable."

We also returned to the young people in the neighborhood and again asked them to take pictures and explain what the photo represented to them. Of course these were a different group of teenagers from the ones that took photos in 2009. I share a few of their photos here, which suggest that in the eyes of some young people the park and their neighborhood are healing (Figure 4.5a–c).

As I stood near the Elm zip line talking with James, he turned to me

Figure 4.5a "What I see here is a park. What is happening here is that there is kids playing and having fun. This relate to our life because this is a safe and fun place for kids to go in our community. This condition exist in our lives because of the park that we have in our community. What I would do to support this is have more parks like this in our community."

Figure 4.5b "In this picture I see the apartments that are being built nearby the park. This apartments are meant for low income families. This apartments wouldn't come here if the park didn't improve the area. Now more and more development is coming, and I see new stores and people want to stay here. Before, all we talked about was leaving this place."

Figure 4.5c "In this picture, I see a picture of the creek in the park. It symbolizes peacefulness and it shows that there is a place in the community just to sit down, chill, and take a breath. This is important to me because everyone needs a space to just sit and think or to relax in peacefulness, even if its not being used it's good to know its there. This is like this because the Pogo Park team was thinking of others that might be stressed or would just need a spot to relax. If I was in charge, I would make more spaces like this for people to relax in with more shade."

and reflected on what the park and the organization have meant to him and the community: "I wouldn't be here right now if not for this place. I mean, it has changed my life. I got new skills, a steady job and I even got to go to Africa. This place here, we are all better because of what has happened to this park. Fewer people killin' each other, less crazy stuff goin' on; it's just more peaceful, you know what I mean? This place has helped out a whole lot of people around here."

Urban Acupuncture in San Javiar, Medellín

The neighborhood of San Javier, or Comuna 13, in Medellín, is a lot like Richmond's Iron Triangle, with a legacy of trauma and a need for healing. San Javier is located in the Center-Western Zone of Medellín along a rugged hillside, making the area prone to landslides, difficult to navigate because of the steep streets, and leaving many without access to basic services like water, sanitation, and waste collection.[42] Some of the basic infrastructure challenges facing San Javier mirrored those in Nairobi's Mukuru informal settlement.

In the early 1980s, youth gangs in Comuna 13 tried to fill the voids left by the absence of the state by providing some services and even enforcing their own code of justice.[43] Soon, a more organized urban militia, called Comandos Armados del Pueblo (United Commandos of the People [CAP]), claimed control of Comuna 13 and other poor, hillside neighborhoods in Medellín. These militias became powerful by being the enforcers of local rules, acting as local police and juries, but also by delivering services and controlling land-use development.[44]

On October 16, 2002, Operación Orión (Operation Orion) took hold of Comuna 13. Orion was a national government military campaign to rid the area of gangs. The conflict lasted 4 days, and it is estimated that over 1,500 troops entered on foot, in tanks, and from helicopters, killing tens, wounding hundreds, and displacing untold numbers. Months of surveillance in Comuna 13 followed the military campaign. Arrests were frequent, and a state of terror was imposed on the remaining residents. The National Commission for Historic Memory (Comisión Nacional de Memoria Histórica) reported that following Operation

Orion, the government imposed a new social order, limiting social interactions, and fomenting distrust among neighbors.[45]

The scars of Operation Orion ran deep in the memories and bodies of local residents. As recounted by the National Center for Historical Memory report on the "Impacts and Harms Caused by Conflict in Colombia," including Comuna 13: "Thus, being exposed to situations characterized by high levels of terror and defenselessness almost always amounts to experiences that go beyond men´s and women´s capacity to deal with the events. This causes traumas and psychological harms, the most frequent signs of which, according to the victims, are serious sleeping disorders marked by persistent insomnia and nightmares, depression, anxiety and somatization disorders."[46] The conflicts in Comuna 13 left many residents feeling fearful, experiencing anxiety, depression, and a sense of hopelessness.[47]

The Museum of Antioquia invited various organizations, including the Corporación Región, to acknowledge the atrocious violence, trauma, and displacement suffered by residents of Comuna 13. They launched the Memory and Reparation project, which included an art and cultural exhibit that stimulated social reflections.[48] The reflection process stimulated a series of proposals for healing, including significant investments in education, culture, housing, and other life-promoting services.

Education was one priority for addressing inequities and the legacy of violence in Comuna 13.[49] In 2004, a program called Medellín, la más educada (Medellín, the most educated), began guaranteeing early childhood and primary education to all residents. The city began training and hiring over 20,000 new teachers. Every child was guaranteed after-school programs, so learning continued outside the classroom. The program also needed to build new community schools for the new teachers and programs to be housed, and a major initiative was launched by then mayor Sergio Fajardo. Subsequent leaders in Medellín continued the "social urbanism" ideal started by Fajardo, which included a public participation process whereby residents could define their needs and codesign projects, and the city would commit to building the most beautiful of the new projects, from schools to community centers to libraries and parks, in the city's poorest and previously most violent neighborhoods.[50]

As we exited the cable car at the top of the San Javier neighborhood, Aníbal Gaviria, the mayor of Medellín from 2012 to 2015, explained to me that even constructing the most beautiful school or community center wasn't enough to rebuild communities hit hardest by violence like Comuna 13. "What residents told us they needed was places to learn and work, but also opportunities and programs, and that they wanted to be leaders in these investments," he described to me.

Gaviria was giving me a personal tour of the Colegio Maestro Lusitania Paz de Colombia,[51] which was one of those new, beautiful schools. He described the school as a place for equity investments: "Equity is written with the 'E' of education. We wanted to offer the poorest children the most beautiful facilities and the most technologically advanced opportunities for learning. This is about investing in life, all lives, and especially those that have been hurt by violence and inequality. Education is an important transcendent tool."

The round courtyard was vast and from every angle I could look up into the classrooms. The school includes preschool, primary, and secondary school classrooms for 1,400 students. The circular design invites collaboration and sharing, with the glass walls giving students and faculty soothing views of the surrounding parks and natural preserve. It was a curious, albeit beautiful, design. Gaviria explained part of the architectural significance: "This area used to have a 'plaza de toros' or bullring here. It was a place where the mafias came and animals were slaughtered. It was a ring or place of death. Today, the same courtyard is for athletics and play. We have tried to turn a place of violence into one of peace" (Figure 4.6).

From the school we took a short walk to the newly renovated Nuevo Occidente hospital unit. The new hospital had all the latest technologies, seventy beds, operating rooms, a lab, and an emergency department, all things that this poor, peripheral community had been lacking. The hospital is focused on *preventing* illness, not just *treating* it. As I entered the lobby, it looked more like a computer start-up company than a hospital. Children and adults were crowded about workstations.

Figure 4.6 Former bull ring now playground at Colegio Maestro Lusitania Paz de Colombia, Medellín.

An attending physician told me: "The labor and delivery area will ensure women don't have to travel hours to get prenatal and newborn care. The clinic will screen for breast cancer. We have counseling and mental health services. We went from having seven patients in one room to now having only two, and allowing us to provide all the tools of twenty-first-century medicine right in this community." I was convinced that more people were visiting the hospital for its internet-café-style lobby than for primary care.

Gaviria and I crossed the street from the hospital and entered the UVA Nuevo Occidente. Unidades de Vida Articulada (UVAs) (Articulated Life Units), are former hillside water storage tanks that were opened up and turned into public spaces. Through a partnership with Medellín's utility company, Empresas Públicas de Medellín, the city and residents reclaimed these spaces but designed each in a unique way to reflect the local culture and needs. Each UVA is intended to offer public gathering and recreation space in neighborhoods that mostly lack these amenities.

Figure 4.7 The author (left) and former mayor Aníbal Gaviria (right) in San Javiar neighborhood. (Source: Jude Johnson, used with permission)

The UVA Nuevo Occidente is close to the city's Metrocable line J, and has a swimming pool, a large library, performance space, classrooms for adults and childcare, and basketball and other sports fields (Figure 4.7). The pool was filled with children playing, and later, adults doing laps. We knocked on the door of a classroom with kindergarten children. The kids barely noticed that the former mayor was at the door, but the eyes of the teachers lit up, and they beamed with smiles. One teacher described how the UVA provided her with a formal paying job for things she had already been doing informally. It was a community center roaring with life.

Medellín's approach to education and community building draws from the Latin American traditions of learning-by-doing and education as power. As I walked the neighborhood, visited these public facilities, and met the people working and playing there, I couldn't stop thinking of Paulo Freire's *Pedagogy of the Oppressed*: "Education as the practice of freedom—as opposed to education as the practice of domination—denies that man is abstract, isolated, independent, and unattached to the world; it also denies that the world exists as a reality apart from people. Authentic reflection considers neither abstract man nor the world without people, but people in their relations with the world."[52]

It was clear that rehabilitative education didn't stop inside the classroom. Medellín's cultural and education leaders seemed invested in remaking public spaces in neighborhoods as part and parcel of the education system.

Leaving the classroom and the UVA, Gaviria and I took the gondola, or Metrocable, down to San Javier station. In 2008, the city government built a cable car network connecting the steep, isolated Comuna 13 to the rest of the city. In 2011, the city finished Las Escaleras (electric escalators) that climbed 984 meters to the highest parts of Comuna 13 with the aim of improving mobility and urban inclusion for all residents. The escalator project, the first of its kind in the world, has become a source of both local pride and controversy over whether it has helped reduce inequalities or just attracted international tourists and made Comuna 13 a 'brand name'"[53] (Figure 4.8).

We soon arrive at Parque Biblioteca San Javier (San Javier Library Park). The park is one of ten "library parks" in Medellín. This was the first one, consistent with the aforementioned Medellín philosophy of social urbanism, which meant redistributing wealth by investing in and building the most beautiful and catalytic projects in the poorest communities first.[54] The Library Park was codesigned by residents. Gaviria described how residents changed significant aspects of the design working with architects and planners, and wound up suggesting creative performance spaces, adding green space, and including a bridge over Calle 44 to provide safer access.

It feels more like an open-air theater and art gallery than a library. Giant steps like wide outdoor staircases and ramps create a tiered, auditorium-like feeling. The walls are covered with local art and kids race up and down the stairs. There is an adult literacy class taking place the day we are there, a room full of what looks like new mothers with infants, and a workshop led by local social workers teaching conflict resolution. According to Johana Pabon, a member of the teaching staff at Parque Biblioteca San Javier, "This is a safe space for the

Figure 4.8 Las Escaleras in Comuna 13, Medellín. (Source: Judea Johnson, used with permission)

community. Before there was nothing like this. There was no place that was safe."[55]

As Gaviria engaged one of the social workers at the center, she explained, "What happens here isn't just inside the walls of the center. Social workers employed here go into the community to support people to get rights and services, like titles to their house. We enroll families in food supports, after-school programs, or to get government loans to start a business. Conflict resolution of domestic and other violence is also done in the community, not just in the class. We take the services of the center to the people who need them the most."

Between 2002 and 2017, communities with library parks in Medellín saw their employment rate increase 17 percent more than neighborhoods without the parks.[56] The San Javier Library Park and neighborhood UVAs have helped create a stronger sense of community cohesion among residents in a place that was severely traumatized by Operation Orion and related gang violence.[57]

By literally removing walls that separated poor, hillside communities and state- and government-owned facilities, the UVAs are acting to physically and socially remove barriers between government and the most vulnerable places. This was an intentional objective of the UVAs, as Gaviria reflected with me, suggesting that committing to new and beautiful spaces was a recognition that government had been part of damaging trust, and trustworthiness needed to be rebuilt. He told me, "We didn't look to the latest technologies or an App where people would need their phones to connect with one another. Instead, residents were rightly skeptical of these projects and whether they would really benefit. Government and powerful institutions that historically were part of fostering fear and exclusion needed to take the lead, redistribute resources, and listen to residents on how to encourage inclusion. There is a conscious attempt to redefine how the city takes responsibility for dismantling inequities."

Building City Safe Sanctuaries: Ciudadela Universitaria

As Gaviria and I continued through the neighborhood, it became increasingly apparent that for almost every physical project there was a social and symbolic meaning. We soon reached a block of buildings with high walls surrounding them in a dormitory-style layout. Gaviria informed me that this was the new Ciudadela Universitaria,[58] a former women's prison called El Buen Pastor: "It is not by accident that we chose to turn a prison into a space of learning, hope, and freedom of ideas. This was obviously a place of pain and suffering, much like our city's past. The idea is to turn that into hope; higher education offers hope for thousands of young people. We can also hopefully host international universities here, to open up the world of knowledge to our students."

During construction, we walked through the gates and immediately workers rushed to Gaviria to shake his hand and take pictures with the former mayor. The workers, men and women and many Afro-Colombianos, were almost all from the surrounding community. The project was committed to hiring over 500 local people in various construction jobs. As one worker explained to me, "This is my opportunity to rebuild my community from a place that housed violence to one that will house the free minds and bodies of students. We are helping build

Figure 4.9 Street life in Comuna 13. (Source: Judea Johnson, used with permission)

this future for all of us and the city." The university campus will also have community-accessible classrooms, computer labs, sports areas, a jogging track, and green spaces.

There Is Love Here

A part of what makes all these projects and the people who build, maintain, and work at them healthy and promote healing is that the past is not forgotten. Memorials to the missing and slain are everywhere in this community. Street art and murals communicate messages of hope and peace, while honoring slain or disappeared activists (Figure 4.9).[59,60] Medellín has an important museum, called the House of Memory, dedicated to collective sharing and healing over the years of violence and conflict. In neighborhoods like Comuna 13, art seems to be helping to reunify a traumatized place.

I meet up with Ciro Censura and Kbala, coleaders of Casa Kolacho, an NGO community group using music and art to memorialize violence and heal from its impacts.[61] The group was founded after the murder of Héctor Pacheco "Kolacho," a community leader who supported and developed artistic processes with local youth. A group of youth came together at his memorial and recorded a hip-hop song entitled, "Aquí sí hay amor," or "There is love here." Censura explains to me that "Casa Kolacho was created out of a need for a cultural center where people can use art as a creative outlet, and make friends with each other. Casa Kolacho is responsible for 90 percent of the murals in the neighborhood, with frequent common symbols like white sheets representing a desire for peace and eagles representing freedom and elephants as the only animal that cries.[62] "Through art and music" explains Ciro, "they no longer see us as guerrillas or gangsters, but as positive people working to transform and heal this place. Music and murals come from within each one of us, and that helps transform me and this reality" (Figure 4.10).

Casa Kolacho is leading tourists on a graffiti tour of the neighborhood, but also working on a project called Techo, where they paint colorful art on the tin roofs of informal settlement houses, with the aim of raising resources to build more permanent roofs. Their art is visible throughout the city from the aerial Metrocable cars.

Casa Kolacho mixes hip-hop and street art as a form of memory, resistance, and hope. As Ciro tells me, "The music is an antidote to violence and the murals make public our message and legitimacy. It was this way with the armed groups, who would use walls to mark their territory and tell everyone how to behave. We are reinterpreting the walls for liberation and peace."

They explain to me that there is a long way to go in Comuna 13 to achieve peace and offer gang alternatives for young people. Their NGO makes little money compared to what they could in a gang, but they explain, "There is no way out of that lifestyle except in a body bag." Ciro says that Casa Kolacho cultural center tries to offer young people an alternative to violence through music and art, "but before forming artists we want to train critical, supportive and constructive human beings," he explains.

Figure 4.10 Mural of youth hope and love in San Javier. (Source: Judea Johnson, used with permission)

The ongoing work in San Javier seems to be reducing violence and creating greater opportunities. There were 243 homicides in Comuna 13 in 2010, 21 in 2015, but 91 in 2018. Overall, Medellín had 173 homicides in 2015, and that number had reached 301 by 2019, but homicides were expected to return to historic lows in 2020, largely due to the pandemic.[63]

After leaving Comuna 13, I travel toward the University de Antioquia, where I will meet some colleagues. Around the corner from the university is a unique place that brings together many of the objectives of the UVAs, the library parks, the schools, and the community initiatives. It is called Parque de la Vida (Park of Life), a community center created through an alliance between the University of Antioquia and the mayor's office of Medellín to train residents in conflict resolution and citizenship; offer programs that promote health; house innovative life-supporting technologies, such as telemedicine; and ultimately reduce inequalities through the implementation and monitoring of public policies that support life. It takes an explicitly "intersectional" approach to inclusion, recognizing the unique needs of young people and older adults, Indigenous and Afro-descendants, people with disabilities, and members of the LGBTQ populations. The Parque de la Vida has been recognized by the World Health Organization and the Latin American Network for Social Innovation as one of the most innovative and health-promoting initiatives on the continent.[64] One program, called Recreado para la paz y la convivencia (Re-created for peace and coexistence), works with children and adolescents to develop nonviolent communication, tolerance, and conflict-resolution skills. Another program trains community residents how to mobilize and meaningfully engage in Medellín's participatory budgeting process. The Parque de la Vida has also created over 1,000 jobs, some at the center but many in the neighborhoods. Julieta Mosquera, coordinator of Parque de la Vida, told me that the objectives of the place were to "reach every resident with a message that well-being begins in your place and participating in policy and place-making can improve health for everyone."

Places That Heal

What can we learn from Pogo Park and the social urbanism in and around Comuna 13 in Medellín for how places can help those in cities heal?

First, a space in the city becomes a place when it is made and remade by people. A park, green space or community center is insufficient by itself to promote health and healing. People, particularly local people, must be involved in creating, shaping, and working those spaces.

Second, the health and healing benefits of urban places come largely from the social interactions and networks among neighbors and even "weak ties," or those that can offer us social benefit but are outside our usual social, political, and economic networks.[65]

Third, there is such a thing as a "concrete peace," or the notion that health and healing rely on concrete both literally and metaphorically, to combine physical improvements with lasting social institutions and community relationships. Roads, water, sewers, schools, and community facilities have become as important as meaningful participatory processes, the rule of law, and good governance.[66]

Fourth, relational investments matter. What this means is that Elm Playlot and Pogo Park were successful because they combined lifting up people, providing new green infrastructure, stabilizing housing, providing childcare services, distributing food, and a host of other strategies. Pogo Park, like the projects in Comuna 13, worked to physically connect one transformative space to others, such as through their Yellow Brick Road initiative. In Comuna 13, the integrated and connected projects linked transport, such as the Metrocable and electric escalators, to schools, libraries, health care, and employment opportunities.

Fifth, projects must redistribute wealth to truly heal those that have been traumatized and marginalized. In both Richmond and Medellín, job creation, employment training, and investments of significant amounts of capital ensured that the initiatives were helping to heal people and the place. Too often, parks, schools, and other place-based investments do not guarantee jobs and economic benefits to the communities that need them the most. Government resources are key, since traumas created by years of government divestment cannot be healed by volunteerism, charity, or nonprofit initiatives alone.

Chapter 5

Resilience and Climate Justice in Medellín

As former mayor Aníbal Gaviria and I walked along Medellín's river, viewing the riverside park that was under construction, he explained that we were strolling right where a multilane highway had once passed. As a child growing up in Medellín, Gaviria had thought the river was just like a sewer. The highway was all that he remembered. Yet we were walking through one of the most beautiful riverfront parks that I had ever seen. The park, part of the Parques del Río project, was launched by Gaviria during his tenure as mayor and was expected to be completed by 2027. The project had already accomplished what few in this City of Eternal Spring had ever imagined possible, putting its largest, most polluting roadway underground and building a multiuse public park with trails, playgrounds, kiosk shops, and low-income housing in its place (Figure 5.1). Gaviria's plan was to connect this city to the long-forgotten river, to green the Aburrá Valley and the Medellín River banks, and to ensure that the poor and those living in precarious peripheral communities at risk of landslides and other hazards, could live here.

While Medellín, Colombia, has become known for its innovative and equity-focused urban planning, including using ski-lift gondolas as part of its public transport system to reach impoverished hillside

Figure 5.1 Parques del Río, Medellín. (Source: Jorge Pérez-Jaramillo, used with permission)

communities and constructing its most architecturally beautiful and functional schools, libraries, and community centers in communities such as San Javier (see chapter 4), the Parques del Río seemed like one of its most ambitious projects to date. It was also controversial. It turned out that even in Medellín, both the rich and the poor were skeptical of the parks project.

We were soon joined by a few young people wearing yellow hard hats and Jorge Pérez-Jaramillo, the former planning director of Medellín under Gaviria. The young people were freshly graduated design students who were part of the team that designed the riverfront park. They had brought other young people together to dream up a new park in their city that focused on revitalizing ecosystems, encouraging social inclusion, and building resilience to climate change, especially for the city's poorest and most vulnerable groups. It was an approach called social urbanism—enlisting residents to define their needs, and codesigning solutions that brought social, economic, and environmental benefits to the poorest communities. The idea first emerged in this city in the mid-2000s and now seemed deeply ingrained in the minds, hearts, and actions of designers, activists, and political leaders.

One aspect of the Parques del Río project that made it so controversial, according to the young designers, was that neither the poor nor the rich considered the riverfront as a place where people would want to live. The years of highway expansion and dumping had turned the entire city away from its river. As a result, small industries were located adjacent to the river, and very few people lived there. Jorge chimed in: "The vision was to return a revitalized, clean and green river to the people, and prevent sprawl by densifying one area of the city yet to be built up, namely the valley floor."

Most of Medellín's wealthy live in its southeastern neighborhoods, or comunas, such as El Poblado, in high-rise buildings with beautiful views of the mountains. The city's poor live on the hillsides in the northern and western comunas, with the least expensive housing on the steepest slopes. The sprawl along the hillsides is an ecological and social danger to the poor and the entire city. Development was putting the poor in danger of landslides and contributing to downstream flooding, longer bus trips, air pollution, and increased segregation between the well-off and the poor.

"The housing will be for the poor, but some also for the wealthy, and this will help subsidize the affordability and the costs of maintaining the riverfront park," Gaviria described to me. And this, it seemed was a key controversy of the Parques del Río: a plan to bring rich and poor together, but to have the market-rate housing support the social housing. This was an all-too-familiar reaction in city planning projects that aim to create mixed-income communities. Here, a highway was being diverted underground, and those living in already vulnerable areas were being given the opportunity to live in what might become the city's most desirable, and expensive, area.

"Why shouldn't the poor live near the city's most beautiful ecologic asset?" one of the designers asked me. "It's like putting social housing on the banks of the Seine or the beach of Los Angeles, but doing this in conjunction with a citywide, coordinated climate change resilience strategy. By doing this we can reduce air pollution and carbon emissions, create more walking and cycling trips, plant thousands of native species, and help the river's habitat return," they explained to me.

Medellín is aiming to combine ecological and social projects to construct climate justice. I call it climate justice because many of the strategies, like the Parques del Río, combine environmental, economic, and social components, with an explicit commitment to improve the lives and living conditions of the urban poor. Medellín has been recognized for its transformation from one of the most violent cities in the world to a city with beautiful and functional new infrastructure, but could all these projects, plans, and programs also promote greater health and healing?

Making the Medellín "Miracle"

The changes in Medellín didn't occur by a miracle; they were actively created and constructed by people coming together, despite their fears and differences, and building a vision for a new future (see Box 2 and chapter 4). The history of the city remains an important factor in understanding its transformation and actions today, since it was in public reflections and contentious dialogues over how to best respond to the overlapping crises of violence and inequality in the 1990s that activists, academics, government, and business elites came together into what was described to me by Jorge Pérez-Jaramillo as a "collective project." This project, according to Pérez-Jaramillo, included difficult dialogues about the city's identity, who was responsible, and what an equitable response might look like. Pérez-Jaramillo described it to me: "We all grew up with fear and turning away from the public space and the 'other.' The constant stress from the unknown of encountering violence really brought us together. We came together in the university in spaces across the city. There was a lot of pain, fear, and uncertainty. The dialogues created a collective vision. It wasn't about just building new projects, it was about a collective response and a new social contract between the city and the people."

The social contract Jorge Pérez-Jaramillo refers to seemed to be driven by the idea of social urbanism, since the community and governmental responses prioritized social and physical inclusion, not the heavy hand of the state reflected through police and military force.[1] He recalled the social contract emerging from the public processes organized by the Presidential Council for Medellín in the 1990s. He reflected on the tens of community forums held across Medellín's neighborhoods and a large workshop with local and global participants in November 1995, called the Future Alternatives Seminars for Medellín and the Metropolitan Area.[2] The global workshop galvanized public and private institutions, academics, and influential organizations, such as Corporación Viva la Ciudadanía and Corporación Región, to agree on a collective way forward for rebuilding Medellín.[3]

A new political movement, Movimiento Compromiso Ciudadano (Citizens' Commitment Movement), also emerged from this process. This movement capitalized on the democratic and community-based spirit of the dialogic process, and it brought together social movements with leading academics. The leader of this movement was a university professor turned politician named Sergio Fajardo. Fajardo launched campaigns for elected office and eventually won the mayoral race in 2004.

According to Jorge Pérez, the significance of this time cannot be overlooked: "It's important that this wasn't the result of one leader. It was a movement and process. Compromiso Ciudadano emphasized dialogue and social processes and ensured those happened in the barrios, not corrupt halls of power. The people's process continually emphasized that long-term security needed to be built into the work of education, housing, and even the private sector. Improving public space was also identified as critically important, but it wasn't the end point. The redevelopment of public spaces was intended to be the glue for social inclusion and widespread opportunity."

Taking an Integrated Approach to Peace and Resilience

By the time Fajardo was elected, some public space innovations and projects had already been built. For example, the first ski-lift gondola that became Medellín's first Metrocable line had already been completed in Comuna 1, also called Popular. The Metrocable was both innovative and socially just, since it reduced travel times for and improved access to resources in the central city for hundreds of thousands of *paisas* (what residents of Medellín call themselves) in the lowest *estrato* (stratum). Estratos were created in Colombia by a law in 1994 and forced municipalities to rank housing on a scale from 1 to 6, with 1 being the lowest and 6 the highest, based on the structure's building materials and the quality of infrastructure in the area, such as roads and access to education. The estratos system classifies which areas of the city, and the residents living there, should receive government subsidies to reduce their utility bills; the lower the estrato, the higher your subsidy and the less you pay for electricity, water, garbage collection, and even your cell phone service.[4] More than 75 percent of Medellín's residents live in estratos 1, 2, or 3, but two comunas, Popular and San Javier (Comuna 13) have the greatest percentage of estrato 1 areas and people. This is one of the main reasons why Medellín's social urbanism projects focused on those neighborhoods first. The first Metrocable line built to reach the hillside community of Popular has helped reduce their travel time into the city from a 1-hour walk to a 10-minute cable car trip. Yet it was a change in governance that ensured the physical infrastructure was tied to social justice objectives.

After Fajardo took office, one of his first steps was to decouple the planning department, which was viewed as captured by elite interests, and the city's Urban Development Corporation (or EDU). This allowed his administration to further their social-urbanism objectives. Practically, this meant that new positions were created for "social managers" within the EDU to work in the neighborhoods to facilitate workshops with youth, adults, and different constituencies to imagine what the city could be. Emerging out of these workshops were community desires to combine physical infrastructure improvement, environmental quality, and social programs.[5]

The new integrated community development strategy linking physical, environmental, and social justice was called the Proyectos Urbanos Integrales (Integrated Urban Projects) (PUIs).[6] Consistent with the social urbanism ethos of investing in the poorest areas first, all the PUI locations at this time were in the city's lowest-income and most violent neighborhoods, and included spatially connected investments in transportation, education, health care, security, and economic and environmental quality.[7] In Popular, the PUI resulted in the construction of a beautiful new library park, pedestrian bridges, new schools, sports facilities, and offices to help stimulate local economic development,

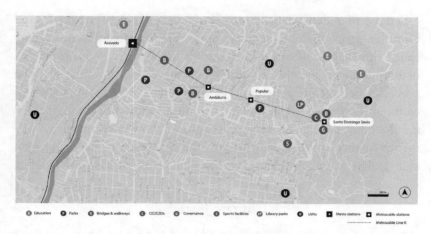

Figure 5.2 Map of Comuna 1 in Medellín, the Metrocable, and other Proyectos Urbanos Integrales (Integrated Urban Projects) (PUIs). Unidades de Vida Articulada (UVAs) (Articulated Life Units), are former hillside water storage tanks that were opened up and turned into public spaces. (Source: Urbam, EAFIT University, 2014. Map: proyecto urbano integral PUI Comuna Nororiental. https://www.eafit.edu.co/wuf/guia-medellin/Paginas/pui-nororiental.aspx)

called Centers of Zonal Development (CEDEZOs) (Figure 5.2). The CEDEZOs are community offices that bring together support from the government and the private sector, including banking. At each CEDEZO, staff help local residents access loans, learn about other small business development strategies, acquire necessary permits, and offer classes in fiscal and organizational management.[8] Among the results of the PUIs were the creation of 125,000 square meters of new public spaces. Neighborhood parks increased from three to seventeen in nine neighborhoods, and 3,439 new jobs were created and 290 programs were provided in education, health, social welfare, recreation, and sports.[9] The participatory program built community kitchens and football parks and also financed 1,200 scholarships for young people to pursue university studies.

The PUI stimulated a new generation of community leaders who brought this integrated planning approach to other efforts. This was formalized in 2002 with the city's long-term comprehensive plan, called the Plan de Ordenamiento Territorial (POT) (Territorial Land Use Plan), and a complementary short-term implementation strategy called the Plan de Desarrollo. Together these plans would provide a new roadmap for the physical and social redevelopment of the city. The processes behind the generation of these plans included hundreds of community workshops and public meetings, and it was through community input that the plans began to focus on how to improve environmental quality in the poorest areas of the city. In short, the plan began to articulate an environmental and climate justice vision for Medellín.

Climate Justice

Climate justice recognizes that there is a global-to-local "climate gap," or that the impacts of an altered climate are disproportionately affecting already vulnerable populations that were not responsible for, or made little contribution to, greenhouse gas emissions. This is climate injustice, since those experiencing the most severe consequences of climate change, such as extreme heat and weather events, drought and food insecurity, and flooding-induced displacement, also have the fewest resources to cope with these impacts.[10] Climate justice is a process that calls for a new science of risk management, where those communities that are already vulnerable, such as Indigenous Peoples, racial and ethnic minorities, and the landless urban poor, are at the center, rather than being an afterthought, of mitigation and adaptation strategies. In the urban context, climate justice is increasingly focused on how existing everyday risks, from physical hazardous exposures to social inequities that make populations vulnerable to displacement, disease, and death, are exacerbated by climate change.[11] Importantly, a central aspect of urban climate justice is the meaningful participation of the most vulnerable in the measurement of risk, generating risk-mitigation strategies and monitoring progress toward increased resilience and lowered vulnerability.[12]

Urban climate justice raises important questions for health and healing in cities. In fact, it confronts and integrates questions about how cities can mitigate or adapt to climate change, and the ways in which cities can be modified in response to climate change. Climate justice also challenges urban resilience, which is frequently defined as the ability to bounce back from shocks and stresses, by claiming that justice demands not returning to unjust systems that often created vulnerability in the first place but developing new, more equitable approaches to resource management and wealth distribution.[13] Climate justice is also attentive to and aims to avoid "green gentrification," or the displacement of the poor that can happen when environmental conservation and natural resources, like a new park or a revitalized riverfront, come to a community.[14] Green gentrification is an environmental justice concern, since the poor, Indigenous, and People of Color tend to be the most adversely impacted from projects and the least able to garner the power to shape projects and guarantee their "right to remain."

A key tenet of climate justice is the *precautionary principle*, or the idea that we already know enough, both technically and socially, about who and what is vulnerable to a changing climate, and we should act to improve those places now to avoid potential future impacts.[15] In cities like Medellín, urban climate justice means investing in those living in informal settlements or self-built communities who already experience multiple vulnerabilities, such as living in poverty, working informal jobs, relying on daily wages for food, and lacking basic services. These same communities are also vulnerable due to their location on steep slopes subject to landslides, on or adjacent to waste dumps, and in flood zones. Communities like Mukuru in Nairobi (chapter 3) and the Iron Triangle in Richmond (chapter 4) are both climate justice communities due to the overlapping social and environmental risks the poor and already vulnerable residents face.

Climate justice is about health and healing. In cities of the Global South, heat events pose a major climate injustice for the poor and those living in already precarious housing and on marginal land. Warming global temperatures and related changes in weather patterns are suspected of increasing the spread and exposure to the *Aedes aegypti* mosquito and related viruses, including dengue, yellow fever, chikungunya, Zika, and Japanese encephalitis.[16] Heat events in cities can combine with short-lived, climate-active pollutants, such as black carbon, and contribute to increased incidence of heart attack, asthma, and other cardiopulmonary diseases.[17]

Food insecurity can also be exacerbated by climate change; for example, when droughts alter food production and distribution, the urban poor can be disproportionately impacted. There are also important gender dimensions to climate justice, since women and girls may be responsible for collecting water and preparing foods, which can take longer during droughts. In some cases women may be forced to forgo education or skip meals in times of scarcity, making them more vulnerable as resources are impacted due to climate change.[18]

Localized flooding is another urban climate justice and health issue. Floods from increased frequency and severity of rain events, combined with slum populations being forced to live in flood-prone areas, can cause substantial physical damage to urban slum structures and displace residents. Flooding in urban slums can cause bacteria and hazardous materials to contaminate water supplies, elevating the risk of waterborne, respiratory, and skin diseases. Flooding displaces and disrupts residents' livelihoods and their access to health care, schools, jobs, clean water, food, roads, infrastructure, and service provision. Flooding can also increase psychological trauma, exposure to vector and gastrointestinal diseases, and food insecurity that puts children at higher risk of malnutrition.[19] The Intergovernmental Panel on Climate Change suggests that there are significant mental health consequences for residents in areas subject to chronic flooding since these events contribute to residential and economic (livelihood) displacement, psychosocial stress, and disruption of school attendance and health care services.[20]

Debate emerged in Medellín over the extent to which the "social" should be included in projects promoting ecosystem services, such as urban greening, land conservation, and water management. During Medellín's Territorial Plan–making process, or POT, questions arose over what areas in the city should receive these projects first, and whether groups that had been denied access to quality environments or were suffering the adverse consequences of exposure to toxic environments should be prioritized. There was some concern about the greening or "green infrastructure" focus and whether the environment would be prioritized over people.[21] Residents and activists demanded that a restorative justice approach to urban greening also be used, so that historical environmental harms would be reversed and those harmed communities would be left better off.[22]

Cocreating Climate Justice in Popular

During a community meeting in one of Popular's community centers constructed as part of the PUI, a group of women community leaders were discussing what issues to prioritize for the upcoming Participatory Budgeting (PB) cycle and how resources might be allocated to improve well-being in their barrio. PB is an annual part of Medellín's policy making and ensures that neighborhood residents can gain access to the city's resources to build and maintain projects and deliver social programs in their communities. The PB process requires that 5 percent of the city's annual budget is reserved for comuna councils to determine its allocation.[23] From 2005 to 2015, the annual participatory budget increased from roughly 60 to 151 million Colombian pesos. The allocation of the participatory funds for community-driven projects is managed by a group of popularly elected neighborhood planning representatives, called Juntas Administradoras Locales (JALs) (Local Management Boards).[24]

One woman participating, Yesly, also a student at the university, described the following: "Violence in the household and mental health is our concern. Sometimes this violence comes when women are blamed for the garbage that brings rats into the household. So when the environmental problems in the community are not addressed they can create mental health issues for women."

Blanca, one of the leaders of another break-out group, reported back about their discussions: "The water supply is not regular and the EPM storage tank overflows, flooding some areas. Water affects growing food, which for some they rely on local gardens. Without enough food, we can't take medications such as for HIV. You need food to take the medicines, and when there isn't enough it goes to the children first."

One participant stated, "Mira [look], we spend a lot of time outside these meetings talking to people and letting them know what we are doing. We hear about problems and most I hear is about public space and mental health. We have to be realistic that this one processes isn't going to solve all our issues."

Students from the Universidad de Antioquia (UdeA) working with facilitator David Hernandez had listed all the projects the group came up with on poster paper, which covered the walls. The students were busy passing out sticky notes for the group to place next to their priority projects. The group had already created a Community Health Plan, which had identified existing health issues and included a number of short- and longer-term interventions that they believed would help their community heal. These projects would decide what would get done in the coming year.[25]

The Health Plan was completed in 2015 as part of a citywide strategy to inject health into the Territorial Plan. The local plans, or Plan Comunal de Salud, allowed residents to develop strategies which ensured that built-environment changes were delivering health benefits to all. According to Eliana Martinez, a professor of epidemiology at the UdeA and an adviser to the health planning processes, women were most often the ones leading the efforts and generating social justice solutions. She told me, "The plans started in the places with the greatest health challenges and of course, these were, like Comuna 1, the most violent, greatest poverty and most segregated place. The plans are only effective when their recommendations are implemented with the community. This is what makes these ongoing dialogues important. Also things change in the community and health priorities can change too. Since this one [Comuna 1] was one of the first, they are furthest along and others look to them for inspiration. Now, with the participatory budgeting coming, the project can get city money for implementation."

Martinez had led the process to integrate all the comuna health plans into a citywide vision and strategy for the Healthy City plan. What I found interesting was that the Healthy City vision for Medellín started with emphasizing public space and "healthy environments," decent work, coexistence or social connection, and food security. Another aspect of Medellin's Healthy City plan that was unique was its explicit commitment to "a society that reconciles, that builds collectively and that overcomes difficulties." I asked David Hernandez about what this meant in practice, and he recalled, "It is a way to not forget the violence, the hardship and inequalities that people have faced and continue to struggle with. It says we must acknowledge and heal from that past and rebuild together. It means health starts in public space and coming together to rebuild the things that support quality of life, food, housing, employment and security."

A collective healing project that Hernandez pointed to was the cleanup of the city's former garbage dump, which involved residents redefining the space and turning it into Moravia Garden, one of the city's most important ecological restoration areas.

From Waste to Life: Moravia Garden

Moravia Garden was once the city's dump site, and a large community lived on and adjacent to the dump, picking whatever waste they could to survive.[26] After the dump closed in 1984, a large informal settlement emerged on top of the landfill. It was, according to Hernandez, a violent place, largely because of the poverty and pollution. By 2005, the area was extremely overcrowded, unsafe, and leaching chemical poisons. Almost everyone living there was classified as in the first or second estrato, meaning they were some of the poorest in the city with the worst physical and social infrastructure.[27]

The Territorial Plan (POT) made the remediation of Moravia a key priority. According to Jorge Pérez, the POT had human security and ecosystem integrity as its objectives. He described it to me: "Displacement is forcing people into precarious conditions and onto land that presents a high risk to them and threatened the regional ecosystem. Moravia was threatening people, the river and the region's sustainability."

By 2006, the strategy outlined in the POT was for improving the neighborhood surrounding the dump site through small urban development projects, and moving people on top of the landfill to the neighboring communities. Over 4,000 families were relocated to newly constructed social housing. In addition, new educational, cultural, and economic development projects were constructed around the site. One project included a series of large greenhouses where native flowers

Figure 5.3 Moravia after restoration, 2015. (Source: Alcaldia de Medellín)

could be grown. The entire project to remediate and redesign the landfill and the surrounding area was called, Moravia: Florece para la Vida (Moravia, flower or blossom into life).[28] Through a collaborative planning process, engineers, designers, and residents developed the plan that turned the dump site into a new site for bioremediation, social housing, and environmental education. The plan, consistent with the integrated projects and social urbanism ideals, included training by the Instituto Popular de Capacitación (Popular Training Institute), for hundreds of *promotores* (community health workers) to mediate domestic and street conflicts, as well as deliver health services to the new housing development. There was also an employment program for women established at the greenhouses. Today, the Moravia Cultural Development Center has become a community (and tourist) destination, as it demonstrates how to rebuild a community that was literally treated as garbage, into a culturally vibrant, environmentally sustainable, and healing-focused place (Figure 5.3).

A project like Moravia addressed what might seem like a more obvious environmental and climate justice issue; the poor were forced to live on a dangerous waste site. The response was less conventional, since housing and jobs came first, cultural preservation was a priority that ran throughout the project, and the remediation of the waste site came last. Perhaps the technical challenges of environmental restoration are not that difficult to address. The challenges are ensuring that the ecosystem objectives do not run roughshod over poor communities and their culture. What emerged from the Moravia project was a new aspect of Medellín's climate justice strategy, called the Urban Adaptation Action Plans (Los Planes Acción de Adaptación Urbana). These plans were to use participatory methods to assess each community's vulnerability to climate-related risks and identify ways to improve their "adaptive capacity" that also reduced existing vulnerabilities.[29] In almost all the plans, the impoverished hillside communities were identified as extremely vulnerable, and a set of strategies were put forward to protect hillside communities and promote their well-being.

Greening for Community Resilience and Climate Justice

A key project to protect hillside communities and promote climate justice was Medellín's greenbelt, Cinturón Verde. This was a strategy that would use a number of interventions to limit new development along the steep slopes while also delivering infrastructure and services to these same peripheral communities to ensure that they weren't vulnerable to landslides and other social and environmental risks. The greenbelt included new, hillside-stabilizing, paved pathways, tree planting, food gardens, as well as community centers and housing. The set of integrated projects came to be known as the Jardin Circunvalar (Circumvent Garden).[30]

I visited Comuna 8, one of those vulnerable hillside communities, with former mayor Gaviria, to see just what this project was aiming to do and how it was attempting to promote climate justice. He took me to the high edges of the city to see the Circumvent Garden as it neared completion. We wound our way up the mountainside in a 4x4 past where the small buses could reach and seemingly where only motorcycles or donkeys could navigate the steep hillside paths. We were in the far reaches of Comuna 8, on the urban fringe. We reached a pathway where people were riding bikes and walking alongside ter-raced gardens. Gaviria explained, "This used be known as the Camino de la Muerte—the 'path of death'—because it was where gangs would hang the bodies of their enemies." As we walked further in silence, I saw a sign announcing the trail as El Camino de la Vida, "the road of life," which is now a 12-kilometer trail connecting formerly discon-nected neighborhoods along the mountainside.

The Circumvent Garden project had already planted over 40,000 native trees on the hillsides, developed new community waste manage-ment plans, and built this pedestrian and cycle pathway as part of the boundary for the greenbelt.[31] Local community organizations, such as the Displaced Persons Board and the Commune Housing Board 8, ensured that any environmental and greening projects also included strategies to prevent displacement, integrated local agricultural and cultural practices, and the involvement of local people in defining what they needed for dignified housing.[32] As Gaviria explained to me, "We recognized that the greenbelt would only work, especially for those living on the hillsides, if we improved their communities and living conditions. The residents were leaders in defining what infrastructure and services they needed. It wasn't a one-size-fits-all climate change resilience strategy."

The Circumvent Garden project has three zones reflecting differ-ent climate change resilience objectives. First is the Protection Zone, where natural habit preservation, ecological restoration, and tree plant-ing as carbon sinks were prioritized. A second area was a transition zone where informal settlements would remain but be served with new municipal services including gardens, green spaces, and paths. A third zone would link the peripheral paths to the city's public transport net-work, formalize communities with land titles, and improve municipal facilities like schools, clinics, exercise areas, playgrounds, and commu-nity centers. Together, these levels of intervention were intended to build climate resilience, support communities, and act as a long-term ecological preservation strategy.

In climate change resilience planning, preventing violence is rarely a central concern. Nor is preserving the well-being of the informal, self-built communities like much of Comuna 8. In climate adaptation planning, green infrastructure like the Circumvent Garden might displace the poor living in risky areas in the name of ecological preservation or even public health.[33] This project was explicitly driven by a commitment to make Medellín more inclusive and climate change resilient, in that order. As Gaviria described to me, "Climate change has contributed to more severe rains and weather in Medellín. The threat of landslides is increasing. These hillsides have always been disaster-prone areas. We have many areas with underground streams and a complex ecosystem of drainage. The trees and plants on the hillside stabilize the environment and feed the region's ecosystem. But we first needed to recognize these communities were excluded from the city and its services, and this made them more vulnerable. They were trying to sustainably manage the local ecosystem, so they were experts in the planning process. However, in some cases the land is too risky, and that is why the River Parks project (Parques del Rio) will offer them housing."

It wasn't so much climate change, but "green gentrification" that seemed to be on the minds of residents in Barrio El Faro in Comuna 8 when I visited and asked about the Circumvent Garden. Juan Camilo Molina Betancur, a student at the UdeA in Medellín who spent many years in the informal settlement of El Faro, was describing to me the processes residents of this community used to prevent green gentrification. Juan Camilo noted that while living in a precarious area, the residents identified the assets in their community that they wanted to preserve and explored how the Circumvent Garden project could support, rather than threaten, their community. He described it to me: "This is a community with self-built houses and community designed water and sewer system. There are no schools or clinics here, and they have been building their own paths, streets and cultivating the land. They are skeptical of government since they are always threatened with evictions. So, they formed their own process."

The residents of El Faro organized and shared the aspects of their lives and community that they thought promoted health. What they generated were descriptions of both social and physical assets that they wanted to be preserved and not threatened by the Circumvent Garden. As Juan Camilo told it to me, "We did community asset mapping and residents said that their collective organization was one of their greatest assets for well-being. These included what they call the Work Table, a place for community decision making. Another is the Illegal Element Collective, a youth hip hop school that creates opportunities for young people to develop their vision for the community through art and music. These are community institutions of resistance and hope. These institutions created the physical assets, like sports and cultural activities. They also said partnerships with outside organizations, such as Techo,[34] the Housing and Public Services Board, and Corporación Volver, have made improvement projects, like Tavo court, urban agriculture, and hillside stabilization walls possible."

To highlight the participatory process and the level of engagement used in El Faro, Juan Camilo showed me an asset-and-network map from a neighboring community, and described how the plotting of physical assets stimulated a conversation about how the community interacted with the spaces and the organizations that were needed to really promote well-being. He elaborated: "In the community mapping process, the members would point to the aqueduct as an asset, but then describe how it is a site for collective work and management. They pointed to the Working Group as a collective that defends life in the territory. When they pointed to the Circunvalar Garden, they not only labeled the physical projects, but their ability to resist the removal of houses. The mapping was a way assets were identified along with the groups that made the community assets work."

As Gaviria told me, Medellín's Department for Social Inclusion and Family (Secretariat de Inclusion Social y Familia del Alcalde de Medellín [SISF]), was also active in El Faro. The SISF supports food security and coordinates school food programs through which all students in the city receive fortified milk and lunch every day. In El Faro, the SISF is helping urban farmers coordinate their crops to take produce to a farmer's market that is held in a wealthier part of the city, called El Poblado.

For Juan Camilo and the El Faro residents, climate change resilience meant strengthening their collective support institutions and processes that keep them safe, as much or more than the physical infrastructure delivered by the city.

Healthy Resiliency Hubs

As Gaviria and I departed Comuna 8, we boarded the Metrocable as it headed back down the mountainside toward the center of the city. He described the larger vision of the city, and that no one project should be viewed in isolation. He noted, "Our government's strategy was Medellín, a "City for Life," which put life and equity at the center of municipal governance (see Figure 5.4). Even this cable car, sure it makes travel more efficient, but more importantly it serves the life of these communities—access to jobs, goods and services, inclusion. The city is foremost about its people, not its projects. So every plan, every project, every policy is aimed at supporting a vibrant, safe, and inclusive life for the people."

Gaviria's eyes lit up, and he pointed toward a large, round structure in the distance. "UVA," he said, "another one of our strategies to create an inclusive city for all."

The Articulated Life Units (Unidades de Vida Articulada [UVA]), are public community spaces reclaimed from previously fenced-in, private utility land, most of them water storage tanks. The idea was that the hillside poor communities didn't have adequate green or play space. Instead of moving housing to create open space, the residents suggested the city open up its property and turn it back over to the people. The sites were collected by Empresa Publicas de Medellín (EPM), the city's utility company. Local design processes were held to decide how best to redevelop these walled-in spaces. Jorge Pérez described it to me: "The UVA design process was also of co-creation. Residents said 'take down the walls and fences to bring people together.' It was young, local designers that helped dream up how to turn something that was a symbol of power and exclusion, to one that was open for all. What emerged is nothing like what a team of city planners or architects would have come up with. I mean maybe we would have some interesting green or play spaces, but not this!"

What 'this' was, were UVAs that are some of Medellín's most beautiful and creative public spaces. At one UVA, water and light are combined to create a play and performance space. At another UVA water fountains were created in areas for both children and adults (Figure

Non – violence   Innovation

Figure 5.4 Me-
dellín, a City for
Life. (Source:
Alcaldia de
Medellín)   **Participation**   **Transparency**

5.5). Other UVAs included art and music spaces, classrooms, swimming pools, libraries, gardens, and recreation spaces. Many UVAs have
won international design awards. For instance the UVAs won the
global Holcim Award in 2015 given to the best project in sustainable
construction and were featured in the 2016 Venice Art and Architecture Biennale. Importantly, the new public places are bringing people
together to play, learn, create, or just be together in a safe space day
and night.

The UVAs act as "resiliency hubs" for the city's most vulnerable residents. Community resilience is often defined as the ability of communities to withstand, recover, and learn from climate-change-induced
adverse impacts and strengthen responses and recovery efforts. Yet,
what Medellín has recognized in the planning of UVAs, its greenbelt
strategy, and integrated territorial planning, is that climate justice demands a more focused attention to *healthy resilience*, which I define as
a commitment to addressing the everyday stressors that compromise

Figure 5.5 Children playing at one of Medellín's UVAs. (Source: Judea Johnson, used with permission)

health, security, and well-being, that are exacerbated by a disaster or climate change–induced event. In this way, Medellín is working to build healthy climate change resilience by strengthening the everyday social connections, physical assets, and economic resources within communities. Healthy climate change resilience promotes greater justice—or climate justice—when it begins to achieve real, measurable changes in communities that reduce and eliminate the inequalities that make the poor extremely vulnerable to climate change–induced shocks and events.

The UVAs are "healthy resiliency hubs" because they anchor a network of resiliency infrastructure in Medellín's poorest areas. At least eighteen UVAs have been developed across the city, and all are physically and socially (through culture, programs, and services) linked to educational, health, parks, transportation, and other healthy development. The UVAs are anchor institutions in their communities, since they offer the types of everyday supports that build resilience and adaptive capacity—from access to food and recreation, to employment and learning, to violence mediation and peace-building services, to invest-ment in local arts and culture. Importantly, according to Jorge Pérez, the cocreation process and the opening-up of EPM infrastructure to community uses has "helped rebuild trust within the community and between the city and communities." While community organizations create the programming, and many local people are employed at each UVA, the utility company EPM pays for the operation and staff, just like they would if the walls were still up.

In climate resilience the driving approach is adaptation and respond-ing to emergencies, while healthy resilience places primacy on current everyday emergencies that are already making urban communities and places vulnerable. A climate resiliency approach also tends to focus on the hazards and risks in a community, while a healthy resiliency strat-egy works to lift up and build on existing community strengths and assets. A third aspect of climate resilience is that it tends to emphasize and focus on ways to "bounce back better," but not on transforming communities and dismantling the structural inequities that tend to make places unhealthy and vulnerable in the first place. Fourth, climate resilience and healthy resilience share in their commitments to learn-ing by doing, but differ in that climate resilience is driven by analyses done by outside experts, often using quantitative modeling to identify places of vulnerability, while healthy resilience emphasizes the impor-tance of evidence, such as lived experiences, observations, and local knowledge. Finally, the driving institutions for climate resilience tend to be national and municipal governments and their environmental agencies, while healthy resilience is led by community-based organiza-tions focused on such social determinants of health as housing, food security, violence prevention, and economic development, with govern-ments and others playing a supporting role (Table 5.1).

Measuring Resilience and Healing in Medellín

Many of the projects and initiatives mentioned here were financed through Medellín's public utility company, EPM. Voters decided in the 1990s to require that 30 percent of the utilities' profits must go back into public use projects, and this created about USD 450 million per

Table 5.1 Healthy resilience vs. climate resilience.

Feature	Climate Resilience	Healthy Resilience
Principles	Adaptation to future shocks	Eliminate everyday vulnerabilities
Focus	Hazard mitigation	Enhance assets and community strengths
Orientation	"Bounce back better"	Dismantle structural inequities
Expertise	Technical outsiders	Lived experiences
Change leaders	Government environmental agencies	Community groups and residents

year.[35] Another insightful innovation by the people of Medellín was that their own public company should redistribute resources back to the people, especially those most in need.

The private sector also plays a significant role providing finance for Medellín's transformation. A group called the Sindicato Antioqueño and the ProAntioquia Foundation both donated buildings, subsidized projects, and offered strategic direction for some public-serving projects. They also began to reshape Medellín's economy toward more professional services, health tourism, and information technology.[36]

Yet, with all the different projects and programs in Medellín, what is the best way to measure whether they are positively impacting health and healing? We want to be cautious with health outcomes, since there isn't a short-term dose–response relationship between such things as building a community center or new public transportation and changes in diabetes, infectious disease rates, or improved mental health. However, conventional public health indicators can give us some clues about the likely impacts of changes. For example, life expectancy in Medellín has increased from 75.2 years in 2006 to 78.2 in 2019, with women living on average 3 years longer than men.[37] The infant mortality rate for Medellín decreased from 14.3 per 1,000 in 2004, to 10.1 in 2011, to 8.3 in 2015, to 7.3 in 2019.[38] The mortality rate for children under 5 due to respiratory infections declined from 24.5 per 1,000 in 2006 to 6.8 in 2016. The prevalence of chronic malnutrition for children under 6 has declined from 10.8 per 1,000 in 2011 to 7.4 in 2019. Violence as a cause of death in Medellín has declined since 2012, but respiratory diseases and hypertension-related deaths have increased (Table 5.2).

Table 5.2 Medellín: Leading cause of death, 2012–2019 (% of total).

	2012	2014	2016	2018	2019
Primary Cause	Heart disease (15.5)	Heart disease (15.1)	Heart disease (14.4)	Heart disease (14)	Heart disease (13.4)
2nd cause	Violence (8.6)	Lower respiratory disease (7.9)	Lower respiratory disease (7.3)	Lower respiratory disease (7.5)	**Lower respiratory disease (8.2)**
3rd cause	Lower respiratory disease (6.9)	Cerebrovascular diseases (6.5)	Cerebrovascular diseases (6)	Cerebrovascular diseases (6.4)	**Hypertensive diseases (5.9)**
4th cause	Cerebrovascular diseases (6.8)	**Violence (5)**	Pneumonia (5.1)	Hypertensive diseases (5.2)	Cerebrovascular diseases (5.7)

Source: Medellin *Como Vamos,* https://www.medellincomovamos.org/system/files/2020-10/docupri
vados/MCV%20Informe%20de%20indicadores%20objetivos%20sobre%20c%C3%B3mo%20vamos%20
en%20salud%20en%20Medell%C3%ADn%2C%202016-2019.pdf

Since at least 2010, Medellín has been using an index of well-being called the Multidimensional Index of Living Conditions (IMCV). This index combines survey data and census-type data on such measures as household economic status, educational attainment, housing quality, use of the social security system, number and type of connected utility services, feelings of security in one's neighborhood, perceptions of environmental pollution, ratings of public transport, levels of civic participation/voting, access to health services, participation in recreation, and overall perception of the quality of life.[39] These data are gathered at the household level so analyses by community are possible.

The IMCV data from Medellín, "Como Vamos?" (How are we going?) suggest that not much has changed in each of the sixteen comunas between 2010 and 2019 (Figure 5.6). Yet my research team at UC Berkeley looked at some individual measures within the index and found some significant improvements in the Popular and San Javier Comunas. For example, the responses of good or excellent self-rated health (the answer to the question "How would you rate your health?"), increased by 6 percentage points from 2011 to 2018 in Comunas 1, 8, and 13 (some of the poorest areas) but stayed the same or decreased between 2 and 4 percentage points in Poblado and Laureles (Comunas 14 and 11, respectively), two of the wealthiest areas.[40]

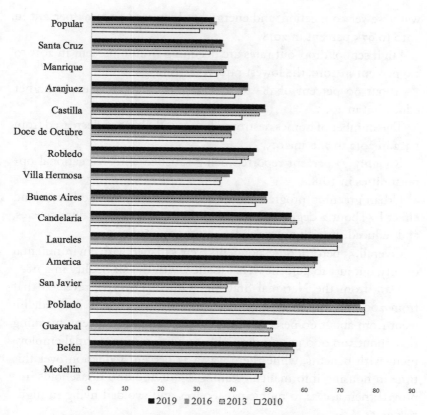

Figure 5.6 Medellín comunas: Multidimensional Quality of Life Index, 2010–2019.

Other social indicators suggest the resources for health and healing may be improving in Medellín. The Gini Index—a measure of income inequality—has declined in Medellín since 2010 (with a brief uptick in 2014). The lower the Gini the less inequality, and in Medellín it was 0.56 in 2003 but fell to 0.46 in 2017, according to data from DANE, the Colombian statistics agency (for comparison, the Gini in the US is about .41 and in South Africa it is .65).[41]

Poverty rates have dropped from 36.5 percent of the population in 2002 to less than 14 percent in 2018.

The percentage of households that received municipal services of water, sewer connection, and energy has increased from 94 percent in 2010 to 97.5 percent in 2018.

High school drop-out rates are declining from 9 percent in 2015 to 2.9 percent in 2019, the lowest rate in 14 years.[42]

About 60 percent of 18- to 24-year-olds were enrolled in higher education in 2017.

The number of homes destroyed by natural disasters decreased from 1,322 in 2012 to 790 in 2015.

Roughly 77 percent reported being satisfied with recreational opportunities in 2018.

Urban greening programs since 2012 have reduced the heat island effect by about 2 degrees C, doubled the biodiversity of flora species, and reduced the risk of landslides across the city.[43]

Overall, 55 percent of respondents were satisfied with environmental quality, but just 10 percent were satisfied with the air quality in 2018.

Data from the National Statistics Office (DANE), revealed that from 2002 to 2018, the percentage of informal workers in Medellín went from about 60 percent of the population to 41 percent, meaning that about 500,000 people were able to acquire more formal employment with benefits, while there was a 33 percent reduction over this time in housing informality, meaning about 200,000 households improved their access to municipal services and avoided living in high-risk areas.[44]

An Ongoing Project

A key aspect of Medellín's approach to constructing climate justice is that it is an ongoing, not static, effort. While most cities would be happy to draft and adopt a climate action plan, Medellín remains committed to continually improving and addressing these challenges. The green belt project has evolved to include the city's Green Corridors initiative, which is planting thousands of trees along roads, creeks, and ecologically sensitive riparian areas within the urban core, not just on the periphery.[45] The city is also investing in the creative economy and innovations of local residents as part of its approach to sustainable development. For this effort Medellín has created the Perpetuo Socorro

Creative District in Comuna 10 to grow the "Orange Economy" where the arts, culture, music, design, gastronomy, film, and other human expressions are fostered through "labs," business supports, tax breaks, subsidies, and innovation spaces.[46]

As respiratory illnesses continue to increase and local air pollution remains an environmental health threat, a network of over thirty-eight community-based air quality sensors across the entire Aburrá Valley (called SIATA) was established to allow for continuous readings of particulate matter pollution. A specific area in the city will be designated in 2021 as a "protected air zone," where a concerted effort will be made to reduce vehicle traffic and associated pollution. An Eco-City Medellín initiative was launched in 2020 as part of the Medellín Future Development Plan, which will build on previous territorial, mobility, and environmental quality plans.[47] According to Medellín's secretary of mobility, Carlos Cadena Gaitán, the Eco-City will link sustainability and biodiversity efforts across the city and the region around Antioquia. It will also include a series of strategic projects that include (1) urban densification, (2) completing the "last mile" of municipal services to those households still not connected, (3) ensuring that a newly proposed underground metro line delivers ecological and health benefits, (4) enhancing electric bus and bicycle mobility and safety, and (5) expanding the Parques del Río project toward the North of the city. Specific indicators for the 4-year, Eco-City plan include expanding bicycle trips from 1 to 4% of daily trips, cutting in half the road death rate from 10/100,000 to 5, expanding the electric bus fleet from 65 to 130, increasing the amount of public space per each resident from 3.7 to 6.1 square meters, and eliminating over 7,000 tons of CO_2 per year and 0.179 tons per year of particulate matter 2.5 (PM2.5).

The River Park: Anchoring Climate Resilience

As we returned to the River Parks project, Gaviria described his vision for an equitable and climate change resilient region. He noted that the River Park was controversial to some, and its expense may make it difficult to implement in other cities of the Global South. Yet, he noted, the idea was not unique, as cities from Paris to Seoul have reclaimed their rivers, reconnected the people to their native ecosystems, and torn down or depressed highways and replaced them with parks and green space. "What is critical" he emphasized to me "is that the momentum continues. The projects and plans with community involvement, must continue to build our resilience. The River Parks project is also about developing a more sustainable, compact city, helping to eliminate the sprawl and offer a vibrant and affordable community where those previously forced to live in precarious areas along the hillsides can relocate." What I have learned from Medellín is that one key ingredient for constructing climate justice is to first focus on social inclusion, then on ecosystems. By late 2019, the green and social transformation along the river was well on its way, as recreation spaces, cafés, and river crossings were complete and residents from all regions of the city were coming to use the space.

The transformation of Medellín has been recognized through numerous global awards, such as the 2012 City of the Year award from the *Wall Street Journal*, Citibank, and the Urban Land Institute, and the 2016 Yee Kuan Yew, World City Prize.[48,49] It has been called the most innovative city in the world.[50] I believe that the innovation and accomplishments of Medellín have more to do with its ongoing commitment to social justice and inclusion. The key principles behind the construction of climate justice in Medellin include the following:

Innovation—with, not just for, people, and prioritizing dialogue over technology

An ethics of aesthetics—putting the most innovative and beautiful projects in the poorest, most deprived areas

Adaptive management—letting local people be stewards and managers of their local ecosystems, supporting them to learn about what is working, and giving them resources to adjust as they go

Social connections—building inclusion through physical projects and services, education programs, and local economic development

Power—reorienting the face of the state, from enforcer of "peace" and planning expert, to convener, facilitator, and collaborator

Institutionalization—ensuring that equity, resilience, and health are not boutique, one-off or disconnected efforts, but are part and parcel of legally adopted plans and public policies, and employing people, for their participation and at the places they cocreate, to recognize the value their work brings to the entire society.

Chapter 6

Putting Health Equity into All Urban Policies

In 2007 African American women in Richmond, California, had the highest maternal mortality rate in the region. Over one quarter of poor children in Richmond were hospitalized for asthma. Rates of obesity were climbing for all groups, and emergency department visits for heart disease were seven times the California average for the city's Latinx, Laotian, and Vietnamese populations. Gun homicides had reached 47 per 100,000 residents, making Richmond one of the most violent cities in America. The city had the lowest life expectancy in the San Francisco Bay Area. A documentary had just been released characterizing Richmond as one of the nation's most violent and unhealthy cites.[1]

This is not what any government officials wanted to hear about their city, especially a city without a public health department. In 2009 I presented these data to Richmond city leaders, showing the persistence of health inequities in the city and their likely causes. I had tried to end on a hopeful note, reminding the audience that only a few years earlier, Richmond had become the first (and at that time only) city in California to adopt a community Health and Wellness Element or chapter into its 2030 General Plan.[2] Breaking the silence, Bill Lindsey, the city manager, stood up, turned to his staff, and said, "We need to find ways to change these outcomes. I want everyone in this room to think of themselves and their departments as 'community clinicians.' From today forward, I want us to see city services through the prism of promoting health."

The declaration was powerful and surprising. It came from a career bureaucrat with an MBA and no prior background in public health. Yet Lindsey would later tell me that he had had an aha moment as we were working with community partners on the health element and related initiatives. His sudden insight was that as a leader in the city, he could use his discretion to ensure that almost all city management practices—from the budget process to street paving to the housing authority to the police department—could be oriented to better promote health and well-being. "Every community meeting, almost every city council meeting I attended," Linsey would tell me after ending his term as city manager, "a resident was concerned with some aspect of health. Whether it was Chevron, air pollution, traffic, noise, housing, jobs, schools, public safety. All of it. Our work made me realize it could all be about promoting health."

Shasa Curl, who was Lindsey's deputy in the Richmond city manager's office, would echo those sentiments, but put a more explicit racial justice frame around the approach. She described the shift in the city in this way: "We are a city of Black, Brown, Asian, and immigrant folks. The residents' and CBOs' [community-based organizations'] demands for services and changes were coming from a space of experiencing institutional racism. The city's response was to own that. Most of us live here and wanted racial and economic justice for our communities too. So it wasn't just about health, but a conscious focus on how racism makes us sick, and that city government and partners must work together to promote social justice."

The city of Richmond didn't just add a new health chapter to its general plan, but developed specific neighborhood-level implementation strategies to put that vision into practice. They created the Richmond Health Equity Partnership (RHEP), with the explicit goal of tackling racial injustice as a way to reduce health inequities. The RHEP, which I helped lead, drafted a strategy and a local law that put Lindsey's vision of "city services through the prism of health" into practice called Health in All Policies. Health in All Policies (HiAP) is an approach to governance that aims to promote health equity by recognizing that the decisions made outside the health care system, many of which cities control, such as land uses, community development, housing, and social services, can be more impactful on our health than medical care. HiAP recognizes that in order to change the dynamic that your zip code is a greater predictor of life expectancy and the probability of disease than your genetic code (introduced in chapter 1), city government policy, planning, and practice work needs to be reoriented to promote health and wellness.

Understanding how Richmond applied HiAP is important for understanding cities for life, since this city's approach was explicitly about addressing health inequities experienced by racial and ethnic groups by changing the institutional practices that have perpetuated the traumas of racism and ingrained these commitments into law.

By 2019, four years after HiAP was adopted as a city ordinance, the outcomes and determinants of health in Richmond had radically improved. Yet very little is known about how this happened or how city governments, even those without a public health department, can promote health and healing.

Life expectancy in Richmond increased from 75.6 years in 2000 to 80.5 years in 2019. Gun homicides were at 30-year lows, reaching 15 in 2019. Unemployment had dropped from almost 19 percent to less than 4 percent. In 2019, almost twice as many residents were homeowners than a decade before. The City and community groups had pressured Chevron Corporation, which operates a large petrochemical refinery in Richmond, to reduce its air pollution emissions and invest in community programs, including the Richmond Promise college scholarship for all graduating high school students. Hundreds of new affordable housing units had been built, and the City was using social impact bonds to purchase abandoned and blighted housing, rehabilitating it, and then reselling the homes to low-income, first-time home buyers. While only 20 percent of residents rated Richmond as a good or excellent place to live in 2009, over 50 percent said it was in 2019.

Richmond, like the entire San Francisco Bay Area, has experienced some gentrification and displacement, particularly of African Americans. From 2010 to 2019, there was an 8 percent decline in the African

American population in Richmond. Of Richmond's 111,000 people in 2019, about 40 percent identified as Latinx, 20 percent as Black, 16 percent as Asian, and 37 percent as White or more than one race.

As in Medellín, Richmond's healing-centered work is ongoing and incomplete. However, both Medellín and Richmond reveal that a focus on meaningful community participation and leadership, government investments in integrated projects, and an explicit focus on addressing structural racism have combined to explain why, as locals say, Richmond is rising.

Environmental Racism and Activism in Richmond

In July 1993, the General Chemical Company, which operated on the same property as the Chevron refinery in Richmond, released a toxic cloud of sulfuric acid. Over 24,000 people from Richmond went to the emergency department complaining of coughing, shortness of breath, runny eyes, nausea, and other symptoms. Activists, community residents, and the city sued General Chemical for negligence, and in May 1994, the company agreed to new reporting requirements, to fund an emergency warning system, and to pay for a new health clinic in North Richmond.[3]

As Greg Karras, a senior scientist with Communities for a Better Environment (CBE), told me, environmental racism was at the root of inequities in Richmond: "Environmental racism defines the corporate–government–community relationship in Richmond and it has for decades. For years Chevron owned the city council, the unions, and controlled local politics. It was the quintessential company town, hidden in plain sight for all the liberals in the Bay Area to ignore. How does a city with a billion dollar multinational corporation in its back yard, be on the verge of bankruptcy? Corruption. They were killing this city, all the while the White corporate leaders lived across the hills in San Ramon." By the 2000s, activist organizations like CBE were building a new coalition to influence decision making and redirect resources to those suffering from historic discrimination.

After decades of citizen activism to address racial and environmental injustices in Richmond (see Box 1), the city elected a Green Party mayor in 2006. A coalition of environmental health activists, labor unions, and immigrant rights groups came together to elect Gayle McLaughlin, and Richmond became the largest city in the US with a Green Party mayor. While Richmond doesn't have a strong-mayor form of government, meaning that the mayor doesn't have the ability to make appointments or dictate the policy agenda, Mayor McLaughlin campaigned against corporate control over environmental health issues. One of the mayor's first tasks was to lead the updating of Richmond's general plan.

Under California law, cities and counties must update their general plans periodically and include a series of chapters or elements. A general plan is supposed to be the policy constitution and development blueprint for local government, but it can just as easily sit on a shelf and be ignored. The required elements at the time included housing, land use/urban design, circulation/mobility, public facilities/infrastructure, open space, public safety, and noise.

A coalition of community groups created the Richmond Equitable Development Initiative (REDI) to influence the general planning process. REDI included environmental justice groups and organizations working to promote affordable housing, employment opportunities, improved access to health services, and violence reduction.[4] According to Juliet Ellis, the former executive director of Urban Habitat, REDI used research, policy advocacy, and organizing strategies to ensure that the growth and development decisions in Richmond benefited the city's low-income populations and communities of color. During some of the first public meetings for the general plan update, REDI members attended and demanded that the plan include environmental justice and health issues. A Technical Advisory Group (TAG) was created to respond to the community concerns and explore how to incorporate community health into the plan.[5]

According to Sheryl Lane, an organizer with Urban Habitat and a leader of REDI at the time, the technical group made explicit the links between land-use decisions and the health inequities that residents were facing. She noted that one result was a draft Community Health and Wellness Element, which "was more than just connecting the built environment to health, but put equity and racial justice issues as a priority for action."

According to another community activist, "The Health Element was a first for any city or county in California, and was a way to hold the City accountable. But, we wanted this to be more than empty promises for racial and social justice, and the pilot implementation phase helped make that a reality."

After the Community Health and Wellness Element was drafted, activists pressured the City to implement some of its recommendations, so the City created a Neighborhood Strategies Work Group. This group of community-based organizations and residents selected two areas in Richmond with the poorest health, social, and economic conditions, called the Iron Triangle and Belding Woods, for pilot interventions. The idea was to "learn by doing," with tangible projects where residents could be active participants. Residents came together at two primary schools in these neighborhoods to create action plans and experiment with what were hoped to be catalytic actions.[6] The idea was very much like the urban acupuncture strategy used in Medellín discussed in chapter 4.

In this pilot phase, local projects included street painting and sidewalk changes at the school sites to slow traffic and make it more pedestrian friendly. Other projects included converting unused tennis courts at two local parks into futsal (soccer) courts, which residents completed with City officials in a weekend. The City also upgraded all lighting so the courts could be used at night. This learning-by-doing approach helped the City rebuild trust with these communities, as Gabino Arredondo, the City of Richmond's coordinator of health initiatives at the time explained to me: "There were many things we as a city could do with little to no cost, that meant a lot to the residents. They also began to see the city as an ally, rather than an institution to fear. The projects gave many families real benefits."

Structural Inequalities Drive the Health in All Policies Strategy

While the neighborhood projects were moving forward, I was asked to bring together a group of community organizations, the City, the county health department, and the school district, to formalize what we were learning from this pilot process into the everyday practices of City decision making.

During the meeting, Shasa Curl, from the Richmond city manager's office, and I proposed a new health equity strategy for Richmond, where the traumas and inequities from institutional racism were made more explicit. We heard from parents that the school district needed more trauma-informed services in schools and built into after-school programs. We asked the county health department to work with the schools to expand school-based health clinics, and open them up to the entire community after school and on weekends. We discussed creating new "health academies" to train high school students in different health career professions. We also asked the county health department to share their epidemiological data to create a health equity report card for Richmond. Community groups supported these proposals and also wanted the City to make health equity a lens for all its departments and procedures. It was at this request that we created the Richmond Health Equity Partnership (RHEP), mentioned earlier in this chapter.

The RHEP held its first meeting in March 2012. We created two parallel work plans that built on previous health equity work. First, the school district and county health department began meeting for the first time to bring new healing and heath-centered programs into the schools. The idea was that schools were to become "health homes" for youth and their families, especially when neighborhoods could be unhealthy and health care was out of reach. A new clinic was opened in Richmond High School, and counseling programs for violence-impacted youth were increased. The second work plan was to develop a plan to integrate health equity into all functions of City government, and this became Richmond's Health in All Policies (HiAP) strategy, (Figure 6.1).

The RHEP organized tens of community meetings to explain why the HiAP strategy was needed and what residents and community groups could gain by participating in its drafting. According to Shasa Curl, "We didn't want to keep focusing on just encouraging people to change their diets or exercise or improving the built environment without also addressing the structural racism that was often underlying whether residents had opportunities. We knew the discrimination in

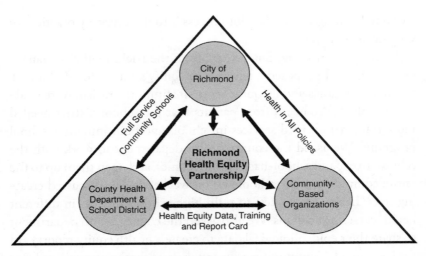

Figure 6.1 Richmond Health Equity Partnership model.

our institutions persisted, but it was often invisible or just had been the way we did business for so long it wasn't challenged. The HiAP process gave us the space to not only identify those practices, but link them to health and well-being for the first time. It was a big step to move us toward being an antiracist institution."

During community-based workshops co-led by Gabino and community-based organizations, we discussed the linkages between experiences with racism and poor health outcomes.[7] Gabino had the idea of creating a poster from an image in one of my presentations of a human skeleton. In community workshops he asked participants to write the stressors they encountered in their lives on the poster (Figure 6.2a and b). Similar workshops were held with City staff.

Richmond's Health in All Policies Approach

After 18 months of workshops, trainings, discussions, and research, a draft HiAP strategy and ordinance were completed. Twelve measures of equity using publicly available data were selected to capture resident's priorities and give the HiAP strategy a clear set of measurable indicators for moving toward greater health equity (Figure 6.3, left

Figure 6.2a and b
Community residents
in Richmond defining
toxic stressors. (Source:
Gabino Arredondo,
used with permission)

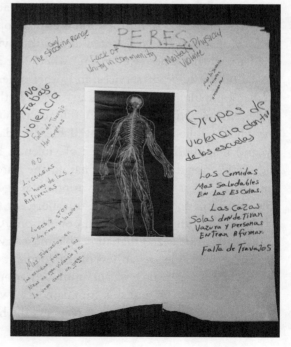

side) and a similar set of indicators were selected as inequities that the group wanted to reduce or avoid (Figure 6.3, right side).

In addition to the indicators, six policy action areas were selected for the HiAP strategy:[8] (1) governance and leadership, (2) economic development and education, (3) residential and built environments, (4) full-service and safe communities, (5) environmental health and justice, and (6) quality and accessible health care. Each action area was framed as a health equity issue, and specific programs, policies, and practices were identified under each area that could address structural racism and move toward greater health equity. The governance and leadership action area was defined as the day-to-day management decisions within the City of Richmond, including but not limited to how inclusive it is to different viewpoints and participants and the degree to which it is committed to shared power in decision making. The economic development and education policy area emphasized that financial status, particularly wealth and relative levels of inequality, are key drivers of health inequities. The economic development and education action area stressed that life-long learning supports critical thinking, and access to information is critical for informed democratic decision making. The residential and built environments action area emphasized that where we live and whether it is affordable, safe, and has culturally relevant services and other amenities or hazards, can predict a population's chances of getting sick, the degree of suffering, and even premature mortality. A full-service and safe community is one where public services were available, affordable, and of high quality, and neighborhoods were free of violence. Environmental health and justice was defined as eliminating the burdens of pollution and improving access to healthy environmental "goods," such as affordable nutritious foods, parks, and transport, for the city's poor, People of Color, and other marginalized populations. Quality and accessible health care emphasized that all people must have their preventive and treatment needs met, regardless of employment or immigration status.

The HiAP Ordinance was unanimously adopted by the Richmond City Council in 2015, and this stimulated a new set of practices, partnerships, and policies all aimed at reaching the health equity goals and indicators mandated by the ordinance.

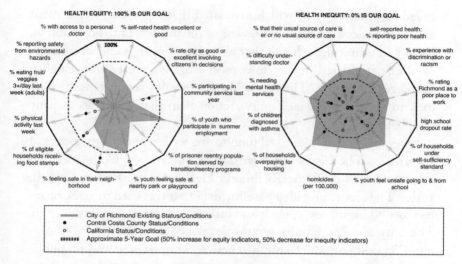

Figure 6.3 Measure of health equity for Richmond's Health in All Policies strategy.

Each polygon includes the existing conditions in Richmond as the shaded gray area, with the dots representing how Richmond compared to the county and state, where data were available. The dashed line reflects the 5-year goal for each indicator, and the arrows on each axis emphasize the direction of progress.

Intervention Area 1: Governance and Leadership

The leadership for implementing HiAP was within the City manager's office, which is the municipal department responsible for budgeting and decision making. A new interdepartmental HiAP Implementation Team was created with representatives from each City department. The Interdepartmental Team also continued to lead trainings about HiAP to City staff and to the community, since HiAP remains an elusive concept and practice.

A key task of the governance and leadership area was to also address structural racism within city government. A team called the Governance Alliance for Race and Equity was established to train City staff in implicit bias, microaggressions, and institutional racism. Emerging out of the work of this group after 18 months were a racial equity law, called Resolution 93-18, which mandated that every City department and council decision include a review of the impacts of the decision on racial and ethnic groups and that all public meetings and documents would be translated in the three most commonly used non-English languages in the city.[9] The resolution was one of a set of steps the City took to develop a Racial Equity Action Plan that would accompany the HiAP Ordinance.

Ongoing measurement and monitoring were also a critical aspect of governance. The City worked with the Contra Costa County Health Department to draft the Richmond Health Equity Report Card in 2016.[10] The report provided baseline data that was used to track progress toward health equity goals and other social determinants of health. The City and community groups developed a Toolkit for Community Engagement, which specified new, more open processes for public meetings, City–community engagement around policy issues, and the responsibilities of the City during public meetings, such as providing child care, food, and other community supports.

Finally, in its continuing effort to ensure transparency and that as much City-collected data as possible is available to everyone, the City of Richmond launched the Transparent Richmond Open Data Platform in 2019. This platform includes data on all six HiAP intervention areas, plus additional information on the city's budget and expenditures, as well as descriptive statistics about the city, such as its changing demographics.[11]

Intervention Area 2: Economic Development and Education

The HiAP Ordinance emphasizes that economic development and educational opportunities are health issues. The HiAP coordinated city investments in four new programs that take an equity approach to economic development and education. The first program, called the Richmond Promise, was created to help pay college tuition for all eligible Richmond graduating high school students. Eligible students receive $1,500 each year for four years of college enrollment. Since the Richmond Promise began in 2016 it has given out over $4.5 million in scholarships to over 1,044 Richmond students. Seventy percent of recipients are first-generation college students, and over 65 percent come from low-income backgrounds. The program also offers mentoring for college students and builds a local network of college mentors for Richmond's college-bound residents.

A second city program, called RichmondBUILD, offers free construction skills and an apprenticeship program to learn how to install solar energy panels on rooftops and buildings.[12] These "green jobs" are offered to youth from public housing, those that have been homeless, and those that are returning from the criminal justice system. According to 2018 data from the RichmondBUILD program, about 90 percent of the participants are People of Color, and 15 percent are women. In over 10 years of operation, there have been over 1,000 graduates, and over 70 percent gain steady employment making at least $25/hour as a starting wage. The founding director, Sal Vaca, described the program as "focused on developing people with talent, to enhance their job skills, to be healthy and earn a high-wage in construction, renewable energy, and related fields."

According to RichmondBUILD's program director, Fred Lucero, "Nothing stops a bullet like a career." Lucero would tell me that the program, in addition to giving young people job training, is "about giving people a chance who haven't had any opportunities. They come to us straight out of jail or from a life on the streets. We invest in their emotional, intellectual, and social development." As one recent graduate of the program described to me, "What this program did was give me a peaceful place to get my mind right. There wasn't no judgment about who we was or came from. They held us accountable and every day we seen the practical skills, but also how to be more professional, know what I mean?"

RichmondBUILD offers wraparound supports to all participants, including basic math and reading skills, computer literacy, résumé building, job interview skills, and others, but also counseling and support for broken family and other relationships. The Healthy RichmondBUILD Academy educates participants about healthy lifestyles, health care, and nutrition. Activities for participants have included exercise classes, cooking workshops, and dental and vision exams.

Figure 6.4 Participants in the RichmondBUILD program. (Source: City of Richmond, used with permission)

More than 1,000 Richmond youth have participated in this program between 2010 and 2019, and over 80 percent of graduates are placed in high-paying union jobs (Figure 6.4). Two related programs, called YouthWORKS and RichmondWORKS,[13] provide career and job preparation services for youth and support adult job seekers with interview skills, small business loans, and employment placement services.

A third initiative is creating jobs and incubating small businesses. A new city law in 2019, called the Local Employment Ordinance, mandates that for all government-funded construction projects in the city at least 25 percent of the employees and total project hours must be for Richmond residents. A new city-supported business incubator space, called CoBiz, provides training and resources for new, start-up business ideas, space for innovators, nonprofits, musicians, and freelance artists to access cutting-edge technologies and use collaborative spaces.[14] The idea is to create a cluster of economic innovation that supports the needs of Richmond while also taking advantage of the technology expertise and resources in the San Francisco Bay Area, according to CoBiz CEO Wesley Alexander.

A fourth initiative is the Environmental and Community Investment Agreement (ECIA), created after the city won a lawsuit against the Chevron Corporation due to the company's chronic violations of its pollution permits. The company and the City negotiated a community benefit agreement in 2014, which mandated that Chevron modernize its pollution control equipment and pay $90 million to the City over a 10-year period to fund the ECIA.[15] The ECIA is supporting a host of community-based greenhouse gas (GHG) reduction programs, direct community grants, and a photovoltaic solar farm. In 2019 the ECIA supported the following:

$2 million to public transit programs

$1 million to the city's Climate Action Plan

$2 million to urban forestry, city tree planting and greening

$6 million to install free rooftop solar and perform energy retrofits for low-income households

$3.7 million to the Richmond Promise college scholarship program

$2 million to job training programs, including YouthBUILD, RichmondBUILD, and the Literacy for Every Adult Program (LEAP)

$1 million on free community internet access

Intervention Area 3: Residential and Built Environments

Housing safety, affordability, and quality, as well as broader neighborhood environments, continue to play a major role in health and well-being in Richmond, California. Richmond has struggled to ensure that all residents are in safe and secure housing, but it has made some progress. A Fair Rent and Just Cause for Eviction Law was passed in 2016 and a Rent Control Program was established in 2017 to ensure that all residents can afford to remain in their homes. In 2019, there were over 543 units of affordable housing built and another 977 units permitted.

The HiAP strategy helped give rise to the Richmond Housing

Renovation Program. In this program, the City of Richmond uses a Social Impact Bond to raise the capital for purchasing abandoned, blighted, and in some cases foreclosed properties within the city.[16] At any one time during the 2015–2020 period, there were an estimated 1,000 blighted properties in Richmond, of which about 150 were abandoned houses, according to Gabino Arredondo, the former housing director. These properties present a fiscal and safety threat to the city, since the city must spend resources maintaining them, and residents frequently complain that illegal dumping, drug use, and sex work can occur at the abandoned structures. The Richmond Community Foundation (RCF), a not-for-profit community entity, works with the City to issue the bonds and eventually uses bond resources to purchase and renovate the blighted homes. RCF also hires construction workers from the RichmondBUILD program to help complete the work, as well as any necessary environmental remediation from potential lead paint, asbestos, and other hazardous materials that might be on-site.[17] The homes are being rebuilt with "zero net energy," meaning that they will generate enough energy for what they use by installing solar power, efficient appliances, and other construction technologies. According to Jim Becker of the RCF, the housing program is innovative and anchored in healing and health. He told me, "We've become too complacent seeing abandoned property in low-income communities and expecting the 'market' to revitalize them. A few abandoned homes on a block, and safety, property values, and neighborhood stability can get bad quickly. This then makes the neighborhood vulnerable to 'block-busting' investors, who can try to come in and buy out everyone at rock bottom. This program isn't just about housing. It's about rebuilding and stabilizing neighborhoods and ensuring working-class people—like teachers, bus drivers, janitors, and small business owners—can afford to live here.

The renovated homes are sold at below-market value to first-time, low-income Richmond residents, who work with RCF, a personal finance coaching organization called SparkPoint, and Mechanics Bank to secure a mortgage and manage monthly payments."[18]

Improving walkability, bicycling, and other opportunities for physical activity have also been a priority of the HiAP work. In addition to investing in small, neighborhood parks like Elm Playlot in the Iron Triangle neighborhood (see chapter 4), the City worked with regional planners to develop a network of paths connecting the city to the region. One connection was creating a new bicycle path over the Richmond–San Rafael Bridge and connecting the city to a series of pedestrian and bicycle paths along the San Francisco Bay Trail. A "wellness" path was also created to navigate from key destinations, like the BART train, through the city's neighborhoods, to these regional trail connections.

Due to poverty, immigration status, and other issues, Richmond residents can be vulnerable to domestic violence and human trafficking. In order to confront this human rights issue and better support victims, the city partnered with social service providers to build and staff the West Contra Costa Family Justice Center, which opened in 2015. The Family Justice Center supports victims of human trafficking, domestic violence, sexual assault, and elder abuse. The Center borrows proven healing-centered practices from other family justice centers around the country, including co-locating trauma treatment with legal protective services, housing assistance, and child protective services in a welcoming and non-law-enforcement setting.[19] The Center coordinates support for victims of interpersonal violence and their children, working to address anxiety, depression, social isolation, and substance use/abuse and to support the success and well-being of children who have witnessed or experienced abuse.

Intervention Area 4: Full-Service and Safe Communities

Throughout the drafting of the HiAP, the impacts of violence on young people and how to make young people leaders in eliminating the root causes of violence were regularly the top priorities for residents. One response was a citizen-led initiative for Richmond to create a Department of Children and Youth that would receive an annual budget allocation from the city. A community-based organization, called the RYSE Center, helped lead the 2018 Richmond Kids First Initiative, which put an initiative on the ballot for all residents to vote whether they wanted a new city department dedicated to the needs of youth and were willing to allocate 3 percent of the city's general fund to this new program.[20] The vote was overwhelmingly supportive and resulted in the creation of a new Department of Children and Youth with a fifteen-member youth board to allocate the resources to community-based programs that they identify as serving their needs.

The RYSE Center was and remains one of the most important community-based, healing-focused organizations in Richmond. It was founded at the request of young people in Richmond needing a safe place to heal from the traumas of poverty, gun violence, anti-immigration policing, and other structural violence issues. RYSE, as it is commonly called, provides direct support to traumatized youth by offering them counseling and case management, but it also offers them a safe, healing space. At this space, a community center in Richmond, youth can engage in arts, media, and culture, as well study, learn, and even incubate a small business idea. According to Kanwarpal Dhaliwal, cofounder and associate director at RYSE, the organization is "a center, a home, a sanctuary and space to create, heal, celebrate, learn and lead. RYSE builds 'beloved community' and is a movement seeking justice, love and joy." A central tenet throughout all the work RYSE does is that young people have the lived knowledge and expertise to identify, prioritize, and direct the programs, activities, and services necessary to benefit their own well-being.[21]

As Kanwarpal was sharing the approach that RYSE takes working with young people to identify and heal from the traumas they experience, she showed me a young person's quote from the organization's recent listening campaign: "My experience with violence is very brutal. . . . I grew up with violence as if it were my sibling." Another youth leader in the report was quoted stating, "We know we can't run the city—it's too complex—but our experience and our voices should count, especially because we're the most affected." Yet another RYSE youth member stated, "Realizing institutions don't work for you but against you, is the first step to healing your community."

RYSE has been instrumental in holding the city accountable and recentering the HiAP work around the needs of young people. For RYSE, a healing-centered approach includes multiple strategies that acknowledge the dehumanization and racism inherent in current systems and working toward restorative practices and liberation. As Kanwarpal described it to me:

"Building Beloved Community is what we are all about. That means leading with love and justice in everything we do and focusing on changing the systems to support lasting peace and healing. People and relationships come first. Along with that is an intersectional and racism analysis, so we understand positionality and the forces shaping decisions. Healing demands that our social-emotional health and development is supported, or else it can be just bureaucratic change. This makes some uncomfortable, because it means discussing our wounds, making repairs together, and working for reparations and redistribution. Healing outcomes mean that what is created isn't just back to the old way that created trauma, but we cocreate a new, more just way forward."

One new manifestation of this commitment by RYSE is the construction of their RYSE Commons, a new community center, health clinic, performance, and "sanctuary" space in Richmond. My UC Berkeley team worked with groups of young people at RYSE to help them codesign the space, which is now nearing completion. The core values of RYSE drove the codesign process emphasizing spaces for healing, flexible and adaptive spaces, and creativity (Figure 6.5). These same values have shaped the entire HiAP approach in Richmond, since RYSE is one of the key community-based organization partners in the work.

Interventional Area 5: Environmental Health and Justice

Environmental issues, including air pollution, climate change, food security, and energy poverty—or the amount of money low-income households spend on utilities—are some of the leading environmental injustice issues in Richmond. A series of actions, supported by the ECIA resources mentioned earlier, have moved the city toward greater environmental health justice.

The HiAP process set in motion the drafting of the city's first ever Climate Action Plan (CAP), which aimed to reduce local pollution

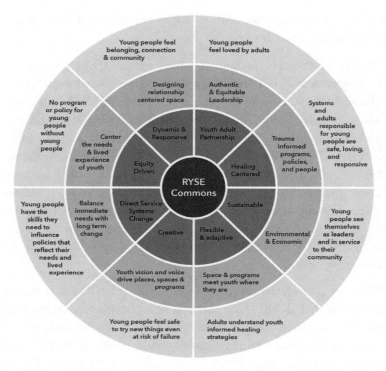

Figure 6.5 RYSE Commons values. (Source: RYSE Center, used with permission)

and mitigate GHG emissions, reduce the energy footprint of the city, and develop an adaptation strategy that protected the city's most vulnerable residents.[22] Richmond has over 32 miles of shoreline along the San Francisco Bay, and projected sea-level rise is expected to adversely impact hundreds of acres of developed land. The CAP strategies focused on stronger regulations of emissions from the Chevron Refinery, one of the region's largest GHG emitters. The CAP also recommended a ban on coal exports through the city's port terminal, aiming not only to discourage the use of coal but to eliminate the health impacts from coal dust coming from trains moving through the city. A pedestrian and bicycle plan, street tree planting, and "road diets," which narrowed the width of streets using angled parking, curb bulb-outs, and other techniques for slowing traffic, were also integrated into the CAP.

Energy Justice

A key aspect of the CAP is to promote energy justice for Richmond's low-income residents. Having consistent and affordable energy for cooking, heating, cooling, electronics, and other uses is recognized as a prerequisite for health and a key climate justice issue.[23] As costs for this basic service as well as household rent and food increase, low-income populations are frequently forced to make choices between paying for energy, or rent, or food, but they can't afford all of these necessities. When energy, like electricity service, is shut off due to nonpayment, low-income households face high bureaucratic and financial barriers in getting service restored amid significant health threats. For example, I heard from residents that when there is a shelter in place order due to an incident at the Chevron refinery or dangerous air from wild-fire smoke, households without electricity or those who can't afford high bills, "just can't shut their windows and turn on the air conditioning." The constant insecurity and uncertainty around energy, and its relationship to housing, food, and thermal comfort, also contribute to significant stress in the lives of the urban poor in Richmond. As one resident described during a workshop for the CAP: "I don't want them (lights) getting shut off. It is stressful. Then I think if I don't pay and they shut off my power, somebody will tell CPS [Child Protective Services] and they might take my kids. I had to send my kids away for a while when I couldn't pay PG&E. That was depressing. I just keep moving to avoid them catching up with me. I used a propane tank for cooking, but I know that's not safe inside."

A related aspect of energy insecurity is when low-income households are forced into older housing that may have structural deficits that contribute to drafts, leaks, and dampness. These issues are known to contribute to increased mold, which can worsen arthritis symptoms, cause headaches, and exacerbate allergies, eczema, and asthma. Climate health justice in Richmond required a concerted effort to promote energy justice.[24]

The HiAP strategy supported the creation of a free solar energy program for low-income households. The city partnered with the non-profit GRID Alternatives to install the solar components with funding coming from the State of California's Low-Income Weatherization Program.[25] As of 2019, 1,718 new rooftop photovoltaic solar energy systems had been installed on low-income households at no cost, and a solar array, or farm, was created in Richmond to deliver free energy to 155 low-income renters that were not candidates for rooftop solar.[26] This project is also hiring the young people trained through the RichmondBUILD program to install the solar and perform the energy-efficiency upgrades in the housing (Figure 6.6). According to Adam Lenz, former environmental services director at the City of Richmond, "The solar projects are saving each low-income family about $1,200 dollars per year, in addition to providing them free electricity, and the city is reducing its GHG footprint by about 20,000 tons."

The City also launched a "citizen science" community air monitoring program in partnership with environmental groups, to continuously monitor the ambient air along the "fence-line" of the refinery and sensitive receptors, such as schools in Richmond.[27] As part of this effort, a series of monitoring locations were selected with a committee of environmental justice organizations, the Bay Area Air Quality Management District, the City, and Chevron. A select set of air pollutants are continuously monitored and reported on a web site.[28] Despite these efforts, air pollution remains a stubborn problem in Richmond, as the community monitoring stations continue to detect hazardous chemicals in the air more often than regional monitoring stations.[29] As Greg Karras from CBE told me, "Monitoring is not bad, but without the hammer of emissions reduction it doesn't accomplish much. We want to decommission the refinery and transition to a clean, non–fossil fuel energy future. That is our proposal and many of the local air pollution problems will only be addressed when there is no longer a refinery in our backyards."

In an effort to pay for the climate change–induced damages to the community's well-being that they allege was made significantly worse by Chevron, the City filed a lawsuit against the company and twenty-eight other fossil fuel polluters. Richmond became one of only seven California cities alleging that these polluters create a public nuisance and are negligent for climate change, and the City was seeking a

Figure 6.6 Solar panels installed on public housing in Richmond, California.

damage payment to cover the costs of climate-change restoration and adaptation.[30]

Food Security and the Grocery Gap

In Richmond, small corner stores outnumber grocery stores by about five to one. However, grocery stores, food access, and employment helped define racial justice activism in Richmond. In 1947, a coalition of Latino and African American activists protested at a White-owned Lucky's grocery store in Richmond near the segregated Canal Housing Projects. Protesters picketed in front of the store and demanded people stop patronizing it until Lucky's hired Black clerks in the same proportion as Black customers that shopped at the store. It was an anti-racism, affirmative action, civil rights claim, but Lucky's filed a lawsuit to remove the picketers, and the courts agreed. John Hughes, a Black protester, sued, claiming picketing was protected as free speech and that the protesters were denied due process under the 14th Amendment. In a 1950 case, *Hughes v. Superior Court*, Justice Felix Frankfurter upheld the court injunction, noting that racial quotas might excite "community tensions and conflicts" and the State should not compel an employer to hire based on racial proportions or quotas.[31]

The private employer, the grocery store Lucky's in this case, was allowed to engage in discriminatory hiring if they chose to do so, and the courts in the 1950s were fine with that. One bit of fallout from this case, along with a more general "White flight" to the suburbs, was that Richmond was left without many full-service grocery stores. Like other low-income, communities of color, corner and liquor stores, and later fast-food chains, became the only food outlets. By 2008 there was an identified "grocery store gap" in Richmond, since there was only one full-service grocery store in central Richmond serving over 20,000 customers, 34 percent of the city was considered critically underserved, and for every farmer's market there were six fast-food restaurants.[32]

"It was beyond a food desert, it was a swamp," said Doria Robinson, a Richmond native and activist who founded Urban Tilth, a local organization that created a farm, community gardens, and supports Black, Indigenous, People of Color (BIPOC) to take back their power by growing food and creating jobs in the food sector. Robinson also revitalized vacant land in Richmond that was sitting idle. She explained, "You have all of these things that have just been completely undernourished—people, places—and we're one of the forces that are trying to bring life back, putting nutrients back into the soil, putting people back on the land and in the process hopefully waking people up. We grow food for the opportunity to grow ourselves."

According to Contra Costa County, over 50 percent of Richmond's residents in 2007 were eligible for food stamps, but less than 20 percent were receiving them. Following the objectives of the HiAP strategy, Richmond created a Food Policy Council, with Robinson acting as its first leader, to make food security a health equity issue. She explained that "food insecurity is a health issue since eating a high-quality and well-balanced diet obviously impacts whether we get the nutrients to live, but it is also a learning and mental health issue, as kids who are hungry can't learn and parents who are hungry are more depressed and stressed out." A first task of the council was an urban agriculture study that produced an assessment of the type and locations of urban gardens and outlined the details of a new urban agriculture ordinance in Richmond. This analysis found that while there was a need for more food production, there was a greater need for accessible, affordable, and culturally appropriate sites of food distribution.[33] "To our surprise, there were a number of community gardens but the food wasn't reaching the poor and most vulnerable groups," Lina Velasco, the lead planner with the City of Richmond, told me about the assessment. The council helped ensure that the West Contra Costa County School District in Richmond could serve salad for all school lunches. In 2016, the mayor's office launched a "food census" where over fifty food outlets in Richmond were visited to assess the type, affordability, and accessibility of food. They found that only seven stores met the California Department of Public Health food accessibility and affordability minimum standards.

At the urging of the HiAP Interdepartmental Group, the city began to work with corner stores to support them to include more produce and fresh foods. Urban Tilth partnered with a regional organization called Growing the Table, which supports small BIPOC farms in bringing their products to low-income urban communities.[34] The City created a new street food vending ordinance that decriminalized the work of many immigrants, particularly women, who were selling street food, and helped them get access to more fresh and organic products at an affordable price. Richmond also created a food production and distribution designation in their land-use zoning, which attracted tens of food-related start-ups to the city. A cooperative industrial kitchen, called the Artisan Kitchen, was opened, and it helped incubate a number of food companies locating their work in Richmond, such as Nutiva, Zoe's Cookies, Galaxy Deserts, and Blue Apron.[35] A regional Whole Foods distribution warehouse also opened in Richmond. According to Miya Yoshitani, executive director of the Asia-Pacific Environmental Network, food security in Richmond is about an integrated strategy that moves toward local ownership and control, not just farming or grocery stores. She described the importance of centering immigrants and People of Color in the movement, stating that part of the work included "informing the immigrant community about the health impacts of subsistence fishing in the Bay, and about lead in dishware. We had a community garden, where seniors would come and garden and interact with the young people in our youth program, teaching them about the herbs and vegetables they had brought over from their home countries. . . . APEN [Asia-Pacific Environmental Network] and its allies have been innovating and experimenting with new models—like Cooperation Richmond, which builds local wealth by incubating worker- and community-owned co-ops; and locally owned community-run renewable energy systems; and new food systems that are democratically run and serve the interests of local communities."[36]

Intervention Area 6: Quality and Accessible Health Care

The HiAP Ordinance also recognized that many Richmond residents were delaying or avoiding medical care due to lack of insurance, fear of deportations, or lack of resources. Further exacerbating the challenge of seeking medical care, one of Richmond's hospitals that served the poor and those without health insurance, called Doctor's Medical Center, was forced to close in 2015. One response by the City was to work with the State of California to increase enrollment in the state's free medical care program, called Covered California. Identifying a site for a new community clinic was another response by the City; in partnership with an experienced community clinic operator called LifeLong Medical Center, a site was identified. The new clinic, called the LifeLong William Jenkins Health Center, opened in 2019. The new health center expands pediatric services currently offered at the site and will feature primary care, obstetrics, dental services, and urgent care for families. Importantly, as Julie Sinai, the director at LifeLong told me, the clinic mandates that all its staff members are trained in the science of childhood adversity and trauma-informed practices, including knowledge of and responses to adverse childhood experiences (ACEs) and toxic stress, as well as how to screen and refer patients. "We want to ensure all our clinicians, nurses, social workers, everyone, can identify and help address the traumas our patients arrive with, not just patch them up and wait for them to return," she described to me.

The Impacts of HiAP on Urban Health and Healing

There are a number of projects, partnerships, and programs that fall under the HiAP umbrella in Richmond. Thus it is hard to pinpoint exactly which efforts are having an impact on health and healing. However, my team used a biannual community survey administered to all Richmond residents that began in 2007 to help us understand if all these efforts were having an impact on the perceptions of well-being, the perceived quality of one's neighborhood, feelings of safety, and whether residents trusted the local government to be a part of the solutions. The Richmond Community Survey (RCS) results suggest that more residents responded "good" or "excellent" when asked to rate the quality of their neighborhood, Richmond overall, their own quality of life, Richmond as a place to raise children, and the city's overall image in 2019 rather than around the time the Health and Wellness planning began in 2007 (Table 6.1). Since 2009, new questions were added to the survey, and those also offer clues into how residents perceive their well-being. For example, between 2009 and 2019, the percentage of residents rating their health as good or excellent has increased by over 80 percent. During this same time, there were significant increases in residents responding "good" or "excellent" to the way they perceived the overall quality of development, Richmond as a place to live, recreational opportunities, and the ease of bicycle travel. Perceptions of citizen involvement in decision making have improved by over 60 percent, and the number of those stating that they regularly experience discrimination has decreased, as have gun homicides.

There are other, more qualitative examples of how the HiAP strategy has helped shift policy and practice in Richmond toward an ethos of health and healing. For example, the Richmond Police chief rejected a proposal to expand the West County Detention Facility in Richmond. According to Adam Kruggel, executive director of Contra Costa Interfaith Supporting Community Organization, a group organizing for violence reduction and city programs to support people not prisons, the decision by the City of Richmond was "a great example of elected officials really, truly listening to the voice of the community and responding."[37] A San Francisco Bay Area newspaper described the

Table 6.1 Richmond community survey results.

Community characteristic	Percent rating good or excellent		% Change*
	2007	2019	
How I rate my neighborhood	49	65	**+33**
Richmond as a place to live	20	47	**+135**
My overall quality of life	17	38	**+123**
Richmond as a place to raise children	9	24	**+166**
Richmond's overall image	4	13	**+225**
	2009	**2019**	
Self-rated health	36	65	**+81**
Quality of development	33	71	**+115**
Richmond as a place to work	21	36	**+64**
Recreational opportunities	23	49	**+113**
Ease of bicycle travel	35	44	**+26**
Citizen involvement in decision making	23	47	**+104**
Experiences with discrimination or racism	42 (2013)	24	**−43**
Gun homicides	47	15	**−68**

* Significant at 95% confidence interval (CI).
Source: https://www.ci.richmond.ca.us/1871/Community-Surveys

changes in Richmond as a renaissance: "A new spirit in city government has helped transform industry, the quality of life in the city, and Richmond's grim reputation. The city has undergone a facelift, citizens are attending community meetings and events in unprecedented numbers, and new businesses—many of them green—are bringing economic opportunities back to town. While other cities are desperately contending with debilitating budget deficits and struggling to maintain public safety and other basic services, Richmond has produced balanced budgets and enjoys a full complement of police officers. The combined efforts of city departments and community members have resulted in meaningful reductions in violent crime. And the city has completed numerous civic and neighborhood revitalization projects that have given Richmond a new air of vitality and community health."[38]

Institutionalizing Healing through Health in All Policies

Richmond's HiAP strategy is a work in progress, but it is helping to create projects, partnerships, and policies that support health and healing. The HiAP was not a top-down idea; it emerged out of long-standing activism by residents and community-based organizations demanding racial and social justice. These same activists confronted the corporate hold on decision making in Richmond, took back power through elected office, and directed resources toward healing for working-class and immigrant communities.[39] The success of Richmond's healing-centered work also has to do with its approach to learning by doing, where neighborhood-scale projects were implemented and built toward larger policy changes. Importantly, HiAP is not just governmental action. Community-based organizations, such as RYSE, were already taking a healing-centered approach to their work, and the city followed their lead, rather than trying to reproduce this work. So a key aspect of the success of HiAP in Richmond is the City knowing when to get out of the way of innovative and successful community-led initiatives and strategies, such as the Office of Neighborhood Safety and others, but be willing to partner and provide resources to these organizations and programs. The work continues today, and tracking progress, through such initiatives as the Transparent Richmond data portal, will be necessary to ultimately decide the success or failure of the HiAP investment.[40] Yet there is no denying that what has happened in Richmond, California, is a model for other cities around the world who are prepared to commit to investing in their often traumatized residents and redeveloping communities to promote health and healing.

Conclusion

Toward Cities That Heal

The rains that had flooded the St. Elizabeth Primary School in Mukuru had ended, but I could still see the waterline along the walls where the river had inundated classrooms. Flooding from the same river had contributed to a nearby cholera outbreak. It was early December 2019, and I was taking a break during a community meeting discussing the redevelopment of the community and how to stop the risks from flooding. The outside air reeked of burning plastic, likely from the industries across the road. Inside the school, the walls were covered with maps proposing road improvements, river crossings, and flood protections. The meeting was full of planners from the county government, engineers, NGO leaders, health care providers, and community elders.

One of the youth leaders in the community, Nelmo Munyiri, approached me while he was eating his *mandazi* (fried dough). I had known Nelmo for a few years—a charismatic leader, artist, musician, and community organizer. He founded and directed an organization called the Mukuru Youth Initiative, which was helping to redefine how Kenyans saw the young people from the slums. Nelmo and his group created exciting radio and TV shows, wrote and directed films, and produced and starred in music videos, all about life and the living conditions in Mukuru. They started a popular film festival in the community, organized an awards show, and sponsored a beauty pageant. Nelmo and his crew were helping thousands of Mukuru youth, and those outside the slum, see their beauty, talent, and humanity.

Nelmo pulled out his phone and started playing a video for me. It was his group singing about the risk of cholera in Mukuru. It was powerful, heartbreaking, and a beautiful piece of art. His crew, dressed in all white, sang about government neglect that allowed the community to face risks from dangerous toilets, lack of water, and unknowingly consuming contaminated food.[1]

I asked him to play the video for the group when the meeting resumed.

Nelmo found the largest laptop in the room and turned the volume all the way up. As the video played, everyone in the meeting was glued to the laptop, and most heads, shoulders, and some hips were rocking to the beat. A woman from the community spoke out as the music subsided. "These youth are telling the real stories we face. They are the ones who speak to the people in a way everyone can understand. But why aren't they in this plan? Who are we developing this community for, after all?"

The meeting was silent as the adults seemed to realize that the voices of the talented youth hadn't been included. Nelmo wasn't trying to speak for all youth, but his art was inclusive and spoke truth to power, like the quote from Bob Marley's "Redemption Song" outside the entrance to his organization: "Emancipate yourselves from mental slavery, None but ourselves can free our minds."

Nelmo had also done what the activists in Richmond and Medellín were doing, namely revealing that those most impacted by urban inequalities, trauma, and related stress often aren't at the center of decision making. They also surfaced that the expertise we often rely on isn't easily inclusive of what young people know or experiential knowledge more generally. Nelmo and his group—similar to residents in Richmond and Medellín—used art and music, as well as local and cultural knowledge, to highlight to those leading the Mukuru redevelopment process that they were valuable but largely overlooked experts. They were bridge builders between the youth in the community and the power structures with the resources to make lasting change. Nelmo and his group helped change the course of the project because their voices were not just included but valued as a way to bring important dimensions of urban healing—such as art, play, emotion, and feelings—into what was a pretty boring and technocratic redevelopment planning process.

The experience reminded me of how important centering previously marginalized and excluded voices can be for public decision making focused on healing. Nelmo and his socially conscious music also took me back to the Office of Neighborhood Safety in Richmond and the Peacemaker Fellowship, and how it centers traumatized young people in cocreating a pathway toward peace. The outreach workers in Richmond are "street credible," like Nelmo, but they also help connect traumatized young people to services and resources outside the neighborhood. Similarly, the Pogo Park team refused to accept the city's "just good enough" play equipment, and took over the space and collectively redeveloped it with practical (bathrooms) and fun (zip line) activities. In Medellín, the youth artists from Casa Kolacho in San Javier and others pushed back to ensure that City-sponsored new development reflected community needs, including jobs and spaces to collectively heal, while bringing color, life, and humanity to their formerly violent place.

The cities for life approach is fundamentally about addressing the tensions over what to do, whom to include, and how to redevelop people and places. It is not about eliminating those tensions. City making and community development must acknowledge the harms they have created, put those most harmed in the center of new decision making, and provide real economic and social benefits to those harmed people and communities.

The lessons from Richmond, Nairobi, and Medellín can help cities everywhere see a path to building communities that promote health and healing—not harm. There are five key lessons for moving toward cities that heal:

1. Redefining urban expertise
2. Healing people and places

3. Institutionalizing equity
4. Practicing urban acupuncture
5. Adopting a new urban science

Redefining Urban Expertise

If we carry the trauma of structural violence in our bodies, then we can also hold the wisdom of healing. By this I mean that those living with trauma and related inequalities have unique insights into how to survive, and often thrive. The fellows in the Peacemaker Fellowship, founded in Richmond, and their formerly incarcerated adult mentors, have survived the streets, traveled the difficult path of self-healing, and actively work to embody peace every day, even with a multitude of forces working against them. The fellows and mentors are experts in healing.

When community expertise is combined with, but never relegated to, professional knowledge, healing can be most effective. The social urbanism approach in Medellín, including ongoing practices like participatory budgeting and the comuna health plans, suggest that professionals and the state have a role to play in ensuring that local and community expertise is valued and incorporated into decision making. This is not to say that the urban expertise of those traumatized has to "fit" professional modes of decision making. Rather, the oppressive and often dehumanizing decision-making processes common in cities and public health agencies should be challenged.

New forums and methods for incorporating urban expertise are needed. In Mukuru, the slum scientists were able to use professional tools in new ways, but they also upended professional processes of data gathering, such as making films and music videos about their experiences with environmental risks. The women in the Mukuru community collected stories about their experiences with unsafe toilets, which challenged the well-funded twenty-first-century toilet program offered by international donors and tacitly endorsed by the government and many NGOs.

New expertise can create the need for new, radically democratic processes. This may not be easy for privileged professionals who are accustomed to controlling the narrative and public processes. The restorative justice approach used in the Advance Peace model and the participatory design strategies of Pogo Park offer potential models for more democratic decision making. To be successful, these democratic processes must be ingrained into urban institutions and laws, rather than ad hoc, and given the power to allocate municipal resources (an important way to get people to pay attention). This is what has already happened in Medellín, with their mandate for participatory budgeting. In Richmond, the creation of the Department of Children and Youth has the power to convene and allocate money from the city's general fund toward programs and projects that lift up existing community assets. We must recognize that professionals get paid to offer their expertise to public decision-making processes all the time, so too should community residents.

This new urban expertise isn't really new. It is new for professionals and governments that for too long have dismissed the experiential wisdom of Black, Indigenous, People of Color (BIPOC), the poor, and marginalized groups who have faced discrimination and dehumanization, but have found ways to survive. This community expertise is intended to challenge unacknowledged White privilege that can dominate urban decision making. Insights and expertise needed to heal often already exist in communities, as shown in Medellín, Nairobi, and Richmond. Professionals need to stop, sit, and listen.

Healing People and Places

The investment in both people and places is necessary to reinstate the full humanity and agency for every person and every place that has been dehumanized and traumatized. Absent these parallel investments, those harmed are unlikely to be able to fully participate in society, and neighborhoods will not recover from decades of decline.

In Medellín, the UVAs (Unidades de Vida Articulada [Articulated Life Units]), which reclaimed and improved public space, are a great example of how a city can invest in simultaneously healing people and places. The UVAs are community centers codesigned by local residents that turned formerly walled and fenced-off land into beautiful and functional public spaces. Inside the UVAs, job-training classes are held alongside child care, social workers are trained to serve people in the surrounding neighborhood, and performance and play spaces welcome people of all ages, abilities, sexual orientations, and ethnicities.

Too often, there is a tension in public policy, and especially municipal governments, over whether people-focused or place-based investments are most effective for reducing inequality. Economists have long debated whether people-based welfare, such as transferring resources to individuals or households, or place-based strategies, such as building public housing or creating special economic investment districts, are more effective for reducing poverty. In a now classic example from the United States, the Moving to Opportunity Program gave vouchers to a group of low-income public housing residents to move to high-income areas. The lives of the families that received the vouchers and moved into wealthy places did not significantly improve. Why? One in-depth analysis found that when low-income (largely People of Color) families moved to wealthy (largely White) neighborhoods, they were more socially isolated from supportive and culturally competent networks. They also didn't benefit from the access to information, employment, and other networks that their White, wealthy neighborhoods could have shared with them, and which generally help the rich stay rich.[2] In short, being physically in a neighborhood didn't translate to being *in a community*. The people-focused approach didn't help participants heal, and it surely didn't help those left behind.

However, narrowly defined place-based strategies can miss opportunities to heal people. Researchers in Philadelphia have shown a statistically significant correlation between cleaning up vacant lots, such as removing garbage, planting grass, and adding benches, and neighborhood reductions in gun violence.[3] These are important findings and suggest ways that investing in places can be part of an effective approach to public safety. However, they are dangerously limited and run the risk of environmental determinism, or the notion that if we change the physical environment human behavior and outcomes, such as disease, will also change. This can miss the role of institutions, or public policies, as well as the people living in those places. How does improving vacant lots address the historical trauma and chronic stress impacting the people living in those neighborhoods? As importantly, if we only focus on some aspects of places, such as vacant lots and abandoned buildings, we will fail to address the related, more deeply seated traumas from racial residential segregation and may ignore the institutional decisions that likely contributed to creating the vacant lots in the first place.[4] An alternative that improves both people and place was the transformation of Pogo Park in Richmond, which was done by and for community residents. They learned new construction skills and were paid to rebuild the park, transforming their lives and the conditions in their community.

The takeaway from the cases in Richmond, Nairobi, and Medellín is that we can simultaneously focus on people and places (and the institutions that make unhealthy traumatic decisions). For example, the Muungano Alliance is ensuring that youth get jobs and opportunities while simultaneously rebuilding the infrastructure of their community. A new policy, the Mukuru Special Planning Area, was adopted by the Nairobi government ensuring that the improvement practices are institutionalized. The RYSE organization in Richmond is providing healing supports to young people, providing a multiuse community center, and working to change public policy, such as helping to create the Richmond Department of Children and Youth.

Richmond, Medellín, and Nairobi also suggest that the relational view of people and places is crucial for addressing the "pair of ACEs"— the adverse childhood experiences and the adverse community environments—that contribute to trauma. As I discussed in chapter 1, the relational view avoids the reductionist idea that, for example, one traumatic exposure should be addressed at a time. Instead, the relational view recognizes that we are stressed by multiple, overlapping hazards. It also demands that we recognize that people and places are more than their traumatic experiences. The cases here reveal that there are always multiple, overlapping, toxic stressors in communities, and, if we are open to looking for them, beauty, humanity, and assets as well. This means taking an intersectional and antiessentialist approach to healing, since no one group or community has a single, easily stated, unitary identity.

By relational, I also mean relationships. Improving the built environment doesn't necessarily improve relations between neighbors or between communities and dehumanizing institutions. As Kazu Haga, in the book *Healing Resistance*, notes, "We heal society not only through individual resilience, but by healing our relationships to each other. Because we are harmed in relationship, we need to heal in relationship."[5]

Institutionalizing Equity

In Richmond, the City adopted a Health in All Policies law to ensure that their commitment to equity and social justice ran through all their decision making. In Medellín, city-endorsed plans and legal requirements for participation have shaped the government's long-term investments in social urbanism. In Nairobi, the city's legal designation of Mukuru as a Special Planning Area, and policies such as the National Hygiene Program (Kazi Mtaani), are delivering employment to young people and rebuilding slum communities with life-supporting infrastructure. These examples highlight how cities must institutionalize equity for healing.

Institutionalizing equity means that urban healing cannot be expected to occur on the backs of nonprofit, civil society organizations or only with financing from private philanthropy. While these groups are the crucial "connective tissue" for healing in communities, the sustaining investments need to come from government institutions. These investments include new public policies and law, as well as norms of governance. Boutique projects and community organization initiatives may even retraumatize communities when expectations are raised but not delivered.

One example of this phenomenon is the "broken windows" theory of crime fighting adopted by many cities. This theory enlisted the institutions of law enforcement and criminal justice to deliver harsh punishments for nonviolent crimes, like loitering, littering, and unlicensed street vending, with the hope that this would deter more serious crime later. The approach criminalized those accused of contributing to neighborhood "blight," such as failing to manage trash or remove graffiti, with the idea that clean and orderly places deter crime. The institutionalization of broken windows has devastated urban Black and Latino communities and decimated any trust between these communities and city institutions.

Institutionalizing means more than just policy or practices, it means redistributing resources. This is what some have called a "justice reinvestment," or taking from those institutions that have benefited from creating trauma and perpetuating disinvestment and paying that debt back to harmed communities. Cities like Richmond continue to spend a disproportionate share of their tax dollars on policing. Richmond spends over 40 percent of its annual budget, about $70 million in 2020, on policing, while spending less than $1.7 million on the Office of Neighborhood Safety. Few cities are redistributing justice and healing to the extent needed. While Richmond's budget is still skewed toward policing, the City is reinvesting significant tax dollars in youth and employment programs, rehabilitating housing, and providing free solar installations for low-income households. Creating wealth, through transfers of land, jobs, and direct payments must all be considered as part of urban healing strategies. In Medellín, participatory budgeting is redirecting a proportion of the city's budget to communities, and the public–private utility, EPM (Empresa Publicas de Medellín), is required to reinvest a percentage of its profits into community-based projects.

Institutionalizing also means making explicit how racism has and continues to influence government and private sector decisions and formalizing antiracism approaches within these institutions. One example is when urban policy works to build more affordable housing in an area but fails to acknowledge the historical legacy of racist banking institutions that denied access to capital for BIPOC. Accounting for history in urban healing can also help identify what interests may want to maintain a status quo that is harmful, such as resistance to restorative justice as an alternative to a city's heavy-handed, militarized policing, or when wealthy communities resist the siting of new community centers, public transit, or public housing. A critical engagement with history can rehumanize those that have been harmed and communities that have been traumatized and force us to ask what happened here, who has been hurt, and who has a stake in the trauma-producing practice.

Practicing Urban Acupuncture

In Medellín, the social urbanism approach to redevelopment meant that the city would invest in community-based processes in the poorest, most violent neighborhoods, allow residents to dream up the most impactful projects and programs, and build the most beautiful and functional architecture in these same, poor communities. This has been defined as urban acupuncture.[6] Former Medellín mayor Aníbal Gaviria described this to me as the "ethics of aesthetics," or investing with intention and beauty in the places suffering the most.

Urban acupuncture is crucial for healing since it does a number of things. First, it gives agency to local people to define what they think will be catalytic projects. Second, urban acupuncture aims to implement the selected projects incrementally, learning what aspects are beneficial and catalytic and for whom. Importantly, local people must be paid to do this social and community-building work. This is what Pogo Park in Richmond did with their pop-up Elm Playlot. Learning by doing can be healing when people see themselves having ownership over what happens in their place and realize benefits through their own participation.

When government is involved in and committed to urban acupuncture, as was the case in Richmond and Medellín, this can reorient the role and function of government toward traumatized communities. This means that the cocreation and participatory development aspects of urban acupuncture can allow communities to engage with the state as a partner, where trust can be rebuilt as decisions are made. This can be radically different than seeing the state solely as the enforcer of safety, such as through militarized policing, or as an institution that is inefficient and disinterested in community well-being. The Empresa de Desarrollo Urbano (Company of Urban Development), was created by the City of Medellín to institutionalize resident participation and have a constant presence for planning in communities. The EDU helped ensure that when the city's greenbelt or Circumvent Garden threatened to displace El Faro residents in Comuna 8, residents demanded that they be allowed to be stewards of the greenbelt's food gardens and were granted legal land rights. The process ensured that informal residents had an opportunity to meaningfully engage with government planners.

Urban acupuncture also means investing in multiple "pressure points" to promote healing. In Mukuru, residents crafted their redevelopment plan to address the stressors of unsafe toilets and sanitation, lack of water and energy, unsafe roads and river flooding, industry pollution, and unemployment for youth. In Richmond, Pogo Park used Elm Playlot as the "heartbeat" of the Iron Triangle neighborhood and is connecting this catalytic project to new "arteries" that will promote safety as part of their Yellow Brick Road safe streets project. A series of catalytic projects, networked across space, constructed and operated by local residents, is transforming Richmond's most stressed community.

Urban acupuncture for healing doesn't always have to be a physical project. The catalytic impacts of the Parque de la Vida (Park of Life) in Medellín are supporting healing through training, popular education, and bringing social programs to community schools and civil society organizations. The Park of Life links community experts in conflict resolution, Indigenous health, and experiential learning, among other things, with the University of Antioquia. This partnership has a two-way catalytic impact; community experts are able to bring their practices to a wider number of places and share among themselves in a safe space, while these same experts are influencing the students and pedagogy in the university's medical and public health schools. One Park of Life project, "recreado para la paz y la convivencia" (re-created for peace and coexistence), sends community experts trained in conflict resolution, social relationships, and elder caregiving to the city's neighborhoods and has reached over 200,000 people, stimulated over fifteen new spin-off projects, and generated over 1,000 new jobs.[7]

Adopting a New Urban Science

All the lessons discussed so far constitute the framework of a new science for healthy cities. Over the last few years, almost all the major scientific and public health journals, such as *Nature*, the *British Medical Journal*, and *The Lancet*, have recognized the need to refocus science and public health on cities.[8,9,10] Some of these articles note that "the places where the best scholarship is being produced are not the places where knowledge is most needed to solve desperate urban problems," and what is needed is a science more able to "promote ethically sensitive and contextually nuanced urban transformations."[11] What they all have in common is that they each call for a new science of and for the city rooted in complex systems thinking rather than linear, machine-like fixing. Yet they each fail to fully engage with the inequities that drive urban trauma, and in fact almost none of these calls for a new urban science makes equity the priority.

Today, many urban health researchers are using big data to understand seemingly unhealthy behaviors and trying to induce people to change them. For example, the data could be used to encourage people to exercise more or use bicycles for transportation. These computational modelers are often overly reductionist and positivist, meaning they tend to characterize "the city" as a set of quantitative variables that can be measured objectively, and predictions can be made using machine learning and artificial intelligence. Absent from these data scientists is a clear conception of historical inequities, community expertise, or the socially situated characteristics of urban exposures. Fundamentally, urban science has not significantly grappled with how to address the overlapping impacts of interpersonal and community-scale toxic stressors that are driving trauma and the need for healing.

We learned from Medellín that urban innovation does not demand high-tech solutions. Existing technologies, combined with robust community engagement and ownership, successfully integrated the city's cable car, electric escalators, and other transportation innovations. In a similar way, Mukuru women demanded innovation that would deliver them regular access to the twentieth-century toilet, and refused the twenty-first-century technological innovations being thrust upon them.

The three cities in this book highlight that the technologically "smart city" may not be needed to equitably deliver health and healing. The social interactions and nuanced relationships that defined the San Javier community in Medellín cannot be easily reduced to a "resident" constructed by Microsoft, Google, or Facebook variables that characterize people as absent any agency and as passive generators of data. Further, the rapid quest for adopting "smart" technologies in cities has not reduced inequality or segregation—two leading drivers of trauma—but instead seems to be exacerbating the schism between the haves and the have nots. This is perhaps most stark in my own backyard here in the San Francisco Bay Area, as massive wealth was created in Silicon Valley for a few, while an epidemic of homelessness, violence, and gentrification took hold.

Technology is seen as the antidote to unhealthy cities, even in the Global South. "Smart" cities, such as Eko Atlantic in Lagos, Nigeria, India's Palava City, and Kenya's "silicon savannah" outside Nairobi, called Tatu City, all aim to erase the poverty, segregation, and legacies of colonialism that plague those places. These cities will likely be the Brasilia of the twenty-first century; technically advanced, rational, and soulless.

A new urban science for healing will need to be much more adaptive and participatory than the quantitative modeling that seeks to inform the "smart city" with ongoing surveillance and massive data collection that some are calling the "urban genome" project.[12] Instead, I suggest that this new urban science start with the lessons from Richmond, Medellín, and Nairobi, namely, prioritizing the science of eliminating health inequities and toxic stress. This work reveals that only through social change, not digital technologies, can stressors be eliminated. It won't be through laboratory science, vaccines, or biomedicine that we eliminate the sources of urban trauma and toxic stress.

I close with a call for a people's science. This science must be with, not for, urban communities in cities. A people's science must prioritize equity, because today's urban suffering is too great, inequities are growing too fast, and power is being centralized in the hands of too few, to expect that anything less will support healing. We need to stop pretending that neutral, disinterested science will magically reduce the harms and suffering afflicting the poor. Recall that during the global pandemic of 2020, calls for science, not politics, were supposed to save us. Yet this fell on deaf ears for those of us who recognize that these same references to "neutral science," without any meaningful or critical public discourse, were used to underwrite many of the greatest harms humanity has faced, such as slavery, eugenics, and poisonous chemicals.

Pursuing a science and practice of cities for life will mean committing to something like jazz music—always improvisational, respectful of the everyday rhythms of cultures and communities, playful, and most of all committed to the struggle for justice, or what love looks like in public.[13]

Notes

Introduction: Designed for Life or Death

1. "RYSE Commons," https://rysecenter.org/rysecommons.

2. American Public Health Association. Racism is a Public Health Crisis. https://www.apha.org/topics-and-issues/health-equity/racism-and-health/racism-declarations

3. Lois Beckett et al., "Guns and Lies in America: Decoding an Unlikely Gun Violence Success Story," *Guardian*, June 4, 2019, https://www.theguardian.com/us-news/2019/jun/03/guns-and-lies-in-america-decoding-an-unlikely-gun-violence-success-story

4. Bessel van der Kolk, *The Body Keeps the Score: Brain, Mind, and Body in the Healing of Trauma* (New York: Penguin, 2014), 358.

5. WHO, "Health Inequalities and Their Causes," February 22, 2018, https://www.who.int/news-room/facts-in-pictures/detail/health-inequities-and-their-causes.

6. National Academies of Sciences, Engineering, and Medicine, *Communities in Action: Pathways to Health Equity* (Washington, DC: National Academies Press, 2017), 3, "The Root Causes of Health Inequity," https://www.ncbi.nlm.nih.gov/books/NBK425845/.

7. Pan American Health Organization, "Health Equity," https://www.paho.org/en/topics/health-equity.

8 Jo Vearey, et al., "Urban Health in Africa: A Critical Global Public Health Priority," *BMC Public Health* 19 (2019): 340, https://doi.org/10.1186/s12889-019-6674-8.

9. Charles Montgomery, "The Secrets of the World's Happiest Cities," *Guardian*, November 1, 2013, https://www.theguardian.com/society/2013/nov/01/secrets-worlds-happiest-cities-commute-property-prices.

10. WHO, "Depression and Other Common Mental Disorders: Global Health Estimates" (Geneva: World Health Organization, 2017), http://www.who.int/iris/handle/10665/254610.

11. Gregory Trencher and Andrew Karvonen, "Stretching 'Smart': Advancing Health and Well-Being through the Smart City Agenda," *Local Environment* 24, no. 7 (2019): 610–627, doi: 10.1080/13549839.2017.1360264.

12. William Wan, "Coronavirus Pandemic Is Pushing America into a Mental Health Crisis," *Washington Post*, May 4, 2020, https://www.washingtonpost.com/health/2020/05/04/mental-health-coronavirus/.

13. Ed Diener and Martin E. P. Seligman, "Very Happy People," *Psychological Science* 13, no. 1 (2002): 81–84, doi: 10.1111/1467-9280.00415.

14. Institute of Medicine and National Research Council, *From Neurons to Neighborhoods: The Science of Early Childhood Development* (Washington, DC: The National Academies Press, 2000), https://doi.org/10.17226/9824.https://www.nap.edu/catalog/9824/from-neurons-to-neighborhoods-the-science-of-early-childhood-development.

15. Stokely Carmichael, "Black Power, a Critique of the System of International White Supremacy and International Capitalism," in *The Dialectics of Liberation*, ed. David Cooper (New York: Verso, 2015), 150–175, 151.

16. john powell, "Structural Racism: Building upon the Insights of John Calmore," *North Carolina Law Review*, no. 86 (2008): 791–816.

17. Salima Koroma, "Hear Cornel West Recount His First Political Memory," *Time*, October 2, 2014, https://time.com/3453821/cornel-west-first-political-memory/.

18. George Rosen. "Health, History and the Social Sciences," *Social Science & Medicine* 7, no. 4 (1973): 233–248.

19. Shawn Ginwright, "The Future of Healing: Shifting from Trauma Informed Care to Healing Centered Engagement," *Medium*, May 31, 2018, https://ginwright.medium.com/the-future-of-healing-shifting-from-trauma-informed-care-to-healing-centered-engagement-634f557ce69c.

20. Michelle Alexander, *The New Jim Crow: Mass Incarceration in the Age of Colorblindness* (New York: The New Press, 2020).

Box 1: Richmond, California: The Industrial City by the Bay

1. City of Richmond Planning Division, *Preserve Richmond to Interpret and Support Memories*, Project PRISM (Richmond, CA: City of Richmond, 2009), http://www.ci.richmond.ca.us/DocumentCenter/View/7083/Project-PRISM---Historic-Survey-Report?bidId=.

2. Ibid.

3. Shirley Ann Wilson Moore, *To Place Our Deeds: The African American Community in Richmond, CA 1910–1963* (Berkeley: University of California Press, 2000).

4. Ibid.

5. City of Richmond Planning Division, *Preserve Richmond*, 72.

6. Gretchen Lemke-Santangelo, *Abiding Courage: African American Migrant Women and the East Bay Community* (Chapel Hill: University of North Carolina Press, 1996).

7. Richard Rothstein, *Color of Law: A Forgotten History of How Our Government Segregated America* (New York: Liveright, 2017).

8. Contra Costa JACL, "Blossoms and Thorns: A Community Uprooted," Contra Costa JACL, 19:00, January 28, 2013, https://janmstore.com/products/blossoms-and-thorns-a-community-uprooted-dvd.

9. Albert S. Broussard, *Black San Francisco: The Struggle for Racial Equality in the West, 1900–1954* (Lawrence: University Press of Kansas, 1993).

10. Alfredo Morabia, "Unveiling the Black Panther Party Legacy to Public Health," *American Journal of Public Health* 106, no. 10 (October 1, 2016): 1732–1733, https://ajph.aphapublications.org/doi/10.2105/AJPH.2016.303405.

11. Mary T. Bassett, "No Justice, No Health: The Black Panther Party's Fight for Health in Boston and Beyond," *Journal of African American Studies* 23, no. 4 (2019): 352–363, https://doi.org/10.1007/s12111-019-09450-w.

12. Antonia Juhasz, *The Tyranny of Oil: The World's Most Powerful Industry and What We Must Do to Stop It* (New York: Harper Collins, 2008).

13. Jane Kay, "Richmond Plant Safety Pact OK'd," *San Francisco Examiner*, February, 7, 1996, A-5.

Box 2: Medellín, Colombia

1. Forrest Hylton, "Remaking Medellín," *New Left Review* 44, no. 2 (2007): 70–89.

2. Justin McGuirk, *Radical Cities: Across Latin America in Search of a New Architecture* (London: Verso, 2014), 232.

3. "Medellín Rebuilds Its Violent Past and Remembers Its Resistance," *Verdad Abierta*, September 14, 2017, https://verdadabierta.com/medellin-reconstruye-su-pasado-violento-y-hace-memoria-de-sus-resistencias/.

4. Adriaan Alsema, "The National Urban War Front, the ELN's Elusive Urban Terrorist Network," *Colombia Reports*, January 31, 2018, https://colombiareports.com/national-urban-war-front-elns-elusive-urban-terrorist-network/.

5. "Colombia," Operations, The UN Refugee Agency (UNHCR), accessed February 2, 2020, https://reporting.unhcr.org/colombia#:~:text=According%20to%20official%20data%2C%20more,actors%2C%20an%20increasingly%20widespread%20phenomenon.

6. Adriaan Alsema, "Colombia Has Highest Number of Internally Displaced People," *Colombia Reports*, June 19, 2018, https://colombiareports.com/colombia-has-highest-number-of-internally-displaced-people/.

7. Centro Nacional de Memoria Histórica, "Medellín: memorias de una guerra urbana" (Medellín: Memories of an Urban War) (Bogota: Centro Nacional de Memoria Histórica , 2017), https://centrodememoriahistorica.gov.co/medellin-memorias-de-una-guerra-urbana/.

8. Lorenzo Castro and Alejanddro Echeverri, "Bogotá and Medellín: Architecture and Politics," *Architectural Design* 81 (2011): 96–103.http://dx.doi.org/10.1002/ad.1246.

9. Francisco Gutiérrez Sanín and Ana María Jaramillo, "Crime, (Counter-) Insurgency and the Privatization of Security: The Case of Medellín, Colombia," *Environment and Urbanization* 16, no. 2 (2004): 17–30, https://doi.org/10.1177%2F09562478040 1600209.

10. Sibylla Brodzinsky, "From Murder Capital to Model City: Is Medellín's Miracle Show or Substance?" *Guardian*, April 17, 2014, https://www.theguardian.com/cities/2014/apr/17/medellin-murder-capital-to-model-city-miracle-un-world-urban-forum.

11. Alcaldía de Medellín, "Our New Medellín, City for Life 100 Facts 2012–2015" (Medellín: Alcaldía de Medellín, 2015).

12. Ivan Turok, "The Seventh World Urban Forum in Medellín: Lessons for City Transformation," *Local Economy* 29, no. 6–7 (2014): 575–578, https://doi.org/10.1177%2F0269094214547011.

13. Juan Mauricio Rámirez, Yadira Díaz, and Juan Guillermo Bedoya, "Decentralization in Colombia: Searching for Social Equity in a Bumpy Economic Geography" (working paper no. 62 2014-3, Bogotá: Fedesarrollo Centro de Investigacion Economica y Social, 2014), https://www.repository.fedesarrollo.org.co/bitstream/handle/11445/233/WP_2014_No_62.pdf?sequence=1&isAllowed=y.

14. Banco Interamericano de Desarrollo (BID), *Medellín: transformación de una ciudad* (Medellín: Alcaldía de Medellín, 2011), https://acimedellin.org/wp-content/uploads/publicaciones/libro-transformacion-de-ciudad.pdf.

15. Laura Jaitman and Jose Brakarz, *Evaluation of Slum Upgrading Programs*

Literature Review and Methodological Approaches (Washington, DC: InterAmerican Development Bank, 2013).

16. John J. Betancur, "Approaches to Regularization of Informal Settlements: The Case of PRIMED in Medellín, Colombia," *Global Urban Development Magazine* 3, no. 1 (2007), https://www.globalurban.org/GUDMag07Vol3Iss1/Betancur%20PDF.pdf.

17. Ivo Imparato and Jeff Ruster, "Slum Upgrading and Participation: Lessons from Latin America," *Directions in Development* (Washington, DC: World Bank, 2003). https://openknowledge.worldbank.org/handle/10986/15133.

Chapter 1: Cities of Trauma or Healing?

1. Farnaz Fouladi et al., "Air Pollution Exposure Is Associated with the Gut Microbiome as Revealed by Shotgun Metagenomic Sequencing," *Environment International*, no. 138 (2020): 105604, https://doi.org/10.1016/j.envint.2020.105604.

2. Amanda S. Janesick and Bruce Blumberg, "Obesogens: An Emerging Threat to Public Health," *American Journal of Obstetrics and Gynecology* 214, no. 5 (2016): 559–565, https://doi.org/10.1016/j.ajog.2016.01.182.

3. Philippa D. Darbre, "Endocrine Disruptors and Obesity," *Current Obesity Reports* 6, no. 1 (2017): 18–27, https://doi.org/10.1007/s13679-017-0240-4.

4. Michelle S. Wong et al., "The Neighborhood Environment and Obesity: Understanding Variation by Race/Ethnicity," *Preventive Medicine* 111 (2018): 371–377, https://doi.org/10.1016/j.ypmed.2017.11.029.

5. Craig A. McEwen and Bruce S. McEwen, "Social Structure, Adversity, Toxic Stress, and Intergenerational Poverty: An Early Childhood Model," *Annual Review of Sociology* 43 (2017): 445–472, http://dx.doi.org/10.1146/annurev-soc-060116-053252.

6. Thomas F. Gieryn, "A Space for Place in Sociology," *Annual Review of Sociology* 26, no. 1 (2000): 463–496, https://doi.org/10.1146/annurev.soc.26.1.463.

7. Lisa Schweitzer, "Restorative Planning Ethics: The Therapeutic Imagination and Planning in Public Institutions." *Planning Theory* 15, no. 2 (May 2016): 130–144. https://doi.org/10.1177/1473095214539620.

8. Aftab Efran, "Confronting Collective Traumas: An Exploration of Therapeutic Planning," *Planning Theory & Practice* 18, no. 1 (January 2, 2017): 34–50, https://doi.org/10.1080/14649357.2016.1249909.

9. Andy Dangerfield, "Tube Map Used to Plot Londoners' Life Expectancy," *BBC News*, July 20, 2012, https://www.bbc.com/news/uk-england-london-18917932#:~:text=For%20example%2C%20if%20you%20travel,on%20which%20direction%20you%20travel.

10. "Le long du RER B, l'inegalite devant la mort," Urbamedia, accessed February 2, 2020, http://www.urbamedia.com/le-long-du-rer-b-linegalite-devant-la-mort.

11. Matt Wade and Danielle Maha, "A Shame on Our City: The Yawning Gap in Lifespans across Sydney," *Sydney Morning Herald*, January 27, 2021, https://www.smh.com.au/national/nsw/a-shame-on-our-city-the-yawning-gap-in-lifespans-across-sydney-20210124-p56wgp.html?btis.

12. WHO, "Health Inequities and Their Causes," last modified February 22, 2018, https://www.who.int/news-room/facts-in-pictures/detail/health-inequities-and-their-causes#:~:text=Health%20inequities%20are%20differences%20in,right%20mix%20of%20government%20policies.

13. Germán Freire et al., *Afro-descendants in Latin America: Toward a Framework of Inclusion* (Washington, DC: International Bank for Reconstruction and Development/The World Bank, 2018).

14. Sean Fox, "The Political Economy of Slums: Theory and Evidence from Sub-Saharan Africa," *World Development*, no. 54 (2014): 191–203, https://doi.org/10.1016/j.worlddev.2013.08.005.

15. Steven Johnson, *The Ghost Map: The Story of London's Most Terrifying Epidemic—and How It Changed Science, Cities, and the Modern World* (New York: Penguin, 2006).

16. Hull-House, Residents, *Hull-House Maps and Papers: A Presentation of Nationalities and Wages in a Congested District of Chicago, Together with Comments and Essays on Problems Growing Out of the Social Conditions* (Champaign: University of Illinois Press, 1895 [2007]).

17. Angela Saini, *Superior: The Return of Race Science* (Boston: Beacon Press, 2019).

18. Daniel J. Kevles, *In the Name of Eugenics: Genetics and the Uses of Human Heredity.* (Cambridge, MA: Harvard University Press, 1995).

19. W. E. B. Du Bois, *The Health and Physique of the American Negro: A Sociological Study Made Under the Direction of Atlanta University by the Eleventh Atlanta Conference* (Atlanta: Atlanta University Press, 1906), 89.

20. Nelson Peter Lewis. *The Planning of the Modern City: A Review of the Principles Governing City Planning* (New York: Wiley, 1916), 17–18.

21. C.-E.A. Winslow, "Public Health at the Crossroads," *American Journal of Public Health* 16, no. 11 (1926): 1075–1085, https://doi.org/10.2105/ajph.89.11.1645.

22. Christopher Silver, "The Racial Origins of Zoning: Southern Cities from 1910–40," *Planning Perspective* 6, no. 2 (1991): 189–205, https://doi.org/10.1080/0266543910 8725726.

23. American Planning Association, *Planning the Neighborhood* (Chicago: R.R. Donnelly & Sons, 1948), vi–vii.

24. Arnold R. Hirsch, *Making the Second Ghetto: Race and Housing in Chicago 1940–1960*, Historical Studies of Urban America (Cambridge: Cambridge University Press, 1983).

25. Vince Graham, "Urban Renewal . . . Means Negro Removal. ~ James Baldwin (1963)," YouTube video, 1:14, June 3, 2015, https://www.youtube.com/watch?v=T8Abhj 17kYU/.

26. Mindy Thompson Fullilove, *Root Shock: How Tearing Up City Neighborhoods Hurts America, and What We Can Do about It* (New York: One World/Ballantine, 2004).

27. James Greer, "The Home Owners' Loan Corporation and the Development of the Residential Security Maps," *Journal of Urban History* 39, no. 2 (2013): 275–296, https://doi.org/10.1177%2F0096144212436724.

28. Bruce Mitchell and Juan Franco, *HOLC 'Redlining' Maps: The Persistent Structure of Segregation and Economic Inequality* (Washington, DC: National Community Reinvestment Coalition, 2018), https://ncrc.org/wp-content/uploads/dlm_up loads/2018/02/NCRC-Research-HOLC-10.pdf.

29. Nancy Krieger et al., "Structural Racism, Historical Redlining, and Risk of Preterm Birth in New York City, 2013–2017," *American Journal of Public Health* 110, no. 7 (2020): 1046–1053, https://doi.org/10.2105/AJPH.2020.305656.

30. "500 Cities Project: 2016–2019," PLACES: Local Data for Better Public Health,

Centers for Disease Control and Prevention, last modified December 8, 2020, https://www.cdc.gov/places/about/500-cities-2016-2019/index.html.

31. Anthony Nardone, Joey Chiang, and Jason Corburn, "Historic Redlining and Urban Health Today in US Cities," *Environmental Justice* 13, no. 4 (2020): 109–119, https://doi.org/10.1089/env.2020.0011.

32. Joseph P. Fried, "City's Housing Administrator Proposes Planned Shrinkage of Some Slums," *New York Times*, February 3, 1976, https://www.nytimes.com/1976/02/03/archives/citys-housing-administrator-proposes-planned-shrinkage-of-some.html.

33. Deborah Wallace and Rodrick Wallace, *A Plague on Your Houses: How New York Was Burned Down and National Public Health Crumbled* (London: Verso, 1998).

34. Joe Flood, *The Fires: How a Computer Formula, Big Ideas, and the Best of Intentions Burned Down New York City—and Determined the Future of Cities* (New York: Riverhead Books, 2011).

35. Edward H. Blum, "Urban Fire Protection: Studies of the Operations of the New York City Fire Department," R-681-NYC (Santa Monica: The Rand Corporation, 1971). https://www.rand.org/pubs/reports/R0681.html.

36. Wallace and Wallace, *A Plague on Your Houses*.

37. Elizabeth Hinton, *From the War on Poverty to the War on Crime: The Making of Mass Incarceration in America* (Cambridge: Harvard University Press, 2017).

38. Ashley Provencher and James M. Conway, "Health Effects of Family Member Incarceration in the United States: A Meta-Analysis and Cost Study," *Children and Youth Services Review* 103 (2019): 87–99, https://doi.org/10.1016/j.childyouth.2019.05.029.

39. National Research Council (US) and Institute of Medicine (US) Committee on Integrating the Science of Early Childhood Development, "From Neurons to Neighborhoods: The Science of Early Childhood Development. Committee on Integrating the Science of Early Childhood Development," ed. Jack P. Shonkoff and Deborah A. Phillips (Washington, DC: National Academy Press, 2000).

40. Institute of Medicine and National Research Council, *From Neurons to Neighborhoods: An Update: Workshop Summary* (Washington, DC: The National Academies Press, 2012), https://doi.org/10.17226/13119.

41. Elie G. Karam et al., "Cumulative Traumas and Risk Thresholds: 12-Month PTSD in the World Mental Health (WMH) surveys," *Depression and Anxiety* 31, no. 2 (2014): 130–142, https://dx.doi.org/10.1002%2Fda.22169.

42. Andrew F. Clark, L. Barrett, and I. Kolvin. "Inner City Disadvantage and Family Functioning," *European Child & Adolescent Psychiatry* 9, no. 2 (2000): 77–83, https://doi.org/10.1007/s007870050001.

43. Maximus Berger and Zoltán Sarnyai, "More Than Skin Deep: Stress Neurobiology and Mental Health Consequences of Racial Discrimination," *Stress* 18, no. 1 (2015): 1–10, https://doi.org/10.3109/10253890.2014.989204.

44. J. P. Shonkoff, A. S. Garner, and Committee on Psychosocial Aspects of Child and Family Health, "The Lifelong Effects of Early Childhood Adversity and Toxic Stress," *Pediatrics* 129, no. 1: e232–e246, www.pediatrics.org/cgi/doi/10.1542/peds.2011-2663.

45. Arline T. Geronimus et al., "Weathering in Detroit: Place, Race, Ethnicity, and

Poverty as Conceptually Fluctuating Social Constructs Shaping Variation in Allostatic Load," *Milbank Quarterly* (2020), https://doi.org/10.1111/1468-0009.12484.

46. Elizabeth Blackburn and Elissa Epel, The Telomere Effect: A Revolutionary Approach to Living Younger, Healthier, Longer (New York: Grand Central Publishing, 2017).

47. Centers for Disease Control and Prevention (CDC), "What Is Epigenetics," 2020, https://www.cdc.gov/genomics/disease/epigenetics.htm.

48. National Scientific Council on the Developing Child, "Early Experiences Can Alter Gene Expression and Affect Long-Term Development," 2010, Working Paper No. 10, https://developingchild.harvard.edu/resources/early-experiences-can-alter-gene -expression-and-affect-long-term-development/.

49. P. Braveman et al., "Worry about Racial Discrimination: A Missing Piece of the Puzzle of Black–White Disparities in Preterm Birth?" *PLoS One* 12, no. 10 (2017): e0186151.

50. Tomoko Soga et al., "Genetic and Epigenetic Consequence of Early-Life Social Stress on Depression: Role of Serotonin-Associated Genes," *Frontiers in Genetics*, 11 (2021): 601868, doi:10.3389/fgene.2020.601868.

51. Vincent J. Felitti et al., "Relationship of Childhood Abuse and Household Dysfunction to Many of the Leading Causes of Death in Adults: The Adverse Childhood Experiences (ACE) Study," *American Journal of Preventive Medicine* 14, no. 4 (1998): 245–258, https://doi.org/10.1016/S0749-3797(98)00017-8.

52. Madison Armstrong and Jennifer Carlson. "Speaking of Trauma: The Race Talk, the Gun Violence Talk, and the Racialization of Gun Trauma," *Palgrave Communications* 5, no. 1 (2019): 1–11, https://doi.org/10.1057/s41599-019-0320-z.

53. David R. Williams, "Stress and the Mental Health of Populations of Color: Advancing Our Understanding of Race-Related Stressors," *Journal of Health and Social Behavior* 59, no. 4 (2018): 466–485, https://doi.org/10.1177/0022146518814251.

54. Njabulo Ndebele, *Fine Lines from the Box: Further Thoughts about Our Country* (Roggebaai: Umuzi, 2007), 137.

55. Nancy Krieger, "Embodiment: A Conceptual Glossary for Epidemiology," *Journal of Epidemiology & Community Health* 59, no. 5 (2005): 350–355, https://dx.doi.org /10.1136%2Fjech.2004.024562.

56. Enrique Gracia, "Neighborhood Disorder," in *Encyclopedia of Quality of Life and Well-Being Research*, ed. A. C. Michalos (Dordrecht: Springer, 2014), https:// doi.org/10.1007/978-94-007-0753-5_2751.

57. Robert J. Sampson and Stephen W. Raudenbush, "Seeing Disorder: Neighborhood Stigma and the Social Construction of 'Broken Windows,'" *Social Psychology Quarterly* 67, no. 4 (2004): 319–342, https://doi.org/10.1177/019027250406700401.

58. Catherine E. Ross and John Mirowsky, "Neighborhood Disadvantage, Disorder, and Health," *Journal of Health and Social Behavior* 42, no. 3 (September 2001): 258–276, https://doi.org/10.2307/3090214.

59. Tama Leventhal and Jeanne Brooks-Gunn, "The Neighborhoods They Live In: The Effects of Neighborhood Residence on Child and Adolescent Outcomes," *Psychological Bulletin* 126, no. 2 (2000): 309–337, https://doi.org/10.1037/0033-2909.126.2.309.

60. Wendy R. Ellis and William H. Dietz, "A New Framework for Addressing

Adverse Childhood and Community Experiences: The Building Community Resilience Model," *Academic Pediatrics* 17, no. 7 (2017): S86–S93, https://doi.org/10.1016/j .acap.2016.12.011.

61. Kathryn Collins et al., *Understanding the Impact of Trauma and Urban Poverty on Family Systems: Risks, Resilience, and Interventions* (Baltimore: Family Informed Trauma Treatment Center, 2010), https://www.nctsn.org/sites/default/files/resources /resource-guide/understanding_impact_trauma_urban_poverty_family_systems .pdf.

62. J. L. Hirschtick et al., "Persistent and Aggressive Interactions with the Police: Potential Mental Health Implications," *Epidemiology and Psychiatric Sciences* 29, no. 19 (2019).

63. Jordan E. DeVylder et al., "Association of Exposure to Police Violence with Prevalence of Mental Health Symptoms among Urban Residents in the United States," *JAMA network open* 1, no. 7 (2018): e184945-e184945, https://doi.org/10.1001 /jamanetworkopen.2018.4945.

64. Noni K. Gaylord-Harden et al., "Examining the Pathologic Adaptation Model of Community Violence Exposure in Male Adolescents of Color," *Journal of Clinical Child & Adolescent Psychology* 46, no. 1 (2017): 125–135, https://doi.org/10.1080/15374416 .2016.1204925.

65. Rob Nixon, *Slow Violence and the Environmentalism of the Poor* (Cambridge, MA: Harvard University Press, 2011).

66. Audre Lorde, "Learning from the 60s," in *Sister Outsider: Essays and Speeches by Audre Lorde* (Berkeley, CA: Crossing Press, 2007), 138.

67. Danielle Sered, *Until We Reckon: Violence, Mass Incarceration, and a Road to Repair* (New York: The New Press, 2019).

68. Shawn Ginwright, "The Future of Healing: Shifting from Trauma Informed Care to Healing Centered Engagement," *Medium*, May 31, 2018, https://medium .com/@ginwright/the-future-of-healing-shifting-from-trauma-informed-care-to -healing-centered-engagement-634f557ce69c.

69. George Rosen, "The First Neighborhood Health Center Movement—Its Rise and Fall," *American Journal of Public Health* 61, no. 8 (1971): 1620–1637, https://doi .org/10.2105/AJPH.61.8.1620.

70. Eli Y. Adashi, H. Jack Geiger, and Michael D. Fine, "Health Care Reform and Primary Care—the Growing Importance of the Community Health Center," *New England Journal of Medicine* 362, no. 22 (2010): 2047–2050, https://doi.org/10.1056 /NEJMp1003729.

71. Judy Schader Rogers, "Out in the Rural," Vimeo video, February 8, 2010, https:// vimeo.com/9307557.

72. "Metta Health Center," Lowell Community Health Center, accessed February 2, 2020, https://www.lchealth.org/patients/connect-services/metta-health-center.

73. "What Is Community Wealth Building?" Preston City Council, accessed February 2, 2020, https://www.preston.gov.uk/article/1335/What-is-Community -Wealth-Building-.

74. Mark Lipman, "Holding Ground: The Rebirth of Dudley Street," New Day Films, 58:00, 1996, https://www.newday.com/film/holding-ground-rebirth-dudley-street.

Notes 243

Chapter 2: Reducing Urban Violence through Street Love

. United States Department of Justice, Federal Bureau of Investigation, 2019 Crime in the United States, Expanded Homicide Data Table 9 (Murder Victims by Age by Weapon, 2019), 2020, https://ucr.fbi.gov/crime-in-the-u.s/2019/crime-in-the -u.s.-2019/topic-pages/tables/expanded-homicide-data-table-9.xls.

2. United States Department of Justice, Federal Bureau of Investigation, 2019 Crime in the United States, Table 2 (Crime in the United States by Community Type, 2019), 2020, https://ucr.fbi.gov/crime-in-the-u.s/2019/crime-in-the-u.s.-2019 /topic-pages/tables/table-2.

3. United States Department of Justice, Federal Bureau of Investigation, 2019 Crime in the United States, Expanded Homicide Data Table 12 (Murder Circumstances, 2015–2019), 2020, https://ucr.fbi.gov/crime-in-the-u.s/2019/crime-in-the-u.s.-2019 /topic-pages/tables/expanded-homicide-data-table-12.xls.

4. Sara F. Jacoby et al., "The Enduring Impact of Historical and Structural Racism on Urban Violence in Philadelphia," *Social Science & Medicine* 199 (2018): 87–95, https://doi.org/10.1016/j.socscimed.2017.05.038.

5. Michelle Alexander, *The New Jim Crow: Mass Incarceration in the Age of Colorblindness* (New York: The New Press, 2020).

6. Michele R. Decker, Holly C. Wilcox, Charvonne N. Holliday, and Daniel W. Webster, "An Integrated Public Health Approach to Interpersonal Violence and Suicide Prevention and Response," *Public Health Reports* 133, no. 1 suppl. (2018): 65S–79S, https://doi.org/10.1177/0033354918800019.

7. Substance Abuse and Mental Health Services Administration (SAMHSA), *SAMHSA's Concept of Trauma and Guidance for a Trauma-Informed Approach*, HHS Publication No. (SMA) 14-4884 (Rockville, MD: Substance Abuse and Mental Health Services Administration, 2014), https://ncsacw.samhsa.gov/userfiles/files/SAMHSA_Trauma.pdf.

8. Katherine Kirkinis et al., "Racism, Racial Discrimination, and Trauma: A Systematic Review of the Social Science Literature," *Ethnicity & Health* (August 30, 2018): 1–21, https://doi.org/10.1080/13557858.2018.1514453.

9. Sam Vaughn, "Ending Violence with an Empowering Antidote," TEDMED, 12:54, 2015, https://www.tedmed.com/talks/show?id=527628.

10. Yasser Arafat Payne and Hanaa A. Hamdi, "Street Love: How Street Life Oriented U.S. Born African Men Frame Giving Back to One Another and the Local Community," *Urban Review* 41, no. 1 (2009): 29–46, https://doi.org/10.1007/s11256-008 -0098-6.

11. Shawn Ginwright, *Hope and Healing in Urban Education* (New York: Routledge, 2016).

12. Jason Motlagh, "A Radical Approach to Gun Crime: Paying People Not to Kill Each Other," *Guardian*, June 9, 2016, https://www.theguardian.com/us-news/2016 /jun/09/richmond-california-ons-gun-crime.

13. Aaron C. Davis, "Cities Begin to Challenge a Bedrock of Justice: They're Paying Criminals Not to Kill," *Washington Post*, March 26, 2016, https://www.washingtonpost .com/local/dc-politics/cities-have-begun-to-challenge-a-bedrock-of-american-jus tice-theyre-paying-criminals-not-to-kill/2016/03/26/f25a6b9c-e9fc-11e5-a6f3-21ccdb c5f74e_story.html.

14. "Community Surveys," City of Richmond, California, last updated 2020, https://www.ci.richmond.ca.us/1871/Community-Surveys.

15. Jim Herron Zamora, "RICHMOND/ 4 on Council Call for State Emergency/ The Idea Is to Raise $2 Million to Fight Violent Crime Wave," SFGate, January 12, 2019, https://www.sfgate.com/bayarea/article/RICHMOND-4-on-council-call-for-a-state-of-2627613.php.

16. Tim Murphy, "Did This City Bring Down Its Murder Rate by Paying People Not to Kill?" *Mother Jones*, July/August 2014, https://www.motherjones.com/politics/2014/06/richmond-california-murder-rate-gun-death/.

17. Lee Romney, "Suspension Rates for Black Male Students in California Higher for Foster Youth, Rural Students," EdSource, February 20, 2018, https://edsource.org/2018/suspension-rates-for-black-male-students-in-california-higher-for-foster-youth-rural-students/593888.

18. Aliza Aufrichtig et al., "Want to Fix Gun Violence in America? Go Local," *Guardian*, January 9, 2017, https://www.theguardian.com/us-news/ng-interactive/2017/jan/09/special-report-fixing-gun-violence-in-america.

19. David Weisburd, "The Law of Crime Concentration and the Criminology of Place," *Criminology* 53, no. 2 (2015): 133–157, https://doi.org/10.1111/1745-9125.12070.

20. Vaughn, "Ending Violence."

21. Chimamanda Ngozi Adichie, "The Danger of a Single Story," TEDGlobal, 18:34, 2009, https://www.ted.com/talks/chimamanda_ngozi_adichie_the_danger_of_a_single_story?language=en.

22. Anthony Braga et al., *Reducing Gun Violence: The Boston Gun Project's Operation Ceasefire* (Washington, DC: U.S. Department of Justice/Office of Justice Programs, 2001), https://www.ojp.gov/pdffiles1/nij/188741.pdf.

23. Alex Kotlowitz, "Blocking the Transmission of Violence," *New York Times*, May 4, 2008, https://www.nytimes.com/2008/05/04/magazine/04health-t.html.

24. "Our Impact," Cure Violence Global, last updated 2021, https://cvg.org/impact/.

25. Jeffrey A. Butts et al., "Cure Violence: A Public Health Model to Reduce Gun Violence," *Annual Review of Public Health*, no. 36 (2015): 39–53, https://doi.org/10.1146/annurev-publhealth-031914-122509.

26. Lois Beckett, "How the Gun Control Debate Ignores Black Lives," ProPublica, November 24, 2015, https://www.propublica.org/article/how-the-gun-control-debate-ignores-black-lives.

27. "The Opportunity to Help Others," Credible Messenger Justice Center, last updated 2020, https://cmjcenter.org/become-a-credible-messenger/.

28. Insight Prison Project, accessed February 2, 2020, http://www.insightprisonproject.org/.

29. Marieke Liem, Margaret A. Zahn, and Lisa Tichavsky, "Criminal Recidivism among Homicide Offenders," *Journal of Interpersonal Violence* 29, no. 14 (2014): 2630–2651, https://doi.org/10.1177/0886260513517302.

30. Lila Kazemian and Jeremy Travis, "Imperative for Inclusion of Long Termers and Lifers in Research and Policy," *Criminology & Public Policy* 14, no. 2 (2015): 355–395, https://doi.org/10.1111/1745-9133.12126.

31. Thomas P. LeBel, Matt Richie, and Shadd Maruna, "Helping Others as a Response to Reconcile a Criminal Past: The Role of the Wounded Healer in Prisoner

Reentry Programs," *Criminal Justice and Behavior* 42, no. 1 (2015): 108–120, https://doi.org/10.1177%2F0093854814550029.

32. Paulo Freire, *Pedagogy of the oppressed, (New York: Continuum, 1970), 54.*

33. W.E.B. Du Bois, "Strivings of the Negro People," August 1897, reprinted in *The Atlantic,* https://www.theatlantic.com/magazine/archive/1897/08/strivings-of-the-negro-people/305446/.

34. W.E.B. Du Bois, *The Souls of Black Folk: With "The Talented Tenth" and "The Souls of White Folk"* (New York: Penguin, 1903).

35. Bessel Van Der Kolk, *The Body Keeps the Score: Brain, Mind, and Body in the Healing of Trauma* (New York: Penguin, 2014), 97.

36. Joint Economic Committee, *A State-by-State Examination of the Economic Costs of Gun Violence,* U.S. Congress, Joint Economic Committee, September 19, 2019, https://www.jec.senate.gov/public/_cache/files/b2ee3158-aff4-4563-8c3b-0183ba4a8135/economic-costs-of-gun-violence.pdf.

37. Carl Sullivan and Carla Baranauckas, "Here's How Much Money Goes to Police Departments in Largest Cities across the U.S.," *USA Today,* June 26, 2020, https://www.usatoday.com/story/money/2020/06/26/how-much-money-goes-to-police-departments-in-americas-largest-cities/112004904/.

38. Giffords Law Center, "The Economic Cost of Gun Violence in California," Giffords Law Center, March 2018, https://giffords.org/wp-content/uploads/2018/03/Economic-Cost-of-Gun-Violence-in-California.pdf.

39. National Institute for Criminal Justice Reform, "Stockton, California: The Cost of Gun Violence" (Oakland, CA: National Institute for Criminal Justice Reform, 2020), https://nicjr.org/wp-content/themes/nicjr-child/assets/Stockton.pdf.

40. Jeffery A. Kottler, *Travel Change Your Life: How to Create a Transformative Experience* (San Francisco: Jossey-Bass, 1997), xi.

41. David Muhammad and DeVone Boggan, "The Very Essential Work of Street-Level Violence Prevention," The Trace, April 14, 2020, https://www.thetrace.org/2020/04/the-very-essential-work-of-street-level-violence-prevention/.

42. Keosha Valrela, "Death Row Attorney Bryan Stevenson on 4 Ways to Fight Against Injustice," Aspen Institute, July 20, 2016, https://www.aspeninstitute.org/blog-posts/death-row-attorney-bryan-stevenson-4-ways-fight-injustice/.

43. Zack Norris, *We Keep Us Safe: Building Secure, Just and Inclusive Communities* (Boston: Beacon Press, 2020).

44. Ibid.

45. Mariela Antonia Waloff and Rachel Mary Waldholz, *A Confused War* (Berkeley: UC Berkeley Graduate School of Journalism, 2013), https://escholarship.org/uc/item/4txib29p.

46. Motlagh, "A Radical Approach."

47. Patrick Sharkey, *Uneasy Peace: The Great Crime Decline, the Renewal of City Life, and the Next War on Violence* (NY: W.W. Norton, 2018), 54.

48. Clinton Lacey, director of the District of Columbia, Department of Youth Rehabilitation Services, captured the essence of the Advance Peace approach in a 2019 presentation: "We need to shift the conversation to what heals people, what restores people, what empowers people to have options, to make other choices, to be positive parts of the community. . . . Ultimately, we need to reimagine what justice is and what

a justice system can be. We need to suspend reality and imagine something different, something healthy, something caring, something—I'll use an unscientific term: 'loving.' We need to imagine what love can look like in policy and how that can translate into practices and policies." National Academies of Sciences, Engineering, and Medicine (NASEM), *The Effects of Incarceration and Reentry on Community Health and Well-Being: Proceedings of a Workshop* (Washington, DC: The National Academies Press, 2019), https://www.ncbi.nlm.nih.gov/books/NBK555730/.

Chapter 3: Slum Scientists Diagnosing Traumas

1. Eyder Peralta, "Kenya Braced for the Worst. The Worst Didn't Happen. Why?" NPR, September 18, 2020, https://www.npr.org/sections/goatsandsoda/2020/09/18/913937122/kenya-braced-for-the-worst-the-worst-didnt-happen-why.

2. "National Hygiene Program Creates Jobs for Kenyans in Informal Settlements," World Bank, October 12, 2020, https://www.worldbank.org/en/news/feature/2020/10/12/national-hygiene-program-creates-jobs-for-kenyans-in-informal-settlements.

3. Faith Nyasuguta, "City Slums Now Better Places to Live In, Thanks to Kazi Mtaani," *Star Kenya*, September 10, 2020, https://www.the-star.co.ke/counties/nairobi/2020-09-10-city-slums-now-better-places-to-live-in-thanks-to-kazi-mtaani/.

4. Barbara A. Israel et al. "Community-Based Participatory Research: A Capacity-Building Approach for Policy Advocacy Aimed at Eliminating Health Disparities," *American Journal of Public Health* 100, no. 11 (2010): 2094–102, doi:10.2105/AJPH.2009.170506.

5. Sheila Jasanoff, ed., *States of Knowledge: The Co-production of Science and the Social Order* (New York: Routledge, 2004).

6. Ibid., 3.

7. Barbara Goldberg. "Move to Rename Harlem Neighborhood Sparks Outrage over Erasing Black History," Reuters, June 26, 2017, https://www.reuters.com/article/us-new-york-harlem/move-to-rename-harlem-neighborhood-sparks-outrage-over-erasing-black-history-idUSKBN19H2CL

8. Elinor Ostrom, "Crossing the Great Divide: Coproduction, Synergy, and Development," *World Development* 24, no. 6 (June 1996): 1073–1087, https://doi.org/10.1016/0305-750X(96)00023-X.

9. Serrano Sanz et al., *White Paper on Citizen Science in Europe* (EU: Socientize Consortium, 2014).

10. Steven Epstein, *Impure Science: AIDS, Activism, and the Politics of Knowledge* (Berkeley: University of California Press, 1998).

11. Anand Giridharadas, *Winners Take All: The Elite Charade of Changing the World* (New York: Vintage, 2018).

12. Ibid,, 5–6.

13. Katri Betram, Ngozi Erondu, and Madhukar Pai, "Silenced Voices in Global Health," Think Global Health, June 3, 2020, https://www.thinkglobalhealth.org/article/silenced-voices-global-health.

14. Murithi Mutiga, "Pipeline Fire Kills Dozens in Nairobi Slum," *Guardian*, September 12, 2011, https://www.theguardian.com/world/2011/sep/12/pipeline-fire-nairobi-slum.

15. Christopher J. L. Murray et al., "Global Burden of 87 Risk Factors in 204 Countries

and Territories, 1990–2019: A Systematic Analysis for the Global Burden of Disease Study 2019," *Lancet* 396, no. 10258 (2020): 1223–1249, https://doi.org/10.1016/S0140 -6736(20)30752-2.

16. African Population and Health Research Center (APHRC), "Population and Healthy Dynamics in Nairobi's Informal Settlements: Report of the Nairobi Cross-Sectional Slums Survey (NCSS)" (Nairobi: African Population and Health Center, 2014).

17. J. B. Isunju et al., "Socio-economic Aspects of Improved Sanitation in Slums: A Review," *Public health* 125, no. 6 (2011): 368–376, https://doi.org/10.1016/j.puhe.2011 .03.008.

18. Amnesty International, *Insecurity and Indignity: Women's Experiences in the Slums of Nairobi, Kenya* (London: Amnesty International Publications, 2010).

·   19. Mark Anderson, "Nairobi's Female Slum Dwellers March for Sanitation and Land Rights," *Guardian*, October 29, 2014, https://www.theguardian.com/global-devel opment/2014/oct/29/nairobi-slum-dwellers-sanitation-land-rights.

20. Mark Anderson, "Kenyan Women Sue for Ownership of Nairobi Slum," *Guardian*, October 2, 2013, https://www.theguardian.com/global-development/2013 /oct/02/kenya-women-sue-nairobi-slum.

21. Sphere, accessed February 2, 2020, https://spherestandards.org/.

22. "Reinvent the Toilet Challenge & Expo: Strategy Overview," Bill and Melinda Gates Foundation, accessed February 2, 2020, https://www.gatesfoundation. org/what-we-do/global-growth-and-opportunity/water-sanitation-and-hygiene /reinvent-the-toilet-challenge-and-expo.

23. "Innovative Toilet Technology for the 21st Century | Bill & Melinda Gates Foundation," Bill & Melinda Gates Foundation, July 18, 2011, https://www.gate sfoundation.org/Media-Center/Press-Releases/2011/07/Innovative-Toilet-Tech nology-for-the-21st-Century.

24. Vanessa Van Voorhis. "Tech Disruption Comes to Global Sanitation," Boston Consulting Group, November 19, 2018, https://www.bcg.com/en-us/publications/2018 /tech-disruption-comes-to-global-sanitation.

25. "Bill Gates Launches Reinvented Toilet Expo Showcasing New Pathogen-Kill-ing Sanitation Products That Don't Require Sewers or Water Lines," Bill & Melinda Gates Foundation, November 6, 2018, https://www.gatesfoundation.org/Media-Cen ter/Press-Releases/2018/11/Bill-Gates-Launches-Reinvented-Toilet-Expo-Showcas ing-New-Pathogen-Killing-Sanitation-Products.

26. "Start Thinking Peepoo," Pee poople, accessed August 22, 2020, http://www .peepoople.com/peepoo/start-thinking-peepoo/.

27. Sindya N. Bhanoo, "For Pennies, a Disposable Toilet That Could Help Grow Crops," *New York Times*, March 2, 2010, https://www.nytimes.com/2010/03/02 /science/02bag.html.

28. "Business Partnerships," International Aid Services, accessed February 2, 2020, https://sites.google.com/ias-intl.org/lakarmissionen-ias-together/about-ias/busi ness-partnerships?authuser=0.

29. Know Your City TV, "The Unchecked Injustice," YouTube video, 5:05, Novem-ber 21, 2017, https://www.youtube.com/watch?v=OsVuDPQRgdI&t=135s.

30. Sarah E. West et al., "Particulate Matter Pollution in an Informal Settlement in

Nairobi: Using Citizen Science to Make the Invisible Visible," *Applied Geography*, no. 114 (2020), https://doi.org/10.1016/j.apgeog.2019.102133.

31. Maureen Kinyanjui, "Blame Games between NMS, City Hall over Collapsed Mukuru Building," *Star Kenya*, August 5, 2020, https://www.the-star.co.ke/counties /nairobi/2020-08-05-blame-games-between-nms-city-hall-over-collapsed-mukuru -building/.

32. "National Hygiene Program Creates Jobs for Kenyans in Informal Settlements," World Bank, October 12, 2020, https://www.worldbank.org/en/news/feature/2020 /10/12/national-hygiene-program-creates-jobs-for-kenyans-in-informal-settlements.

33. Collins Omulo, "Roads in City Informal Settlements Set for Major Facelift," *Nairobi News*, August 17, 2020, https://nairobinews.nation.co.ke/news/roads-in-city -informal-settlements-set-for-major-facelift.

34. Africa for Africa, "Kenya Begins Construction of Hospitals in Nairobi's Informal Settlements," Construction Review Online, August 12, 2020, https://con structionreviewonline.com/news/kenya/kenya-begins-construction-of-hospitals -in-nairobis-informal-settlements/.

35. Kevin Cheruiyot, "Uhuru Commissions Sh210 Million NMS Slum Hospital Project," *Star Kenya*, August 10, 2020, https://www.the-star.co.ke/news/2020-08-10 -uhuru-commissions-sh210-million-nms-slum-hospital-project/.

36. Julie Owino, "President Kenyatta Commends NMS City Health Expansion Efforts," *Capital FM Kenya*, December 12, 2020, https://www.capitalfm.co.ke /news/2020/12/president-kenyatta-commends-nms-city-health-expansion-efforts/.

37. Macharia Kamau, "State to Put Up 10,000 Houses on Repossessed Land," *Standard*, August 18, 2020, https://www.standardmedia.co.ke/business/article/20013 82884/state-to-put-up-10-000-houses-on-repossessed-land.

Chapter 4: Cocreating Places for Urban Health and Healing

1. John Muir, *The Yosemite* (New York: The Century Co., 1912).

2. Frederick Law Olmsted, "Trees in Streets and in Parks" in *Frederick Law Olmsted: Writings on Landscape, Culture, and Society* (New York: Library of America, 2015), 590.

3. Ibid., 587–594, 589.

4. Frederick Law Olmstead and Laura Wood Roper, "The Yosemite Valley and the Mariposa Big Trees: A Preliminary Report (1865)," *Landscape Architecture* 43, no. 1 (1952): 12–25, https://www.jstor.org/stable/44659746.

5. Deborah Franklin, "How Hospital Gardens Help Patients Heal," *Scientific American*, March 1, 2012, https://www.scientificamerican.com/article/nature-that-nurtures/.

6. Edward O. Wilson, *Biophilia* (Cambridge, MA: Harvard University Press, 1984).

7. Biophilic Cities, accessed February 2, 2020, https://www.biophiliccities.org.

8. World Health Organization, *Urban Green Space Interventions and Health: A Review of Impacts and Effectiveness* (Copenhagen: World Health Regional Office for Europe, 2017), https://www.cbd.int/health/who-euro-green-spaces-urbanhealth.pdf.

9. Terry Hartig et al., "Tracking Restoration in Natural and Urban Field Settings," *Journal of Environmental Psychology* 23, no. 2 (2003): 109–123, https://doi .org/10.1016/S0272-4944(02)00109-3.

10. Terry Hartig et al., "Nature and Health," *Annual Review of Public Health*, no. 35 (2014): 207–228, https://doi.org10.1146/annurev-publhealth-032013-182443.

11. "A Space for Healing: Overcoming Environmental Diseases in National Parks," International Union for Conservation of Nature, June 5, 2019, https://www.iucn.org/news/asia/201906/a-space-healing-overcoming-environmental-diseases-national-parks.

12. Hiromitsu Kobayashi et al., "Forest Walking Affects Autonomic Nervous Activity: A Population-Based Study," *Frontiers in Public Health*, no. 6 (2018): 278, https://doi.org/10.3389/fpubh.2018.00278.

13. Stephen Kaplan, "The Restorative Benefits of Nature: Toward an Integrative Framework," *Journal of Environmental Psychology* 15, no. 3 (1995): 169–182, https://doi.org/10.1016/0272-4944(95)90001-2.

14. Marc G. Berman et al., "Interacting with Nature Improves Cognition and Affect for Individuals with Depression," *Journal of Affective Disorders* 140, no. 3 (2012): 300–305, https://doi.org/10.1016/j.jad.2012.03.012.

15. Andrea Faber Taylor and Frances E. Kuo, "Children with Attention Deficits Concentrate Better after Walk in the Park," *Journal of Attention Disorders* 12, no. 5 (2009): 402–409, https://doi.org/10.1177/1087054708323000.

16. Thich Nhat Hanh, "Thich Nhat Hanh on Walking Meditation," Lion's Roar, May 31, 2019, https://www.lionsroar.com/how-to-meditate-thich-nhat-hanh-on-walking-meditation/.

17. Bessel A. Van der Kolk, *The Body Keeps the Score: Brain, Mind and Body in the Healing of Trauma* (New York: Penguin, 2014).

18. Roger S. Ulrich, "View Through a Window May Influence Recovery from Surgery," *Science* 224, no. 4647 (1984): 420–421, https://doi.org/10.1126/science.6143402.

19. L. McDonald, "Florence Nightingale and Hospital Reform: Collected Works of Florence Nightingale," in *Notes on Hospitals*, 3rd ed., vol. 16 (Waterloo, ON: Wilfrid Laurier University Press, 1863).

20. Marcus Hedblom et al., "Reduction of Physiological Stress by Urban Green Space in a Multisensory Virtual Experiment," *Scientific Reports* 9, no. 1 (2019): 1–11, https://doi.org/10.1038/s41598-019-46099-7.

21. Eugenia C. South et al., "Effect of Greening Vacant Land on Mental Health of Community-Dwelling Adults: A Cluster Randomized Trial," *JAMA network open* 1, no. 3 (2018): e180298-e180298, https://doi.org/10.1001/jamanetworkopen.2018.0298.

22. Kirsten M. M. Beyer et al., "Exposure to Neighborhood Green Space and Mental Health: Evidence from the Survey of the Health of Wisconsin," *International Journal of Environmental Research and Public Health* 11, no. 3 (2014): 3453–3472, https://doi.org/10.3390/ijerph110303453.

23. Jolanda Maas et al., "Morbidity Is Related to a Green Living Environment," *Journal of Epidemiology & Community Health* 63, no. 12 (2009): 967–973, https://doi.org/10.1136/jech.2008.079038.

24. Clare Cooper Marcus and Marni Barnes, *Healing Gardens: Therapeutic Benefits and Design Recommendations* (New York: John Wiley & Sons, 1999).

25. Roslyn Lindheim, "New Design Parameters for Healthy Places," *Places* 2, no. 4 (1985): 17–27, https://escholarship.org/uc/item/3mz7z8pn.

26. Susan Stone, "A Retrospective Evaluation of the Impact of the Planetree Patient-Centered Model of Care on Inpatient Quality Outcomes," *HERD: Health Environments Research & Design Journal* 1, no. 4 (2008): 55–69, https://doi.org/10.1177/193758670800100406.

27. WHO, "Urban Green Space Interventions and Health: A review of impacts and effectiveness," WHO Regional Office for Europe, (2017), 5. https://www.euro.who .int/__data/assets/pdf_file/0010/337690/FULL-REPORT-for-LLP.pdf

28. Jolanda Maas et al., "Social Contacts as a Possible Mechanism behind the Relation between Green Space and Health," *Health & Place* 15, no. 2 (2009): 586–595, https://doi.org/10.1016/j.healthplace.2008.09.006.

29. Nooshin Razani et al., "Healing through Nature: A Park-Based Health Intervention for Young People in Oakland, California." *Children Youth and Environments* 25, no. 1 (2015): 147–159, https://doi.org/10.7721/chilyoutenvi.25.1.0147.

30. Nooshin Razani et al., "Effect of Park Prescriptions with and without Group Visits to Parks on Stress Reduction in Low-Income Parents: SHINE Randomized Trial," *PloS one* 13, no. 2 (2018): e0192921, https://doi.org/10.1371/journal.pone.0192921.

31. Carolyn Jones, "Revitalizing Parks Means New Life for Richmond Neighborhood," SFGate, October 7, 2007, https://www.sfgate.com/bayarea/article/Revitalizing -parks-means-new-life-for-Richmond-2498327.php#photo-2665369.

32. Erin Gilmore, "A Park Grows in Richmond," *East Bay Express*, June 9, 2009, https://www.eastbayexpress.com/oakland/a-park-grows-in-richmond/Content?oid =1370046.

33. Patricia Leigh Brown, " How a Forlorn Playground Became One of America's Most Innovative Public Spaces," *Christian Science Monitor*, May 24, 2017, https://www .csmonitor.com/World/Making-a-difference/2017/0524/How-a-forlorn-playground -became-one-of-America-s-most-innovative-public-spaces.

34. Gilmore, "A Park Grows."

35. "Statewide Park Program (SPP)—Round 4," California Department of Parks and Recreation, last updated 2021, https://www.parks.ca.gov/?page_id=29939.

36. Vanessa L. Neergheen et al., "Neighborhood Social Cohesion Is Associated with Lower Levels of Interleukin-6 in African American Women," *Brain, Behavior, and Immunity* 76 (2019): 28–36, https://dx.doi.org/10.1016%2Fj.bbi.2018.10.008.

37. Lauro Velazquez-Salinas et al., "The Role of Interleukin 6 during Viral Infections," *Frontiers in Microbiology*, no. 10 (2019): 1057, https://doi.org/10.3389/fmicb .2019.01057.

38. Jennifer W. Robinette, Jason D. Boardman, and Eileen Crimmins, "Perceived Neighborhood Social Cohesion and Cardiometabolic Risk: A Gene × Environment Study." *Biodemography and Social Biology* 65, no. 1 (2020): 1–15, https://doi.org/10.1080 /19485565.2019.1568672.

39. Eric S. Kim, Nansook Park, and Christopher Peterson. "Perceived Neighborhood Social Cohesion and Stroke," *Social Science & Medicine* 97 (2013): 49–55, https:// doi.org/10.1016/j.socscimed.2013.08.001.

40. Samson Y. Gebreab et al., "Neighborhood Social and Physical Environments and Type 2 Diabetes Mellitus in African Americans: The Jackson Heart Study," *Health & Place* 43 (2017): 128–137, https://doi.org/10.1016/j.healthplace.2016.12.001.

41. Pogo Park, *Pogo Park Annual Report 2014* (Richmond, CA: Pogo Park, 2015), https://pogopark.org/wp-content/uploads/2018/07/Annual-Report-2014.pdf.

42. Luisa Sotomayor, "Dealing with Dangerous Spaces: The Construction of Urban Policy in Medellín," *Latin American Perspectives* 44, no. 2 (2017): 71–90, https://doi .org/10.1177%2F0094582X16682758.

43. "Desaparecían personas en la Comuna 13 y decían que eran un mito (People disappeared in Commune 13 and said they were a myth)," Verdad Abierta, August 8, 2015, https://verdadabierta.com/desaparecian-personas-en-la-comuna-13-y-decian -que-eran-un-mito/.

44. Ramiro Ceballos Melguizo and Francine Cronshaw, "The Evolution of Armed Conflict in Medellín: An Analysis of the Major Actors," *Latin American Perspectives* 28, no. 1 (2001): 110–131, https://www.researchgate.net/deref/http%3A%2F%2Fdx .doi.org%2F10.1177%2F0094582X0102800107.

45. Yineth Bedoya, "Viaje a las fronteras invisibles de la Comuna 13," (Journey to the invisible frontiers of Comuna 13). *El Tiempo*, October 13, 2012, http://www .eltiempo.com/justicia/viaje-a-las-fronteras-invisibles-de-la-comuna-1_12303318-4.

46. National Center for Historical Memory, *BASTA YA! Colombia: Memories of War and Dignity*, General Report (Bogota: National Center for Historical Memory Colombia, 2016).

47. Grupo de Memoria Histórica (Historical Memory Group), *La huella invisible de la guerra. Desplazamiento forzado en la Comuna 13* (The invisible footprint of the war, Forced displacement in the Comuna 13) (Bogotá: Taurus/Semana, 2011), 122.

48. "We Are: Exile and Reparation Are Everyone's Business," Region, last updated 2016, https://www.region.org.co/index.php/nuestra-historia/item/233-el-destierro-y -la-reparacion-son-asuntos-de-todos-y-todas.

49. Aníbal Gaviria, personal communication to author, August 15, 2018.

50. David H. Freeman, "How Medellin, Colombia, Became the World's Smartest City," *Newsweek*, November 18, 2019, https://www.newsweek.com/2019/11/22/medel lin-colombia-worlds-smartest-city-1471521.html.

51. "Lusitania Paz School of Colombia / Camilo Avellandeda," *ArchDaily Colombia*, last updated August 18, 2016, https://www.archdaily.co/co/793548/colegio-lusitania -paz-de-colombia-camilo-avellaneda.

52. Paulo Freire, *Pedagogy of the Oppressed*, trans. Myra Bergman Ramos (New York: Continuum, 2005), 81.

53. Letty Reimerink, "Planners and the Pride Factor: The Case of the Electric Escalator in Medellín," *Bulletin of Latin American Research* 37, no. 2 (2018): 191–205, https://doi.org/10.1111/blar.12665.

54. Françoise Coupé, Peter Brand, and Julio Dávila, "Medellín: contexto institucional y cambio de paradigma urbano" (Medellín: institutional context and urban paradigm shift), in, *Movilidad urbana y pobreza: Aprendizajes de Medellín y Soacha, Colombia* (Urban mobility and poverty: Learning from Medellín and Soacha, Colombia), ed. Julio Dávila (London: Development Planning Unit, UCL/Universidad Nacional de Colombia, 2012), 47–58.

55. Greg Nichols, "Library Parks Foster Community in Colombia," *Pacific Standard*, June 14, 2017, https://psmag.com/social-justice/library-parks-bring-community -to-colombia-39915.

56. "Quality of Life Survey," Alcaldia de Medellín, last updated February 5, 2021, https://www.medellin.gov.co/irj/portal/medellin?NavigationTarget=navurl:// foea9f10392febab26306c5be3d1bba5.

57. Greg Nichols, "Library Parks Foster Community in Colombia," *Pacific Standard*, June 14, 2017, https://psmag.com/social-justice/library-parks-bring-community -to-colombia-39915.

58. David Calle Atehortua, "Así serán las dos nuevas ciudadelas universitarias que tendrá Medellín," *El Tiempo*, July 30, 2020, https://www.eltiempo.com/colombia/medellin /asi-seran-las-dos-nuevas-ciudadelas-universitarias-que-tendra-medellin-523770.

59. CPI Popular Training Institute, "Youth, Memory and Peace-Book," Instituto Popular de Capacitacion, http://ipc.org.co/index.php/2017/07/juventud-memoria-y -paz-libro/.

60. Juan Diego Jaramillo, *Entrando y saliendo de la violência: construcción del sentido joven em Medellín desde el graffiti y el hip-hop* (Entering and exiting violence: Construction of a sense of youth in Medellín through graffiti and hip-hop) (Bogotá: Pontificia Universidad Javeriana, 2015).

61. Liz Beddall, "Change Gains Momentum in Medellin," *Toronto Star*, April 13, 2017, https://www.thestar.com/life/travel/2017/04/13/change-gains-momentum-in -medellin.html.

62. Lola Iron, "Casa Kolacho: Violence Is Cured with Hip Hop," *El Pais*, June 30, 2016, https://elpais.com/elpais/2016/06/23/planeta_futuro/1466698760_170228.html.

63. Adriaan Alsema, "Homicides in Colombia Reach Hoistoric Low Amid Pandemic," Colombia Reports, December 21, 2020, https://colombiareports.com/homicides-in -colombia-reach-historic-low-amid-pandemic/.

64. Hanier Anturi Ramirez, "El Parque de la Vida en Medellín, una institución aplaudida por la OMS," *El Tiempo*, October 28, 2018, https://www.eltiempo.com/vida /educacion/el-parque-de-la-vida-en-medellin-una-institucion-aplaudida-por-la -oms-286192.

65. Mark S. Granovetter, "The Strength of Weak Ties," *American Journal of Sociology* 78, no. 6 (1973): 1360–1380.

66. Jan Bachmann and Peer Schouten, "Concrete Approaches to Peace: Infrastructure as Peacebuilding," *International Affairs* 94, no. 2 (2018): 381–398, https://doi .org/10.1093/ia/iix237.

Chapter 5: Resilience and Climate Justice in Medellín

1. Jason Corburn et al., "The Transformation of Medellín into a 'City for Life': Insights for Healthy Cities," *Cities & Health* 4, no. 1 (2020): 13–24, https://doi.org/10 .1080/23748834.2019.1592735.

2. Consejeria Presidencial para Medellin y su Area Metropolitana, *Seminario Alternativas y Estrategias de Futuro para Medellín y su Area Metropolitana* (Presidential Advisory Office for Medellin and its Metropolitan Area, Seminar on Alternatives and Future Strategies for Medellín and Its Metropolitan Area) (Medellín: Lealón, 1995).

3. "Four Steps Up to the Plan," Region, accessed February 2, 2021, https://www .region.org.co/index.php/nuestra-historia/item/223-cuatro-pasos-hasta-el-plan.

4. "Stratification Methodologies," Colombia, National Administrative Department of Statistics—DANE, accessed February 11, 2021, https://www.dane.gov.co/index.php /69-espanol/geoestadistica/estratificacion/468-estratificacion-socioeconomica.

5. Justin McGuirk, *Radical Cities: Ciuad Des Radica Les Cidades Radica Is* (London: Verso, 2014).

6. Fernanda Magalhães et al., *Slum Upgrading and Housing in Latin America* (Washington, DC: Inter-American Development Bank, 2016).

7. Alejandro Fajardo and Matt Andrews, "Does Successful Governance Require Heroes? The Case of Sergio Fajardo and the City of Medellin: A Reform Case for Instruction" (WIDER Working Paper 2014/035, Helsinki: United Nations University [UNU-WIDER], 2014).

8. Milford Bateman, Juan Pablo Duran Ortíz, and Kate Maclean, "A Post-Washington Consensus Approach to Local Economic Development in Latin America? An Example from Medellín, Colombia" (London: Overseas Development Institution, 2011).

9. Gotelind Alber, *Gender, Cities and Climate Change* (Nairobi: UN-HABITAT, 2010), www.mirror.unhabitat.org/downloads/docs/GRHS2011/GRHS2011ThematicStudyGender.pdf.

10. Harriet Bulkeley, Gareth A. S. Edwards, and Sara Fuller, "Contesting Climate Justice in the City: Examining Politics and Practice in Urban Climate Change Experiments," *Global Environmental Change*, no. 25 (2014): 31–40, https://doi.org/10.1016/j.gloenvcha.2014.01.009.

11. Gina Ziervogel et al., "Inserting Rights and Justice into Urban Resilience: A Focus on Everyday Risk," *Environment and Urbanization* 29, no. 1 (2017): 123–138, https://doi.org/10.1177/0956247816686905.

12. David Satterthwaite et al., "Building Resilience to Climate Change in Informal Settlements," *One Earth* 2, no. 2 (2020): 143–156, https://doi.org/10.1016/j.oneear.2020.02.002.

13. Malini Ranganathan and Eve Bratman, "From Urban Resilience to Abolitionist Climate Justice in Washington, DC," *Antipode* 53, no. 1 (2021): 115–137, https://doi.org/10.1111/anti.12555.

14. Kenneth A. Gould and Tammy L. Lewis, *Green Gentrification: Urban Sustainability and the Struggle for Environmental Justice* (London: Routledge, 2016).

15. Linda Shi et al., "Roadmap Towards Justice in Urban Climate Adaptation Research," *Nature Climate Change* 6, no. 2 (2016): 131–137, https://doi.org/10.1038/nclimate2841.

16. Sadie J. Ryan et al., "Global Expansion and Redistribution of Aedes-Borne Virus Transmission Risk with Climate Change," *PLoS neglected tropical diseases* 13, no. 3 (2019): e0007213, https://doi.org/10.1371/journal.pntd.0007213.

17. Nick Watts et al., "The 2019 Report of *The Lancet* Countdown on Health and Climate Change: Ensuring That the Health of a Child Born Today Is Not Defined by a Changing Climate," *Lancet* 394, no. 10211 (2019): 1836–1878, https://doi.org/10.1016/S0140-6736(19)32596-6.

18. Gotelind Alber, *Gender, Cities and Climate Change* (Nairobi: UN-HABITAT, 2010), www.mirror.unhabitat.org/downloads/docs/GRHS2011/GRHS2011ThematicStudyGender.pdf.

19. Ibid.

20. Intergovernmental Panel on Climate Change (IPCC), *Climate Change 2014—Impacts, Adaptation and Vulnerability: Part A: Global and Sectoral Aspects: Working Group II Contribution to the IPCC Fifth Assessment Report* (Cambridge: Cambridge University Press, 2014).

21. Isabelle Anguelovski, Clara Irazábal-Zurita, and James J. T. Connolly, "Grabbed

Urban Landscapes: Socio-spatial Tensions in Green Infrastructure Planning in Medellín," *International Journal of Urban and Regional Research* 43, no. 1 (2019): 133–156, https://doi.org/10.1111/1468-2427.12725.

22. Luis Fernando Restrepo-Betancur et al., "Climate Change in the City of Medellín-Colombia, throughout Fifty Years (1960–2010)," *DYNA* 86, no. 209 (2019): 312–318, http://dx.doi.org/10.15446/dyna.v86n209.69531.

23. Municipal Resolution 43 of 2007 created and institutionalized participatory planning within the municipal planning system.

24. Alejandro Guerrero, "Rebuilding Trust in Government via Service Delivery: The Case of Medellín, Colombia" (Washington, DC: World Bank, 2011), 1–28.

25. E. Martinez-Herrera, D. A. Hernandez, and J. C. Benach, "Advances in an Integrated Evaluation of Community Health in Medellín (Colombia) during 2014–2019," *European Journal of Public Health* 30, no. 5, suppl. (2020): ckaa166-159, https://doi.org/10.1093/eurpub/ckaa166.159.

26. Taran Volckhausen, "Colombia's Climate Change Issues: 180,000 Medellin Families in 'High Risk' of Natural Disaster," *Colombia Reports*, January 27, 2014, https://colombiareports.com/medellin-precarious-position-climate-change-increasing-natural-disasters/.

27. Alcaldía de Medellín, *Moravia una Historia de Resistencia* (Medellín: Alcaldía de Medellín, 2015), http://www.medellindigital.gov.co/Mediateca/repositorio%20de%20recursos/AlcadiaMedellin_Moravia_Resistencia.pdf.

28. Alcaldía de Medellín, Presentación: Mejoramiento Integral Barrio Moravia Medellín (Medellín: Alcaldía de Medellín, n.d.), https://www.medellin.gov.co/irj/go/km/docs/wpccontent/Sites/Subportal%20del%20Ciudadano/Planeaci%C3%B3n%20Municipal/Secciones/Informaci%C3%B3n%20General/Documentos/POT/PPMORAVIA%20D%20TECNICO%20COMPLETO%20DEFINITIVO.pdf.

29. Carolina Pérez-Muñoz, Peter Charles Brand, and Luis Carlos Agudelo, "Action Plans for Urban Adaptation and Vulnerability Analysis for Medellín: A Proposal to Reduce the Effects of Climate Change from a Territorial Planning Approach," *Gestión y Ambiente* 20, no. 2 (2017): 155, https://doi.org/10.15446/ga.v20n2.67538.

30. Laura Vanesa Aguelo Perez, "Urban Experts Know 'Sustainable Neighborhoods,'" *El Mundo*, May 7, 2015, https://www.elmundo.com/portal/noticias/territorio/expertos_urbanistas_conocen_barrios_sostenibles.php#.X7xX0RNKg4s.

31. "How to Avoid Risks," *Semana Sostenible*, May 29, 2015, https://sostenibilidad.semana.com/medio-ambiente/articulo/jardin-circunvalar-medellin-siembra-para-evitar-riesgos/33109.

32. Juan Fernando Oliveros Ossa and Adolfo Eslava, *Políticas públicas desde abajo: Proceso de concertación durante la formulación del programa Barrios Sostenibles en Medellín* (Medellín: Universidad EAFIT, 2016), https://repository.eafit.edu.co/bitstream/handle/10784/11336/JuanFernando_OliverosOssa_2016.pdf?sequence=2&isAllowed=y.

33. Isabelle Anguelovski et al., "Equity Impacts of Urban Land Use Planning for Climate Adaptation: Critical Perspectives from the Global North and South," *Journal of Planning Education and Research* 36, no. 3 (2016): 333–348, https://doi.org/10.1177%2F0739456X16645166.

34. TECHO is a global NGO that works to address poverty with those living in informal settlements using participatory approaches. www.techo.org.

35. Milford Bateman, Juan Pablo Duran Ortíz, and Kate Maclean, *A Post-Washington Consensus Approach to Local Economic Development in Latin America? An Example from Medellín, Colombia* (London: Overseas Development Institution, 2011).

36. Alejandro Guerrero, *Rebuilding Trust in Government via Service Delivery: The Case of Medellín, Colombia* (Washington, DC: World Bank, 2011), 1–28.

37. Medellín Comovamos, *Medellín Quality of Life Report, 2016–2019* (Medellín : Medellín Comovamos, 2020), https://www.medellincomovamos.org/informe-de -calidad-de-vida-de-medellin-2016-2019.

38. Medellín Comovamos, *Medellín Quality of Life Report—Infographics, 2016–2019* (Medellín: Medellín Comovamos, 2020), https://www.medellincomovamos.org /infografia-informe-primera-infancia-medellin-2016-2019.

39. Medellín Comovamos, *Medellín Quality of Life Report, 2016–2019.*

40. "Medellín Comovamos," last updated 2021, https://www.medellincomovamos .org/que-hacemos-en-medellin-como-vamos.

41. The Gini coefficient is a scale of 0 to 1, with 0 implying equality across a population and 1 meaning maximum inequality where one person has all the income. OECD, Income inequality (indicator), OECD, 2021, doi: 10.1787/459aa7f1-en, https:// data.worldbank.org/indicator/SI.POV.GINI?locations=CO.

42. "Aprueban presupuesto 2019 de Medellín y Antioquia ¿en qué se asignará?" (Medellín and Antioquia's 2019 budget approved—what will it be spent on?) *El Tiempo*, November 26, 2018, https://www.eltiempo.com/colombia/medellin/aprue ban-presupuesto-2019-de-medellin-y-antioquia-298240.

43. Agencia De Cooperacion e Invesrion de Medellín y el Area Metropolitana (ACI Medellín), *Link: Medellín: On the Way to the Fourth Industrial Revolution*, no. 7 (Medellín: ACI Medellín, 2019), https://www.acimedellin.org/wp-content/up loads/2019/11/LINKS-web.pdf.

44. "Estadisticas por tema: Pobreza y Condiciones de Vida" (Statistics by Topic: Poverty and Living Conditions) Dane Informacion Para Todos, accessed February 2, 2021, https://www.dane.gov.co/index.php/estadisticas-por-tema/pobreza-y-condici ones-de-vida.

45. "About C40," C40 Cities, accessed August 20, 2020, https://www.c40.org/about.

46. Agencia De Cooperacion e Invesrion de Medellín y el Area Metropolitana (ACI Medellín), *Link: Medellín.*

47. David Alejandro Mercado, "¿Qué significa que Medellín se convierta en una 'ecociudad'?" *El Tiempo*, May 17, 2020, https://www.eltiempo.com/colombia/medellin /que-significa-que-medellin-se-convierta-en-una-ecociudad-496218.

48. "City of the Year—Medellín," *Wall Street Journal*, advertisement, 2012, http:// www.wsj.com/ad/cityoftheyear.

49. "Lee Kuan Yew World City Prize," Lee Kuan Yew World City Prize, last updated January 25, 2021, https://www.leekuanyewworldcityprize.gov.sg/.

50. "Colombia's Medellín Named 'Most Innovative City,'" BBC, March 1, 2013, https://www.bbc.com/news/world-latin-america-21638308.

Chapter 6: Putting Health Equity into All Urban Policies

1. California Newsreel, "Unnatural Causes—Place Matters," California Newsreel, 29:00, 2008, https://unnaturalcauses.org/.

2. City of Richmond, California, "Community Health and Wellness: City of Richmond General Plan Element 11" (Richmond, CA: City of Richmond, 2012), http://www.ci.richmond.ca.us/DocumentCenter/View/8579/Health-and-Wellness -Element?bidId=.

3. Jane Kay, "Richmond Plant Safety Pact OK'd," *San Francisco Examiner*, February 7, 1996, A-5, https://www.sfgate.com/news/article/Richmond-plant-safety-pact-OK -d-3151094.php.

4. The members of REDI include Alliance of Californians for Community Empowerment (ACCE); Contra Costa Faith Works; Contra Costa Interfaith Supporting Community Organization (CCISCO); East Bay Alliance for a Sustainable Economy (EBASE); Greater Richmond Interfaith Program (GRIP); Urban Habitat; Asian-Pacific Environmental Network (APEN); Laotian Organizing Project (LOP); Communities for a Better Environment (CBE). See http://urbanhabitat.org/richmond.

5. The TAG also included representatives from the Contra Costa Health Services Department (CCHS); the Environmental Health Investigation Branch (EHIB) of the California Department of Health Services; and the Department of Public Health, City and County of San Francisco. Members included: Richard Jackson MD, MPH, Adjunct Professor, School of Public Health, University of California, Berkeley; Richard Kreutzer MD, Branch Chief, Environmental Health Investigations Branch, California Department of Health Services; Wendel Brunner, MD, Public Health Director, Contra Costa Public Health; Poki Stewart Namkung MD, MPH, Public Health Officer, Santa Cruz County Health Services Agency and President of the National Association of County and City Health Officials (NACCHO); Dennis M. Barry, Director, Contra Costa County Community Development; Richard Mitchell, Planning Director, City of Richmond; Victor Rubin, PolicyLink; Sharon Fuller, Ma'at Academy; Sheryl Lane, Urban Habitat; Barbara Becnel, North Richmond Neighborhood House; Delphine Smith, Communities for a Better Environment.

6. City of Richmond, California, "Community Health and Wellness."

7. David R. Williams, Jourdyn A. Lawrence, and Brigette A. Davis, "Racism and Health: Evidence and Needed Research," *Annual Review of Public Health* 40 (2019): 105–125, https://doi.org/10.1146/annurev-publhealth-040218-043750.

8. "Health in All Policies," City of Richmond, California, accessed February 2, 2020, http://www.ci.richmond.ca.us/2575/Health-in-All-Policies-HiAP.

9. City of Richmond, California, "Resolution of the Council of the City of Richmond, California, in Support of Systematically and Deliberately Applying a Racial Equity Lens in Decision Making," Resolution No. 93-18 (Richmond, CA: City of Richmond, 2018).

10. Contra Costa Health Services, "The Richmond Health Equity Report Card" (Richmond, CA: Richmond Health Equity Partnership, n.d.), https://cchealth.org /health-data/pdf/Richmond-Health-Equity-Report-Card-Full.pdf.

11. "Transparent Richmond," City of Richmond, California, accessed November 12, 2020, https://www.transparentrichmond.org.

12. "RichmondBUILD Academy," City of Richmond, California, accessed February 2, 2021, https://www.ci.richmond.ca.us/1243/RichmondBUILD.

13. "Career Center Services," City of Richmond, California, accessed February 2, 2020, https://www.ci.richmond.ca.us/661/RichmondWORKS.

14. Cobiz Richmond, accessed February 2, 2020, https://cobizrichmond.com/.

15. "Chevron Environmental and Community Investment," City of Richmond, California, accessed February 2, 2020, http://www.ci.richmond.ca.us/2906/Chevron-Community-Investment.

16. Paul Sullivan, "Adding Good Deeds to the Investment Equation," *New York Times*, March 6, 2015, https://www.nytimes.com/2015/03/07/business/adding-good-deeds-to-the-investment-equation.html?smid=fb-share&_r=1.

17. "Richmond Housing Renovation Program," Richmond Community Foundation Connects, 2021, https://www.rcfconnects.org/community-initiatives/restoring-neighborhoods/richmond-housing-renovation-program/.

18. Mike Aldax, "Your Newest Bay Area Homeowners: A Teacher and Nonprofit Worker," *Richmond Standard*, oust 2, 2018, https://richmondstandard.com/richmond/2018/08/02/your-newest-bay-area-homeowners-a-teacher-and-nonprofit-worker/.

19. Casey Gwinn and Gael Strack, *Hope for Hurting Families: Creating Family Justice Centers across America* (Volcano, CA: Volcano Press, 2006).

20. "Revisions to Richmond Kids First Initiative," City of Richmond, California, accessed December 1, 2020, https://www.ci.richmond.ca.us/DocumentCenter/View/48208/Richmond-Kids-First-Amendment-Measure-K?bidId=.

21. "How It All Began," RYSE Center, accessed September 23, 2020, http://rysecenter.org/about-3/mission-2/.

22. "Climate Action Plan," City of Richmond, California, accessed February 2, 2020, https://www.ci.richmond.ca.us/3313/Climate-Action-Plan.

23. Sonal Jessel, Samantha Sawyer, and Diana Hernández, "Energy, Poverty, and Health in Climate Change: A Comprehensive Review of an Emerging Literature," *Frontiers in Public Health*, no. 7 (2019): 357, https://doi.org/10.3389/fpubh.2019.00357.

24. Sanya Carley and David M. Konisky, "The Justice and Equity Implications of the Clean Energy Transition," *Nature Energy* 5, no. 8 (2020): 569–577, https://doi-org.libproxy.berkeley.edu/10.1038/s41560-020-0641-6.

25. "Solar Savings Reach Renters with LIWP Program," Low-Income Solar Policy Guide, accessed February 2, 2020, https://www.lowincomesolar.org/solar-savings-reach-renters/.

26. "CSD Awards $4.4 Million for California's First Low-Income Community Solar Projects," *California Climate Investments*, accessed February 2, 2020, http://www.caclimateinvestments.ca.gov/press-releases/2019/8/14/csd-awards-44-million-for-californias-first-low-income-community-solar-projects.

27. Mike Aldax, "Richmond's Collaborative Effort to Monitor Its Air," *Richmond Standard*, November 27, 2019, https://richmondstandard.com/richmond/2019/11/27/richmonds-collaborative-effort-to-monitor-its-air/.

28. "About," Chevron Richmond, accessed February 2, 2020, https://richmondairmonitoring.org/about.html.

29. "Air District Announces $146K Settlement with Richmond Chevron Refinery for Violations," CBS SF Bay Area, April 22, 2020, https://sanfrancisco.cbslocal.com/2020/04/22/air-district-announces-146k-settlement-with-richmond-chevron-refinery-for-violations/.

30. Susie Cagle, "*Richmond v. Chevron*: The California City Taking On Its Most Powerful Polluter," *Guardian*, October 9, 2019, https://www.theguardian.com/envi ronment/2019/oct/09/richmond-chevron-california-city-polluter-fossil-fuel.

31. *Hughes v. Superior Court*, 339 U.S. 460 (1950), https://supreme.justia.com/cases /federal/us/339/460/.

32. Social Compact, *Richmond Grocery Gap* (Washington, DC: Social Compact, 2011), http://www.ci.richmond.ca.us/DocumentCenter/View/7976/FINAL-GroceryGap _Report_Richmond.

33. MIG, Inc., *City of Richmond Urban Agriculture Assessment* (Richmond, CA: City of Richmond, 2011), https://www.ci.richmond.ca.us/DocumentCenter/View/8291 /Urban-Ag?bidId=.

34. Growing the Table, accessed February 2, 2020, https://www.growingthetable .org/.

35. Sarah Henry, "The Artisan Kitchen in Richmond: A Cooperative Cooking Space," KQED, April 11, 2011, https://www.kqed.org/bayareabites/26844/the-artisan -kitchen-in-richmond-a-cooperative-cooking-space.

36. Laurie Mazur, "What Does Environmental Justice Organizing Look Like in the Time of Trump?" *Grist*, January 18, 2017, https://grist.org/justice/what-does-en vironmental-justice-organizing-look-like-in-the-time-of-trump/.

37. Julie Brown, "Contra Costa Tables Controversial Jail Expansion," *Richmond Confidential*, September 7, 2012, https://richmondconfidential.org/2012/09/07/contra -costa-tables-controversial-jail-expansion/.

38. John Geluardi, "The Man behind Richmond's Renaissance," *East Bay Express*, May 18, 2011, https://www.eastbayexpress.com/oakland/the-man-behind-richmonds -renaissance/Content?oid=2647128.

39. Steve Early, *Refinery Town: Big Oil, Big Money, and the Remaking of an American City* (Boston: Beacon Press, 2017).

40. "Transparent Richmond," City of Richmond, California, accessed February 11, 2021, https://www.transparentrichmond.org.

Conclusion: Toward Cities That Heal

1. Nelmo Munyiri music video about the risk of cholera in Mukuru, YouTube video, https://www.youtube.com/watch?v=MZAGvx1NxRU.

2. Xavier de Souza Briggs, Susan J. Popkin, and John Goering, *Moving to Opportunity: The Story of an American Experiment to Fight Ghetto Poverty* (New York: Oxford University Press, 2010).

3. C. C. Branas et al., "Citywide Cluster Randomized Trial to Restore Blighted Vacant Land and Its Effects on Violence, Crime, and Fear," *Proceedings of the National Academy of Sciences U S A* 115, no. 12 (2018): 2946–2951.

4. "Segregation Still Blights the Lives of African-Americans," *Economist*, July 9, 2020, https://www.economist.com/briefing/2020/07/09/segregation-still-blights-the -lives-of-african-americans.

5. Kazu Haga. *Healing Resistance: A Radically Different Response to Harm* (Berkeley: Parallax Press, 2020), 225.

6. Jaime Lerner, *Urban Acupuncture: Celebrating Pinpricks of Change That Enrich City Life* (Washington, DC: Island Press, 2014).

7. Hanier Anturi Ramírez, "El Parque de la Vida en Medellín, una institución aplaudida por la OMS" (Parque de la Vida in Medellín, an institution applauded by WHO), *El Tiempo*, October 28, 2018, https://www.eltiempo.com/vida/educacion /el-parque-de-la-vida-en-medellin-una-institucion-aplaudida-por-la-oms-286192.

8. Yvonne Rydin et al. "Shaping Cities for Health: Complexity and the Planning of Urban Environments in the 21st Century," *Lancet* (London, England) 379, no. 9831 (2012): 2079–2108, doi:10.1016/S0140-6736(12)60435-8.

9. M. Ezzati et al., "Cities for Global Health," *BMJ* (Clinical research ed.), no. 363 (2018): k3794, https://doi.org/10.1136/bmj.k3794.

10. M. Acuto, S. Parnell, and K. C. Seto, "Building a Global Urban Science," *Nature Sustainability* 1, no. 2–4 (2018), https://doi.org/10.1038/s41893-017-0013-9.

11. Michael Keith et al., "The Future of the Future City? The New Urban Sciences and a PEAK Urban Interdisciplinary Disposition," *Cities*, no. 105 (2020), https://doi .org/10.1016/j.cities.2020.102820.

12. "The Urban Genome Project," accessed February 18, 2021, https://urbangenome .utoronto.ca/.

13. Cornel West, "Ware Lecture by Cornel West, General Assembly 2015," Unitarian Universalist Association, 2015, https://www.uua.org/ga/past/2015/ware-west.

Index

Page references in *italics* indicate photographs, tables, or charts.

About the Author

Jason Corburn is a professor in the School of Public Health and the Department of City and Regional Planning at UC Berkeley. He Directs the Center for Global Healthy Cities at UC Berkeley and the joint master's degree in city planning and public health. Formerly, he was director of the Institute of Urban and Regional Development and cochair of Global Metropolitan Studies at UC Berkeley. He is cochair of the International Science Council, Committee on Urban Health and Well-Being, an advisory board member of the International Society for Urban Health, and is on the board of trustees of  Slum/Shack Dwellers International–Kenya. He has worked with hundreds of community-based organizations around the world and tens of city governments on conducting action research focused on addressing racial and ethnic health inequities. Professor Corburn is the author of a number of award-winning books: *Street Science: Community Knowledge and Environmental Health Justice* (MIT Press, 2005); *Toward the Healthy City* (MIT Press, 2009); *Healthy City Planning* (Routledge, 2013); *Healthy Cities* (Routledge, 2015), and *Slum Health* (UC Press, 2016). He has received numerous awards for his community-engaged action research, including the UC Chancellor's Public Service Award, the United Nations Association Global Citizenship Award, the Paul Davidoff Best Book Award, and the Environmental Leadership Program Fellowship, and he was named one of the world's Top 40 Thinkers on Cities by Routledge in 2017. Professor Corburn has held visiting faculty appointments at Université Paris Nanterre, the State University of Rio de Janeiro (UERJ), and the University of Nairobi. He received his BA from Brandeis University and an MCP and PhD from MIT. Read more at www.jasoncorburn.com.